RACIST VIOLENCE AND THE STATE

Racist Violence and the State:
a comparative analysis of Britain, France and the Netherlands

Rob Witte

LONGMAN
London and New York

Addison Wesley Longman Limited,
Edinburgh Gate,
Harlow, Essex CM20 2JE, England
and Associated Companies throughout the world.

*Published in the United States of America
by Longman Publishing, New York*

First published 1996

ISBN 0 582 27799-X PPR

British Library Cataloguing-in-Publication Data

A catalogue record for this book is
available from the British Library

Library of Congress Cataloging-in-Publication Data
Witte, Rob.
  Racist violence and the state : a comparative analysis of Britain,
France, and the Netherlands / Rob Witte.
    p. cm.
  Includes bibliographical references and index.
  ISBN 0-582-27799-X
  1. Europe – Race relations. 2. Racism – Europe – History – 20th century.
  3. Violence – Europe – History – 20th century. 4. Great Britain – Race relations.
  5. France – Race relations. 6. Netherlands – Racist relations. I. Title.
  D1056.W58
  1996 323.1'4'09045 –dc20
                                                                    95-48378
                                                                    CIP

Set by 5 in 10/11pt Times
Produced through Longman Malaysia, KPP

This book is dedicated to three young men: Ahmed Iqbal Ullah, Djilali Ben Ali and Kerwin Duinmeijer; and to Marja Veenstra.

CONTENTS

PREFACE

On Sunday, 30 September 1941, my grandfather lay on the wooden slats that served as his bed in the concentration camp of Amersfoort puzzling over members of the Dutch NSB (the Dutch National-Socialist Movement) torn by pity, rage and anger:

Their political thinking has been twisted by years of economic crisis and swept along by a fascist order and race theories. But to simply think of *their* guilt is too superficial. Shouldn't we look for this among those who incited them with their degenerate minds.
(Diary of E. Joh. Bulten, no. 230, *Aaltense Gijzelaars*, 1970: 33)[1]

More than half-a-century later, people in Europe are still confronted by racist terror from individual incidents to long-lasting processes of day-to-day harassment and violence. This violence may be different in intensity, in extent and in scale to the violence which confronted my grandfather and so many others during the Second World War, but the questions he raised are still relevant to our times.

Both then and now, it is not only the vicious leaders of racist extreme-right organisations who incite perpetrators of racist violence. Perpetrators of racist violence are not only 'incited to violent acts', but their actions are also often glossed over, tolerated, sometimes even accepted in the mid-1990s Europe. Authorities in general, and state authorities in particular, have a decisive influence on this. Their responses to the seeds and expressions of racism and instances of racist violence are a definitive factor in the way these phenomena determine the day-to-day life of specific groups within European society.

This study describes and analyses the responses by state authorities to racist violence in Britain, France and the Netherlands since 1945. It would have been impossible without the help and assistance of many. I owe special debts of gratitude to my parents, to my supervisors Frank Bovenkerk and Robert Miles, and to John Schuster, Yücel Yeşilgöz, Jaap van Donselaar, Ben Bowling, Martin Moerings, Tore Björgo, Cathie Lloyd, Paddy Farrington and Bernd Lehmann for our discussions and their advice. Their personal warmth proved to be a special stimulus.

I would also like to thank John Solomos, Paul Gordon, Giles Verbunt, Liz Fekete, Marian FitzGerald, Carol Willis, Jan Rath and all the contributors to *Racist Violence in Europe* (Macmillan, 1993) for their contribution in establishing the theoretical and factual contents of this study. My thanks also go to Alison Bieker, Anne Shaw and Lisa Chason for their assistance with the language.

Science without any actual feeling for, or communication with, people involved in the field of study is the ivory tower kind of science

x   *Preface*

of which I do not approve nor wish to take part in. Therefore I would like to thank all of those in the numerous anti-racism organisations with whom I spoke and worked in these past years, especially those at the *Anti Racisme Informatie Centrum* (ARIC, Rotterdam) and at the Dutch *Landelijke Vereniging van Anti Discriminatie Bureaus* (especially at RADAR-Rotterdam and ADB-Noord Kennemerland). Although I am indebted to many people, everything in this volume is my responsibility.

Finally, I would like to thank the people at the Willem Pompe Institute for Criminal Sciences of the University of Utrecht, especially those at the reception, for establishing a good working climate and the people of the Centre for Research in Ethnic Relations at the University of Warwick for my early appointment to an EU fellowship which enabled me to complete my dissertation without worries about employment in the near future.

This book is dedicated to four people. Ahmed Iqbal Ullah (1973–86, Manchester), Djilali Ben Ali (1956–71, Paris) and Kerwin Duinmeijer (1968–83, Amsterdam) were three young persons in each of the countries involved in this study, representing all those who had and have to cope with racist violence, from day-to-day harassing terror to the murder that ended their young lives.

The fourth person to whom this book is dedicated is Marja Veenstra, for coping with me when this study carried me away completely, for discussing every thought, for inspiring me and, most importantly, for just being there.

Rob Witte

Note

1 This diary has not been published.

Acknowledgements

The publishers are indebted to the following for permission to reproduce copyright material: The Macmillan Press Ltd for the figure 'Different types of state responses in the four phases of the idealised process of racist violence "on its way" to the formal agenda' in *Racist Violence in Europe*, T. Bjorgo & R. Witte (eds), 1993. All rights reserved.

CHAPTER 1

Introduction

In the early 1990s, racist incidents in Europe increasingly attracted international attention. Specifically, the violent attacks against African street vendors in Florence, Italy (1990), the desecration of Jewish graves in Carpentras, France (1990), the racist attacks in Germany against asylum-seekers in Hoyerswerda (1991) and Rostock (1992), and the racist murder of Turkish residents in Mölln (1992) and Solingen (1993) were widely publicised, and stimulated the increasing number of reports of racist incidents in all European countries. Whether there really was more racist violence or not, state authorities were forced to formulate policies and implement measures. This was not limited to local and national authorities; even at a European level initiatives were taken. At the Corfu summit in June 1994, for instance, government leaders of the European Union decided to set up a European Advisory Commission on Tolerance and Understanding of Foreigners. One of its tasks was to formulate general strategies to combat racist violence and expressions of xenophobia.[1]

However, the increasing attention cannot be explained by the severity and level of racist violence since the mid-1980s in European countries alone. In fact, this kind of violence, involving deaths and severe injuries, had been occurring in several countries on a more or less regular basis. Waves of racist violence were reported earlier, for instance, in Britain (the late 1950s, the late 1960s and early 1970s), in France (1973, the early 1980s) and in the Netherlands (the early 1980s). These waves included vicious violent incidents with many casualties, but the attention they attracted was of a different quality and degree in comparison to more recent times.

Approaches, perceptions and definitions

State responses to racist violence

Measured by frequency of expression, severity and level of violence, racist violence did and does differ in each European country. If we look at the reported casualties due to racist attacks, for instance, major differences between countries are obvious. State responses to this violence also differ. The way in which state authorities respond is relatively autonomous and independent of the violence. State responses stem from sources other than the racist violence itself, including historical, political, socioeconomic and ideological processes and circumstances.

The actions of the state do have a major influence on future levels and expressions of racist violence: they may dim or inflame more aggression. If the levels and expressions of racist violence change, the state is then confronted with new facts which will in turn lead to state responses being altered.

In this study, the role and responses of state authorities are singled out from the interactive process of causes and state responses. This is for three reasons: (1) their importance, because national debates and discussions converge on the state; (2) their independent impact; and (3) the responsibility of the state.

The basic theoretical assumption of this study is that state responses are an important, if not decisive, factor in the processes concerning racist violence. The aim of this study is not to describe and analyse racist violence itself, but to analyse the impact of state responses on racist violence. To analyse state responses as a decisive factor on racist violence, an international comparative analysis is executed. State responses in three countries are studied, analysed and compared, to distinguish in these state responses the historically specific processes for each country from the generality of such processes. Doing so, the importance and impact of state responses on the development of the phenomenon of racist violence will be clarified.

International comparative analysis

An international comparative analysis may present better insights into state responses to racist violence. However, comparison of these responses in different countries at a specific moment in time raises difficulties, due to the different situations in each individual country. Already in 1981, for instance, racist violence constituted a topic on the British political agenda, whereas state authorities in France, and more so in the Netherlands, hardly paid attention to this issue until the early 1990s.

Methodologically speaking, one possible way of producing an international comparative analysis is to make use of one country as a frame of reference for studying the situation in the others. In carrying out such an analysis, however, differences in discourses are often overlooked. These differences are important because different ways of perceiving and defining a situation result in differences in policy and practice. In addition to this, the analysis often has an abstract theoretical basis. Therefore the danger of neglecting the specific historical circumstances of individual countries is constantly present (Bovenkerk, Miles and Verbunt, 1990a).

'The quest for both generality and specificity . . . demands a constant shifting between various levels of abstraction. General problems are confronted in specific national situations; solutions are then applied to other instances, thereby creating new general problems, and so on' (Bovenkerk, Miles and Verbunt, 1990a: 386). Therefore, a theoretical framework for an international comparative analysis should include a certain form of discourse analysis and should be formulated on a more abstract level than the phenomenon under study, including explanations of more general processes in the countries involved, as well as of the specific historical elements of each individual country.

The countries and states studied in an international comparative analysis should be those that are most comparable. It is preferable to include countries which make it possible to 'hold constant as many potential explanada as possible in order to maximise the theoretical scope of the analysis' (Bovenkerk, Miles and Verbunt, 1990b: 478). Britain, France and the Netherlands have been selected as the countries in which state responses to racist violence are studied, analysed and compared. There are five main reasons for choosing these three nation-states (Bovenkerk, Miles and Verbunt, 1990b: 478–9):

1 All three have been prominent participants in the historical process of emerging capitalism in Europe, including the creation of nation-states and of imperialist colonial empires.
2 All three remain among the most 'advanced' capitalist countries with comparable modes of production, characterised by the interdependence of capital accumulation and rapid technological change.
3 All three constitute welfare states with a form of representative government based upon universal suffrage.
4 Since 1945, all three nations have witnessed, and have been regulating – albeit to different degrees – four analytically distinct migration movements: (1) owners of wealth, along with managerial and technical staff of international companies; (2) (industrial) workers; (3) subjects from (former) colonies; and (4) asylum-seekers and refugees.
5 In all three countries, the combined numbers of immigrant settlers has been very small, being around 5 to 7 per cent of the total population.

Similarities and differences between the three nation-states are discussed in more detail in Chapter 5 in which the state responses to racist violence in Britain, France and the Netherlands are compared.

In the early 1990s, racist violence in Germany attracted international attention. For reasons of comparability – especially the very different German history in relation to colonialism and post-war migration – Germany has not been chosen as one of the countries in this international comparative analysis.

The concept of the state

'Racial attacks and racial harassment do not occur in a vacuum but take place in a social and political context which can either be more or less favourable' (Gordon, 1990: 36). State responses to racist violence do constitute an important, if not decisive, factor with respect to (future) appearances of, and developments in, this violence. This is shown to be true with respect to individual incidents as well as to the more general patterns of racist violence at a certain time and in a certain place or country (see e.g. Björgo and Witte, 1993).

What do I mean by 'the state' in this study? The concept of the state refers to a complex of institutions or state machineries. The most important state machineries in Western democracies are the central government apparatus, the bureaucratic administration, the police and military, the judiciary, (national and local) representative institutions, and a series of permanent advisory institutions (Stuurman, 1981: 18–19).

The relatively autonomous state, in which freedom of action is limited by national and international economic, political and ideological developments (Stuurman, 1985: 56), should not be perceived as a monolithic unity. State activities comprise a complex series of actions by persons within one or more of the state machineries mentioned. State activities are the result of internal struggle and compromises (Bovenkerk, Miles and Verbunt, 1990b: 480), and are constantly subject to a variety of influences from outside the state. This means that different, even contradictory, state responses to racist violence may and will, logically, be expected to occur simultaneously in any one country. State machineries involve individuals and institutions referred to as internal actors.

For its part, the state is influenced by actors outside the state machineries, so-called external actors. These actors are institutions, national and international organisations, and individuals, such as non-governmental organisations, pressure groups, social movements, lobbyists, and so on.

Imagined community

The state machineries 'collectively claim and use power to structure a particular ensemble of economic, social and political relations within a specified spatial unit to mediate the impact of exterior force upon that unit' (Bovenkerk, Miles and Verbunt, 1990b: 479–80). This notion of unity has an ideologised background. One of the most important mechanisms to structure and preserve the idea of unity consists of the construction, perception and presentation of the imagined community (Anderson, 1983) within dominant popular, political and ideological discourses.

Groups of people are socially constructed by some common origin serving as a basis of community or collective. This origin, real or imagined, can be historically, territorially, culturally or physiognomically based. It can be internally constituted by the group or externally imposed, or both. The terminology 'imagined communities' refers to the assumed sense of commonality with others, since not all members can interact in person to form a real community. In other words, the group of people is constructed to constitute a mythical unity (Anthias and Yuval-Davis, 1993: 4).

The construction of imagined community includes a determination of who belongs to this community. The imagined community is assumed to have a set of collective characteristics and interests. There is a logical other side to the coin: to define who belongs implies describing those who do not belong. The inclusive conception of community (who belongs) necessarily defines a constituency of Others (who do not belong). In other words, a formal dichotomy is developed of Us and Other, for instance national and alien (Miles, 1993: 152).

Three roles of the state

The history of racist violence is closely related to issues of migration and the formation of minorities. The state is here conceived as playing three main roles in relation to these issues (Bovenkerk, Miles and Verbunt, 1990b: 482): (1) the gatekeeper role (the inclusion and exclusion of who is allowed entry to the country); (2) the welfare or collective consumption role (the inclusion or exclusion of people from the distribution of certain resources, goods, and services); and (3) the role of maintaining law and order.

This third role is of eminent importance with respect to racist violence. In the concept of the modern state, the use of violence is monopolised by that state. Any act of violence by private interest group challenges the state in its role as upholder of law and order. The way in which the state will respond to violence in general and to racist violence in particular, however, will differ by state, by situation, and over time.

National versus local state

In international comparative analysis, states are often referred to on the national level. With respect to the state responses to racist violence, however, local authorities often play and have played a very important role. Therefore, the state at the local level should not be ignored in these analyses. Although the main focus of attention will be on the national level, the local level needs to be taken into consideration for six reasons (see also Husbands, 1993: 122–6; Witte, 1993b: 143):

1 Problems, including racist violence, are usually in the first instance perceived to occur at a local level, and are responded to by local authorities.
2 In situations in which racist violence is not perceived as constituting a (major) social problem by the public and political community at large, state responses are mainly visible at the local level (especially the responses by the police as upholder of law and order).

3 In all situations, there are several differences between the national and local level with respect to perceptions of, and approaches and responses towards, racist violence.
4 The differences in intention of policy, and their practical effects, leads one to study the national level at which the intentions of policy are often formulated, as well as the local level at which policies are implemented and have specific effects.
5 Initiatives to combat racist violence, as well as resistance to such initiatives or policies, may be prominent on the local level.
6 In a situation in which racist violence reaches the local political agenda, internal state actors at the local level, for instance councillors, aldermen, police commissioners and mayors, may bring this phenomenon on to the national political agenda, and may have impact on the perception and definition of the problem due to their position within, and (internal) contacts with, state agencies.

The methodological problem then arises of how to compare state responses at both local and national levels in different nation-states and over an extended period of time. I shall turn to this problem later, describing a constructed model of state responses to racist violence. First, I shall elaborate on the importance of problem definition to the process of state responses to a social phenomenon, and present a definition of racist violence.

Problem definition

Why are certain phenomena transformed into political topics while others are not (yet)? Why and how does a phenomenon become an issue at a certain moment in time? Phenomena such as racist violence, as much as incest, child abuse, domestic violence, rape, environmental pollution, and so on, have all existed throughout the twentieth century and before. However, it was not until the 1970s and 1980s that they were transformed into political issues in various countries in Europe, and that policies were formulated, and legislative and other measures taken.

The degree to which a phenomenon occurs does not explain this transformation. Some of the phenomena mentioned did occur to a larger extent earlier this century. However, it was not until the 1980s and 1990s that they received massive public, media and political attention, and were defined as intolerable and unbearable.

This recent attention does not imply that people did not object to these acts of aggression before. However, it was not until the 1980s and 1990s that these phenomena were perceived in mainstream discourses as constituting a social problem, recognised by society as problematic and leading to demands for action. Of course a problem can exist only upon the appearance of a phenomenon which is defined to be problematic. The fact that it is a problem, and is perceived as such, characterises the element of construction (Brants and Brants, 1991: 15).[2] Processes in society in which social definitions of a phenomenon come about are referred to as the social construction of the specific phenomenon by symbolic interactionist theories (see for instance Hester and Eglin, 1992: 27).

This construction has to be perceived as the outcome of processes in society which both influence and are influenced by mainstream discourses. Certain sections of society are very influential in these processes which include changing perspectives, opinions and ideologies. Concerning racist violence, the main sections are the state, science, the mainstream media and the judiciary.

The definition of a problem does not just reflect experiences of the problem. It often presents indications for assumed causes of the problem as well. The problem definition is of eminent importance in every stage mentioned. The likelihood of attracting attention and, for instance, reaching the political agenda, will partly depend upon a definition used or successfully changed. This is particularly true in relation to groups that occupy marginal power positions in society.

Progress in advancing the issue politically will depend upon activities aimed at persuading other 'new' groups to support the demands made. Groups of people who try to increase support for their demands may broaden the definitions used. In the case of racist violence, one may think of definitions including violence against people who are discriminated against on other grounds, for instance, homosexuals, disabled persons, women and homeless people.

Problem definitions do not simply play an important role in having an issue placed on the political agenda. Symbolic presentations also shape an important part of problem definitions: 'The key to success in each case is to put the appeal in a symbolic context that will have a maximum impact on followers, potential supporters, the opposition and/or decision-makers' (Cobb and Elder, 1983: 150). The use of these symbolic presentations is important in attracting attention, and the role of the mass media is essential. Symbolic presentations are a continuing part of political life. Often expressions such as freedom, justice, tolerance, integration and security are used without any consensus about the content of these terms. They are, however, very important in mobilising people, formulating demands, contacting decision-makers and opposing resistance. Therefore, once an issue is situated on the political agenda, the definition is very important (van der Graaf and Hoppe, 1989). Differences in definitions may lead to a situation in which certain state authorities argue that the problem is being dealt with effectively, while other state authorities and external actors disagree.

At a certain stage, and at a certain moment, different definitions of the phenomenon (i.e. racist violence) may exist among internal actors, as well as between internal and external actors, on both local and national levels of the state. In Europe, the variety of definitions is large. In the 1990s, terms used include extreme-right violence, racist violence, anti-immigrant violence, racial violence, violence against foreigners, and neo Nazi violence (see Björgo and Witte, 1993: 6; Witte, 1995).

The definitions used are important as they imply a mode of action. For instance, anti-immigrant violence can focus and/or limit the discussion to the issue of immigration and exclude violence perpetrated against fellow citizens with a skin colour different from that of the majority of the population. Neo Nazi violence may look at the violence perpetrated by people organised in neo Nazi groups, leaving out racist violence perpetrated by the next-door neighbour. Another example is extreme-right violence, which may include violence against homosexuals, women, and physically disabled persons without paying attention to the specific characteristics of racism. The problem with definitions can be that they are either too narrowly formulated (only directed at victimised immigrants or at violence perpetrated by neo Nazis) or too broad (including all 'weaker' groups of people in terms of power, and, for instance, all political opponents).

Racist violence: a definition

I have argued that phenomena can be perceived as problematic, and may be constructed and defined as social problems. This study will focus on the way state authorities respond to the phenomenon of racist violence, and the way in which their response influences the construction of racist violence as a social issue. To do so, I trace the history of state responses. This includes periods of time in which state authorities do not perceive racist violence as a social problem at all. A subject has to be traced back far enough that it is regarded as non-existent at a certain point, or at least is not constructed in similar terms to those used later. Therefore, the past has to be reconstructed by the researcher. With the benefit of hindsight, a definition of racist violence is developed here to refer to the phenomenon to which state responses are studied.

An important element of racist violence is that perpetrators perceive their victims as representatives of a group or community. Whether the victim actually is, or is not, a member of this group/community is not a decisive factor. Therefore, an important element in the definition of racist violence is the recognition that the attacked person is not victimised in his/her capacity as an individual, but as a representative of a real or imagined foreign or strange group. This representative role is not restricted only to people, but may also include buildings, places of worship, and so on. Buildings, properties and institutions may be attacked because they are perceived to represent, or symbolise, these communities or their interests.

Implicitly or explicitly, perpetrators of racist violence define their potential victims as Them who are (to be) distinguished from Us on the basis of phenotypical characteristics, religion, cultural or national origin. Them and Us are regarded as constituting separate groups or separate imagined communities (see pp. 4–5). The main characteristics, by which the Other community is constructed, are perceived to be different-by-definition from Our imagined community to which the perpetrators believe themselves to belong.

Furthermore, the racist nature of the violence is constructed by the signification of the Other collective (see e.g. Miles, 1989; 1993; Rath, 1993). I am aware of the very complex and contested debate about the general concept of racism, as well as of the debate as to whether this signification has to be valuated negatively to be racist (see e.g. Barker, 1981; Miles, 1993). However, in relation to racist violence, the Other (the collective represented by the victim) is always negatively signified. The violence itself is concrete proof of the alleged inferiority of the victim in the perception of the perpetrator. This negative signification is most prominent in the violence carried out against alleged representatives of this Other collective, and implies that the Other is perceived as inferior (by the racist attacker), whether implicitly or explicitly.

The presence of Them is often perceived, experienced and represented as a threat, for instance, to Our culture, life style, welfare or 'race'.[3] In other words, the (increasing) presence of Them is perceived as constituting a threat to certain elements which, in turn, are perceived (implicitly) to be essential to Our community. According to this position, They should be excluded from various aspects of life to varying degrees: from social services, jobs, housing, to even living in the same country. It is important to record that all three nation-states examined in the work include groups of people who, at least legally, constitute an integral part of society as citizens, and who are victimised by racist violence. The most extreme expressions of this racist exclusion are found in racist violence in general, and in racist genocide in particular.

Theoretically, racist positions and behaviour, such as violence, are not reserved for members of majority populations.

It cannot be ruled out that some of the discourses and practices of those committed to doctrines of racial and cultural purity among the ethnic minorities might be regarded in some respects and contexts as 'racist'.

(Rattansi, 1994: 57)

In fact, racism and racist violence also features in the attitudes and ideas of certain sections of minority groups. For example, Yeşilgöz (1993) shows that feelings, ideologies and attitudes of superiority are manifest among specific sections of Turkish minority communities in western European countries. In this study, however, racist violence is understood within the context of a system of unequal power relations (Gordon, 1993: 170–1), as well as in the context of popular, political and ideological mainstream discourses in which certain minority groups are perceived and portrayed as being different by definition. This includes not only theoretical positions and ideological discourses, but also everyday practice in which these minority groups are excluded from equal rights and opportunities in the political field, in the labour market, in the housing market and within the education system.

Understanding racist violence within the contexts of power relations and mainstream discourses does not hold true with respect to the – possibly racist – violence perpetrated by members of ethnic minorities in the three countries studied. Due to their position within the system of power relations, these people by definition are not capable of actually classifying and positioning specific groups of people in a system of unequal power relations, nor of dominating or determining mainstream discourses. Therefore, the definition of racist violence used here does not refer to violence by protest movements of oppressed minorities, such as riots. The definition of racist violence in Western European states in general, and in Britain, France and the Netherlands in particular, has to be limited to violence against individuals because of their real or imagined membership in *minority* groups – in terms of numbers, as well as in terms of power.

For these same reasons, (inter)racial violence as such does not constitute an element in the definition of racist violence here. Racial violence points specifically at the perception that the perpetrator(s) and the victim(s) 'belong' to different groups constructed, and signified, as different 'races' based on phenotypical characteristics or national, cultural or religious origin. In the context of racist violence, this follows 'popular common sense racist ideas which equate attacks on black people with ordinary criminal attacks on white people where the attacker was thought to be black' (Gordon, 1993: 170). This leaves out the context of unequal socioeconomic and political (power) relations in the society in which racist violence specifically takes place, as well as the fact that it perceives racist attacks as just another aspect of crime without reference to the racist background and consequences of this specific type of violence (see also Virdee, 1995).

Included in my definition of racist violence is the violence against people and/or properties because of their real or alleged religious origin. For this reason, anti-semitic violence is included in the concept of racist violence. I am aware of the debates about the relationship between racism and anti-semitism in general (see e.g. Banton, 1992; Miles, 1994b), and between racist and anti-semitic violence in particular. Without going into detail, in this volume I refer to a concept of racisms, one of which is anti-semitism (Cohen, 1988). Therefore, anti-semitic violence is perceived here as a specific kind of racist violence partly because of the similar (not fully the same) mechanisms, perceptions and motives at work, and because the real or alleged membership of victimised Jewish minority communities in the three countries constitutes the key element of categorisation, and in turn of their victimisation.

As to whether victims are selected on the grounds mentioned is an everlasting aspect of debate concerning racist violence. Often a distinction is made between the perception of the victims and the (proven) motives of the perpetrator. I consider violence to be racist when these two distinct factors or circumstantial elements indicate a racist nature to the violence. This definition allows for compounded motives, and does not require perpetrators to have elaborated racist ideologies, and it does not require victims to perceive the violence as racist.

To perceive only those incidents as racist in which the perpetrator(s) support an 'openly' racist ideology, and turn out to be member(s) of a Nazi or racist organisation, is too limited. A vast majority of racist incidents are perpetrated by people not affiliated to any racist organisation, and without clear, elaborated (political/ideological) racist frameworks of thought. These incidents are racist, however, because the victim(s) are attacked because of the colour of their skin, or because of their real or alleged nationality, religion or culture, or because the attacked properties were perceived as symbolising these. Besides, the perpetrators of the vast majority of reported racist incidents are never traced. This would lead to a situation in which a majority of instances of racist violence had to be left out of consideration because real or alleged motives simply cannot be known.

I am aware of the debates about the difficult aspect of defining racist violence. However, the main subject of this study is whether or not, and if so how, state authorities perceive particular violence to be racist violence and how this category is then defined and socially constructed. My main focus is directed at the recognition by state authorities of the phenomenon and their resulting actions, not in registering individual incidents, or determining whether individual incidents are racist.

To sum up, racist violence is defined in this study as *the (threat of) violence in which victims are 'selected'*[4] *not in their capacities as individuals, but as representatives of imagined minority communities based on phenotypical characteristics, and/or religious, national or cultural origin.*

Violence itself is also the subject of much debate and study. This is not the place to discuss these debates, but violence in this study is understood as intentionally causing physical or mental damage to people directly or indirectly. This notion of violence also includes indirect violence by harassment, by threats of such violence or by violent attacks on specific buildings, places of worship, and so on, which are perceived by perpetrator and/or victims as major elements of their personal or community identity. The phenomenon of racist violence is often understood as a phenomenon of separate incidents. The description by Bowling (1993a; see also Virdee, 1995) of racist violence as a process, both in the sense of involving several linked incidents, as well as in the sense of having a social, political and ideological context, is fully taken in the understanding and definition of violence used in this study.

The lists of reported racist incidents in Britain, France and the Netherlands show that all three nation-states are confronted with this phenomenon – albeit to a different extent. All three nation-states include people who are regarded as members of imagined minority communities based on phenotypical characteristics, religion, cultural or national origin different to the imagined majority community. From a perspective of national legislation, as well as of human rights, these people have the right of residence in these three countries. Therefore, the only logical consequence of full recognition of this perception and definition of racist violence is that state responses to this violence indicate the view that the victimised groups constitute an integral part of society, and that these responses include measures directed against perpetrators, as well as against circumstances in which this violence is perceived to flourish. However, it turns out that for the state this is just one possible response. To these possible responses we shall now turn.

To study state responses

State responses to racist violence

Racist violence has increasingly surfaced all over Europe, but has not followed the same course everywhere. As mentioned before, state responses to racist violence differ in each country and at each moment of time. Specific historical circumstances and discourses of each of the countries involved can not be ignored. Therefore, the preconditions and restrictions of an international comparative analysis must be kept in mind when state responses to racist violence are compared and analysed.

The main focus of this study is directed towards the role of state authorities in relation to racist violence. As mentioned before, state responses to racist violence in the three countries studied were different in time and content. To analyse these responses, the descriptions are structured by means of a model of state responses to racist violence, which is constructed with the help of the so-called political agenda approach (van der Eijk and Kok, 1975; Cobb and Elder, 1983; Cobb, Ross and Ross, 1976; Benyon, 1987b; van der Heijden, 1990; Studlar and Layton-Henry, 1990; Hisschemöller, 1993). This approach – in all its diversity (see e.g. Studlar and Layton-Henry, 1990 for a short overview) – is directed at the processes through which (political) issues are transformed into issues on the formal political agenda, and how these are dealt with once they reach this agenda. In the literature concerning this approach, attention is drawn to the role in these processes played by internal actors (the elitist approach) as well as that by external actors (the pluralist approach). In this study, the role of both will be examined in relation to the processes which either brought or failed to bring racist violence as an issue on to the formal political agenda.

In the idealised process of entering the formal political agenda,[5] four stages are distinguished (Cobb, Ross and Ross, 1976: 127–8): initiation, specification, expansion and entrance of the issue. With these four stages in mind, four phases have been distinguished here in which a problem or topic can develop from an individual problem to a political issue on the formal agenda.

From individual to political issue

'Social problems are only then problematic, when (groups of) people perceive and define them as such' (Brants and Brants, 1991: 23). An individual may experience racist violence, but the occurrence of the violence by itself does not necessarily have to be perceived in this fashion.

Even if a certain group of people shares the same experiences, racist violence does not have to present a social problem in mainstream perceptions. Whether it does or does not depends, among other things, on the position of the group(s) experiencing the problem within the power relations of society. The power position is important also with regard to the perceived causes of the violence. This position is crucial in relation to the success or failure of people striving for (or preventing) the acknowledgement that a phenomenon constitutes a social problem, and to attract public and political attention necessary for this acknowledgement.

Perceptions of the need to solve a specific social problem may be transformed into political demands (i.e. specification), and the problem may become a political issue (van der Eijk and Kok, 1975: 282–3). Often the actual transformation into a political issue coincides with an event, which leads people to develop initiatives to attract broader media and, as a result, public attention on the local, national or even international level (i.e. expansion). Usually these events are considered shocking. In the case of racist violence such events are incendiary attacks, desecration of graves and places of worship, riots and assassinations. Such events might be defined as accelerators within the social construction process (Beetstra *et al.*, 1994: 240).

In relation to racist violence, examples are the discussions about the New Cross fire in London (1981), the public outrage in France after the desecration of Jewish graves in Carpentras (1990), or the vandalising of, and arson attack against, a mosque in Amersfoort, the Netherlands (1992). These events have influenced the perception of racist violence in each individual country, and – at that time – accelerated the process in which racist violence was constructed as a social problem in the respective societies.

The three Turkish women burned to death in an arson attack by neo Nazis in Mölln (1992), and the five people killed in Solingen (1993), as well as the racist sieges in Hoyerswerda (1991) and Rostock (1992), are examples of racist incidents which surely influenced the perceptions of racist violence in European countries other than Germany alone. All the examples mentioned were not the first instances of racist violence in these countries. Nevertheless, they shocked a majority of the populations, even internationally, and they led to more attention for racist violence, albeit temporarily, as well as to national and international state responses to this problem.

Demands to combat and solve a social problem, such as racist violence, may receive attention from decision-makers (internal actors) when large groups of people turn out in support. Of course, not all those who support it need to have experienced the social problem themselves. They may have different motives for their support. Opposition to racist violence may be motivated by the idea that racism in general, and racist violence in particular, threaten the perceived system of values held by society. Various positions are possible here. The legalist position may define racist violence as being in conflict with human rights. The sociological position defines this violence as being damaging to social cohesion or structures. The cultural position is concerned with degrading the level of 'civilisation'. Another reason people might support demands to combat racist violence may be that a certain definition of, and attention for, this violence may bring other comparable phenomena to the forefront, for instance homophobic violence or violence against women. In criminology debates in the USA, this led to the rather muddled concept of hate crime (see Levin and McDevitt, 1993; Hamm, 1994).

Large groups of people may demand action to combat the problem. In many cases, people will consider it to be within the power of state authorities to do something about it and this view may be shared by internal actors, such as politicians or civil servants, for various reasons. This may be due to a common perception of the phenomenon, but it may also be based on the idea that adopting this perception may help them to reach personal or organisational goals which have little to do with the actual problem. Of course, these internal actors may themselves venture the opinion that the state has to take action. Cobb and Elder refer in this case to the inclusion of an issue on *the (popular) public agenda*. This agenda includes 'all issues that are commonly perceived by members of the political community as meriting public attention, and as involving matters within the legitimate jurisdiction of existing governmental authority' (Cobb and Elder, 1983: 85).

The authors mention three conditions for placing an issue on this public agenda. It should meet with the requirements that (1) broad public attention and (2) a shared concern by the public are both present, and (3) that shared opinion agrees that proper action is required by the state, and that this lies within the boundaries of state authority. Issues brought forward by groups of people and individuals within the power centres will need to conform less strictly to these conditions before entering the public agenda (van der Eijk, 1975: 353). However, groups of people with marginal positions of power, such as most groups victimised by racist violence, definitely need to meet these conditions before issues may be brought to the surface by them.

A place on the public agenda, however, is no guarantee for state action. The agenda includes a list of issues which the public and the political community more or less agree require attention and action by decision-makers. Many of these issues are formulated rather abstractly in general terms, like the need to fight unemployment, oppose pollution, improve safety for women and combat discrimination.

Issues receiving serious active attention by decision-makers form the basis of the so-called formal or political (government, institutional, official) agenda. I shall refer to this as *the formal agenda*, because both the formal as well as the public agenda are political. The formal agenda includes specific, concrete issues which are often few in number. Benyon (1987b: 168–9; see also Cobb, Ross and Ross, 1976: 126–38; Studlar, 1986: 159–86) distinguishes three ways in which an issue may be placed on this formal agenda. The first two refer to initiatives by internal actors. An internal actor may initiate proceedings to have an issue put on this agenda immediately (i.e. the inside initiative model). This may be motivated by the belief that a particular situation is getting out of hand. Sometimes the opposite may occur: an explicit intention to keep it from the public agenda in order to prevent the problem from getting even worse – for instance to avert a general panic. This internal initiative may involve a form of legislation, for instance the introduction of a Bill, or piece of legislation. Initiatives by internal actors may also be carried out to arouse public attention in order to get the issue on the public agenda to mobilise support for the implementation of their policies (the mobilisation model).

Thirdly, external actors may initiate activities to put an issue on to the formal agenda (the outside initiative model). Examples of this might be organising mass demonstrations, publishing documents, and various other ways of attracting public attention and building up pressure. When an issue is finally placed on to the formal agenda, the state may implement measures intended to solve the problem.

The role of the media and of academic social studies is of unequivocal importance. In relation to racist violence (law and order), the same is also true of the police, the judiciary and legal professions. In addition to their contribution to raising general consciousness about specific phenomena, and bringing the issue to the surface, their role is important in relation to the way a phenomenon is perceived and defined and its 'topicality'. However, they may also play an important role in hindering or preventing a phenomenon from being perceived as a social problem or as a political issue.

This theoretical process or these ideal-type phases, as mentioned, do not depict the route that all social phenomena follow before they reach the formal agenda. Not all issues on the formal agenda go through all the phases identified. This is reflected in the three models mentioned according to which a position on the formal agenda may be achieved, that is, the inside initiative, the mobilisation and the outside initiative models. Some of the issues are put on to the formal agenda directly by internal actors and/or in the course of certain events. Nor will all phenomena reach the formal agenda in the end. A phenomenon may often enter a certain phase, and then disappear from public view.

The process described here is usually not a continuous process. An issue may reach the formal agenda, action may be taken, and the issue may disappear from the agenda, only to re-occur at a later time. This may be the case when action taken by the state does not achieve the results expected and demanded by the relevant audience. This may be due to differences in problem definitions between initiating actors and official decision-makers.

In the historical accounts of responses to racist violence in the three countries, it is obvious that processes through which racist violence reached the formal agenda occurred at different times. In other words, the distinguished phases do not occur at the same time in Britain, France and the Netherlands. However, the distinction of the four phases itself enables us to study responses by state authorities for each of the four phases – whether or not these have occurred at the same historical moment. By means of this political agenda approach, a model is developed (see also Witte, 1993a; 1994a) of possible state responses to racist violence in each of these four phases. With the help of this model, comparison and analysis of state responses in each phase in three countries are made possible.

The main subject of this study consists of state responses to racist violence in Britain, France and the Netherlands, and the ways in which these responses developed. It should be noted that this study does not have the intention of testing the political agenda approach. This approach has merely been used to set up a model of state responses in order to structure the descriptions of these responses in three countries over a period of time, as well as to make possible a comparison of these responses.

A model of state responses

In analysing the ways in which phenomena (may) reach the formal agenda, four phases of racist violence can be distinguished:

A   racist violence as an individual problem
B   racist violence as a social problem
C   racist violence on the public agenda
D   racist violence on the formal agenda

Figure 1 is derived from the earlier mentioned process of political agenda-building, and sums up the different types of state responses to racist violence in the different phases.

Phase A: racist violence as an individual problem

In the first phase, in which racist violence constitutes an individual problem, the main focus for state responses has to be directed at the local situation. A distinction in state responses may occur with respect to the question of whether the racist nature of an incident has been recognised – implicitly or explicitly. This recognition does not have to be expressed explicitly by state authorities, sometimes it can be deduced

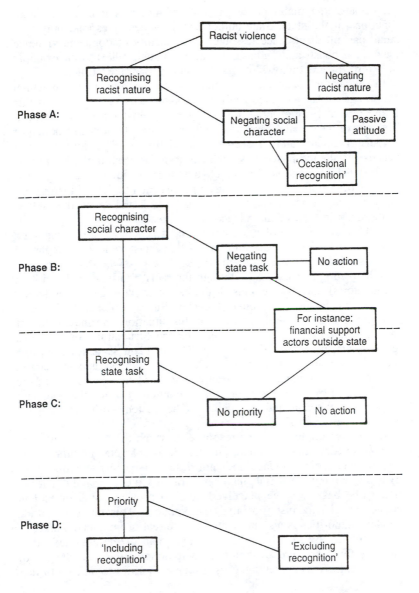

Figure 1.1 **Different types of state responses in the four phases of the idealised process of racist violence 'on its way' to the formal agenda.**[6]

only from a lack of further practical action.

There are many examples in which the violent character of a racist incident is the only element to which state authorities respond. The racist nature of these incidents is totally ignored. However, it would be naive to say that state authorities will always respond to a violent act because the maintenance of law and order is one of the main functions of the state. State authorities, in general, respond only to a small part of all violence in society. The history of domestic violence (see e.g. Dobash and Dobash, 1992; Sheptycki, 1993) is an example of a form of violence which was neglected for a long time.

In relation to racist violence, many examples are known in which action against the violence itself is not assured. An illustration of this is the refusal by the police on occasion to register a racist incident. There have been many cases in which the police did not take notice of a racist incident, and prosecuted the victim who made the report because of alleged provocative behaviour or for wasting police time. A third series of examples in which the racist incident was neglected consists of cases in which victimised people tried to defend themselves against what they believed to be a racist attack and found themselves in the dock instead of the alleged racist attackers.

If the racist nature of a violent incident is recognised in the state response, then the next question is whether racist violence is regarded as constituting a social problem. If not, two possible state responses may be distinguished. First, although the racist motives of the violent perpetrator(s) may be recognised, the case may be regarded as an act with an incidental, occasional character. Racist violence as a social problem is then explicitly denied. In this situation one may speak of the '*occasional recognition*' of racist violence. Structural state measures are not considered to be necessary. The incident is handled by the judicial machinery without further state action. This 'occasional recognition' of racist violence is often experienced when racist motives are clearly stated by the perpetrator(s) in a situation in which the dominant discourse of the state and society denies the existence of racist violence as a social problem.

Another example of a state response in which the racist nature of a specific incident is not denied, but the social character is, reflects the opinion that racist violence does not deserve (special) attention. Motives for denying the social character of racist violence may be diverse. It may be based on the perceived need to prevent panic or violent counter-attacks against (potential) perpetrators. This passive attitude by state authorities is also motivated by the real or imagined danger of over-exposure by massive media publicity, and of the assumed influence of this exposure on potential perpetrators (e.g. the danger of copy-catting). This perception causes state authorities to take no further action.

Phase B: racist violence as a social problem

When different groups in society perceive racist violence as constituting a social problem, state action does not automatically follow. Due to the marginal position of most victimised groups, the attention of the public at large, and a widely shared public concern that state action is taken, are essential (Cobb and Elder, 1983: 85). This may be achieved by activities designed to attract public attention, and by formulating demands. Public awareness and pressure on state authorities in favour of these demands may be increased by organising demonstrations, publishing reports, exerting direct influence on decision-makers, and so on.

Of course, this does not mean that racist violence is placed on the public, or even the formal, agenda after every demonstration. Often demonstrations and other activities receive very little (media) attention; if they do, their importance is often trivialised. Sometimes, these activities do attract a lot of attention, only to be portrayed as a danger in themselves with effects contrary to those intended. This seems to be the case especially when state authorities, and for instance the mainstream media and the public, disagree with the demands of the activists. Small disturbances during these activities may even be enough to criminalise the activists, and to depoliticise and trivialise their demands. Examples in the following chapters will include demonstrations in which the demonstrators, partly as a result of over-policing, were perceived as constituting the main problem, instead of the issues of racism or racist violence against which they were demonstrating.

Registering racist incidents, publishing criticism of the (lack of) responses to incidents, and publishing reports are other ways of increasing pressure and drawing attention to racist violence. Sometimes this increase in attention and pressure is realised by internal actors, such as politicians and civil servants. All of these activities may contribute to a perception of racist violence as a social problem in local or national society.

In a situation in which the specific nature and the social character of the phenomenon of racist violence are recognised, state action seems to be inevitable. Counteracting the racist nature of this violence, however, may be regarded as a task outside the legitimate boundaries of the state authority and as a consequence they may reject further action. For the same reason, state authorities may support external actors in propagating anti-racist activities. Examples of this might be donating financial support to organisations for potential victims, anti-racism organisations, and institutions concerning cross-cultural education.

Phase C: racist violence on the public agenda

If racist violence is recognised as a social problem which needs to be dealt with by the state, it has entered the public agenda. There may however be a number of reasons for the state deciding not to give priority to the fight against racist violence.

State authorities may refer to other issues which, implicitly or explicitly, are regarded as deserving higher priority – for instance unemployment, housing conditions, policing and community relations. On the other hand, state authorities may argue that combating racist violence is merely a matter of being watchful. For the time being, no further state measures are implemented, nor is any other action taken by the state.

Another possible response by state authorities consists of setting up a special inquiry. Often this type of state response is a policy aimed at gaining time to avert panic and anger – whether intentional or unintentional. Whether racist violence will then be put on the formal agenda, and whether concrete state action will follow, remains uncertain. The issue may eventually disappear from the public agenda without ever reaching the formal agenda.

Phase D: racist violence on the formal agenda

Once racist violence is regarded as constituting a social problem to which priority is given, and which needs to be dealt with by the state, the issue of racist violence constitutes a topic on the formal agenda. Racist violence in this phase constitutes an issue of active and serious state action.

Again, two types of state responses can be distinguished here: the '*including recognition*' and the '*excluding recognition*' of racist violence by state authorities. The terminology, 'including recognition' versus 'excluding recognition', refers to the position in society of those groups who are potentially victimised by this violence as indicated (either implicitly or explicitly) by the state response.

State responses to racist violence may indicate the view that these victimised groups constitute an integral part of society (inclusion). State actions, whether these are symbolic or concrete policies and measures, will therefore be directed against (potential) perpetrators of racist violence, as well as against circumstances in which this violence is perceived to flourish. In this case, we may speak of the 'including recognition' of racist violence by state authorities. An example of the 'including recognition' is the implementation or improvement of legislation under which perpetrators can be prosecuted on the basis of the racist nature of their violence. Other examples include state activities designed to prevent demonstrations by racist organisations or firm statements against the expression of racist views. The latter show that the 'including recognition' does not by definition have to lead to legislative action.

However, state responses to racist violence may also indicate the view that the victimised groups are (or should be) isolated, (partly) outside society or separate from the imagined community (exclusion). Causes of the existence of racist violence are perceived to be due to the presence of victimised minorities, the increasing influx of them, to their alleged behaviour, and so on. In these instances, we may speak of the 'excluding recognition' of racist violence. State action to combat racist violence, here, will be directed against the (increasing) presence of the victimised groups.

An example of the 'excluding recognition' of racist violence is the tightening up of asylum policies in the immediate aftermath of racist attacks on asylum centres. Another example is when politicians express their understanding of racist behaviour by people who are assumed to be pressured by inner-city problems, like unemployment or bad housing. These arguments refer to the belief that such 'problems' inevitably lead to violent behaviour directed against specific minority groups who are perceived to be the cause of these problems, and this position is then implicitly recognised by concrete measures or statements.

Examples of both types of state responses will be reported in Chapters 2–4 concerning the state responses to racist violence in Britain, France and the Netherlands. The model constructed here makes it possible to compare state responses to racist violence in different nation-states over a period of time, and bearing the limitations of an international comparative analysis in mind, to analyse three main areas of study:

1 What are the similarities and similar developments in state responses to racist violence? Is there a general perception of the problem?
2 What are the differences? Are these specific national responses? How can they be accounted for?
3 Are there trends in the development of state responses in the three countries?

Source material and time period studied

Racist violence has been the subject of research in Britain since the late 1970s, while this has hardly been the case in France and the Netherlands. This situation has at least two consequences for this study: (1) lack of sources limit the researchability of the subject, and (2) the availability of sources itself reflects state responses in these three countries.

In studying the British situation on racist violence in general, and the state responses to this violence in particular, a vast majority of the sources used include earlier studies and literature. The insights and points of view presented by these studies and literature constitute a significant part of the description of the state responses to racist violence in Britain in this study. Of course, the interpretation and presentation of this literature in the context of this study remains my own responsibility.

For France and the Netherlands very little secondary material exists, thus insights and points of view have to be extracted from newspaper articles and a few background articles. The limitations connected with the use of news items are due to the fact that often racist violence receives only temporary media attention. Because of certain events which attracted national media attention, waves of attention to racist violence are visible in both countries. Whether or not these waves of attention coincide in fact with real waves of racist violence remains a matter of empirical study. Present knowledge about racist violence in these two countries is very scarce and fragmented. This makes it more difficult, but not impossible, to study and analyse state responses to racist violence in these two countries in comparison to Britain.

The main sources of information originate from the three countries (see list of references). In one or two cases concerning the description of certain facts of actual events in France, newspaper articles are used as they appeared in the Dutch press. To describe and analyse state responses and implicit discourses, French as well as British and Dutch references and other literature have been used.

In France and the Netherlands, and to a much lesser degree Britain, racist violence is not yet a major issue for research. Racism, discrimination and extreme-right politics and ideologies are specific subjects within sociology and political science, and much academic research is carried out in this respect. Racist violence would also make a perfect subject for criminology, but surprisingly little research seems to have been done here.

On an international level, racist violence is hardly studied. Nationally, some countries have published a number of studies, especially in Britain and Germany. However, most research in this field is limited to specific case studies of one incident or studies into a specific aspect of racist violence, for instance the response of the police. In France and the Netherlands little research into the subject has been carried out.

In this comparative study, state responses to racist violence are described and analysed for the period between 1945 and 1994. The starting date does not imply that this kind of violence did not occur before 1945. In fact, the history of racist violence in general, and in the three countries involved in particular, shows examples of much earlier violence (see e.g. Lucassen and Penninx, 1985; Fryer, 1991; Hiro, 1992; Witte, 1992; Lloyd, 1993). However, the end of the Second World War, as well as international socioeconomic and political processes since then, have had a major influence on the developments and expressions of racist violence, and the state responses to this violence, which justify starting this study in 1945. The time period studied ends in 1994, the year in which – on the initiative of French President Mitterrand and German *Bundeskansler* Kohl – European government leaders decided to set up a European Advisory Commission (see p. 1). This initiative was one of several actions by European political authorities to discuss and study measures against racist violence on the European level in the early 1990s (see Ford, 1990; Oakley, 1992; Brundtland, 1993).

Initiatives on the European political level are not included in this study. First of all, this study deals with state responses in three individual nation-states, and not with cross-national initiatives. However, more important is that the recent European initiatives predominantly include exchanges of national perspectives, information and measures. These European initiatives have not reached the point of a concrete European action plan to combat racist violence. In the present stage of this international political process, a comparative analysis of state responses and measures in three individual European countries – as the present one – may be of use. This study is the first of its kind, and it presents developments and changes within state responses to a phenomenon increasingly prominent all around Europe. My aim and the specific nature of this study consists of describing and analysing the kinds of state responses themselves, as well as the influences of broader political, popular and ideological contexts on the phenomenon of racist violence. First, I shall describe the case studies concerning Britain, France and the Netherlands. The description of each country will be presented over different periods of time. These periods are distinguished because of different key elements in the responses, and in the political, ideological and public discourses that prevail. In Chapter 5, I shall portray the similarities, differences and trends in state responses to racist violence, and compare and analyse the findings with reference to the ideological, political and socioeconomic contexts of the three countries.

Notes

1 *de Volkskrant*, 27 June 1994.
2 All quotations originally in Dutch or French presented in this study have been translated by the author.
3 Due to the construction element of the notion of 'race', both this and the notion of 'race relations' will be placed in inverted commas throughout the text (see Miles, 1989).
4 The term 'selected' is placed in inverted commas, because this 'selection process' does not have to include, nor to imply, a process of firm and long-lasting consideration, but may be 'spontaneous' and without clear structures (see Witte, 1994b).
5 'Idealised' refers here to an ideal type used in its social science sense, meaning 'theoretically pure form', without any positive or negative valuation.
6 This figure is established by T & A Typesetting Services, and first published in T. Björgo and R. Witte (1993) *Racist Violence in Europe* (p. 142), and used here by kind permission of Macmillan Publishers, Basingstoke.

CHAPTER 2

State responses to racist violence in Britain

Introduction

The frequency of such [racist] attacks, often of a particularly insidious nature, and the depth of feeling and concern which they generate in the ethnic minority communities, are a matter of fact and not of opinion.

(Home Office, 1981: 35)

Statements like these have contributed to a common perception that the 1981 report by the Home Office, *Racial Attacks*, constitutes the first official recognition of racist violence by the British state. In his foreword, Home Secretary Whitelaw states that 'racially motivated attacks, particularly on Asians, are more common than we supposed; and there are indications that they may be on the increase' (Home Office, 1981: iii). Although the Home Secretary and the report talk about racially motivated attacks (i.e. racial violence), these predominantly and explicitly include racist violence as defined in Chapter 1.

While the 1981 report constituted an important stage in the British history of state responses to racist violence, it did not represent the first and only instance in which violence against groups or individuals or their property due to their real or alleged membership in imagined minority communities based on phenotypical characteristics, or religious, national or cultural origin, formed a topic on the British formal agenda. Racist violence, as well as both local and national responses to it, have a long history in British society. In actual fact, the 1981 report by the Home Office was not the first occasion on which British state authorities officially recognised racist violence as a serious problem – a problem which had to be confronted by state action. The novelty of the 1981 report was the fact that it constituted the first example of the 'including recognition' of racist violence by the British national state.

Despite all the criticism it received, there is no denying that the 1981 report and the proposed policy measures represented a concerted attempt to deal with the upsurge of racist violence and the circumstances in which this violence was believed to be flourishing.

In the British history of state responses to racist violence since 1945, four periods may be distinguished: the 1950s to the early 1960s; the 1960s; the 1970s; and the 1980s till early 1990s. These periods are defined in accordance with changing key features of state responses to racist violence. Each period, in relation to its specific key feature, is discussed and analysed separately in this chapter. These four periods are not mutually exclusive because at the end of each period trends and signals are noticeable which become apparent in the next period. Therefore, the boundaries of these periods are not strictly given by a certain year. Along with these four periods, the year 1981 is discussed separately, elaborating on the significance of and causes for the 1981 report by the Home Office.

The 1950s to the early 1960s: 'the problem is not white racism, but black presence'

In 1958, several British cities were confronted with riots. These events were caused by anti-black attacks on restaurants, hostels and individuals.[1] During the eighteen months before the disorders, there was a series of attacks on individual black people on the streets of Nottingham, and such attacks were reported to be increasing in number (Fryer, 1991: 377). These racist incidents 'climaxed in the major rioting in August and September 1958 in Nottingham and Notting Hill' (Kettle and Hodges, 1982: 43).

The 1958 riots constituted the event which brought racist violence to public attention and to the formal agenda. In the terminology of agenda setting, they marked the expansion of the issue as well. The violence was recognised as directed towards people, who were being victimised due to their alleged membership in imagined minority communities based on phenotypical characteristics, or religious, national or cultural origin. And the violence was recognised as constituting a major social problem which had to be dealt with by the state.

The riots, however, were not regarded nor responded to as instances of racist violence, but as 'the evidence of the negative and inevitable consequences of black immigration and settlement' (Cook, 1993: 140). Emphasis needs to be put on the fact that this migration and settlement of black communities and the people within them who were being victimised, all held British nationality and citizenship. In short, the responses to this violence were directed against the increasing presence of the victimised British minority communities. This was in itself an implicit recognition of the fact that the violence was perceived to be based on racist motives.

The first period may, therefore, be characterised by the initial appearance of racist violence on the public (phase C) and formal agenda (phase D) in Britain. At the end of this period, the main state responses to this violence were directed towards the people regarded as being victimised. The key feature of this period may be regarded as the 'excluding recognition' of racist violence by the state, and this was translated into policy measures of migration control and restrictions in the early 1960s. The direction of these state responses was fully in line with the mainstream political discourse which had been established in 1945.

The early post-war years

In the first post-war decade, economic, social and foreign affairs constituted the main topics on the British formal agenda. Racist violence was not considered an issue at all. In the autumn of 1947, anti-semitic violence reached a climax with riots against Jews in major British towns, violence that lasted several nights. This violence was explained by the British–Jewish conflict in Palestine and the consequent intensification of anti-semitism in Britain. Responses seemed to have been dominated by the assumption that attention would only cause anti-semitism to spread further (Kushner, 1994: 223).

However, there was racist violence in these years and it was directed mainly against British subjects who had migrated from former colonies. Responses by state authorities to the violence were directed mainly towards the migration of potential victims to Britain. Although this migration was proportionately small and seemed to be of little importance to the formal agenda, these years definitely cannot be described as a period of *laissez-faire*, but rather of internal debate within state institutions about, and attention in public discussion to, the effective influence of migration on British society.

This concerned not only the supposed biological or social characteristics of black people, but also what had been called the racial character of the British people and their national identity (Solomos, 1989: 47). The arrival and settlement in Britain of these groups of British subjects from former colonies were perceived as threats to the racial character and identity of the British people. Therefore, popular discussions and debates within (closed) Cabinet chambers increasingly showed a racialisation of the migration issue (Layton-Henry, 1992: 28–36).

Every now and then, media reports about the arrival of immigrants or about tension and disturbances in British cities aroused public attention. Sometimes, this led to discussions in the media and among the public about the alleged impact of immigration from former colonies on housing, the welfare state, crime and other existing social problems. Such a situation occurred, for instance, upon the arrival of 492 Jamaicans on the *Empire Windrush* on 22 June 1948, and of 180 West Indians on the *Orbita* in October that same year in Liverpool (see Fryer, 1991: 372).

There was a disproportionate emphasis on the publicity and discussions that followed these arrivals compared to the attention given to the far larger immigration from Ireland, the 'white' Commonwealth and European countries, although hostile responses towards European workers were also seen (see Kay and Miles, 1993).

[The] relatively liberal attitude towards the arrival of European workers contrasted sharply with the fears expressed about the social and racial problems which were assumed to be related to the arrival of coloured workers who are British subjects. Both the Labour government of 1945–51 and the Conservative governments throughout the 1950s considered various ways of stopping

or reducing the number of black migrants arriving and settling in Britain.
(Solomos, 1989: 45)

After the Second World War, hostilities against black migrants in particular frequently erupted. On the one hand, this was evident in racist practices in the housing and labour markets; on the other, in violent actions – whether or not overtly racist and whether or not carried out by racist groups or gangs. Primarily, responses at the national state level to major manifestations of racist violence were directed towards the assumed threat from the increasing presence of black migrants. Violent incidents were interpreted primarily within the context of social and political problems which were assumed to be caused by the arrival of 'coloured' immigrants and by the doubtful capability of the host society to absorb and integrate immigrants of 'an alien race and religion', as stated by the Royal Commission on Population (Layton-Henry, 1984: 22).

The Commission on Population was well aware of the fact that the settlement of black immigrants in Britain could and would come up against racist attitudes and behaviour. Violent expressions of this racism were perceived and responded to within this context. Thus, the racist nature of incidents did not form the core of attention and responses, but the fearfully expected, destabilising effects for British society in general, as well as the maintenance of law and order in particular.

Rioting 1948–49

One of the early major post-war manifestations of racist violence consisted of anti-black riots in Liverpool in August 1948. The National Union of Seamen had been trying to keep black seamen from working on British ships. Liverpool and other British ports were declared to be no-go areas for black sailors (Fryer, 1991: 367). The rioting started when 200–300 white men attacked an Indian restaurant, and one day later, a crowd of 2,000 attacked a hostel for black seamen. The immediate local state response, by the police, consisted of forcing their way into the besieged hostel and arresting some of those defending it (Fryer, 1991: 368).

The 1948 example showed a response which proved to be unexceptional in the years to come, including the arrest of the attacked or removing them from the scene without any clear action taken against the attackers. In only a few cases were attackers arrested, but racist motives never played a role in the judicial prosecution. 'Present in this overture were all the themes that the next generation of black people in Britain were to know so well in their daily relations with the police' (Fryer, 1991: 371).

Other manifestations occurred in 1949. In June, fights broke out between white and black citizens in Deptford, London, where a hostel of migrants was attacked by a white mob. This mob finally attacked the police, who tried to set up a cordon around the hostel under attack (Hiro, 1992: 38). During that same summer, on 6–8 August, a series of attacks occurred against an industrial hostel housing Indian workers near Birmingham (Layton-Henry, 1984: 111).

Cabinet discussions

Responses by national authorities to major racist events underlined and strengthened the increasingly dominant opinion that the presence of the victimised minority communities caused the violence. Reports of Cabinet discussions expressed the danger of the confrontation of specific groups of migrants with explicit racist hostility (Layton-Henry, 1992: 30–6), and of creating a minority which was regarded as being non assimilative.

In May 1950, the Secretary of State for the Colonies stated that 'coloured migration was seen as causing problems in the areas of accommodation, employment, and law and order' (Layton-Henry, 1984: 21). Because of the closed, hidden character of the discussions, one might conclude that the authorities at central state institutions were trying to keep the issue off the public agenda (Layton-Henry, 1992: 71) and therefore we might speak of attempts to put the topic of migration on the hidden formal agenda in close relation to racist violence.

Although racist violence was regarded in retrospect, by some, as constituting a regular part of life in Britain in the early 1950s (Sivanandan, 1987: 7; Gordon, 1990: 1), the racist nature of the violence was, then, completely neglected and was described as being racial rather than racist, suggesting that different 'races' were equally involved. Therefore, anti-racist policies were not taken into consideration in the 1950s. In political and public discourses, a link was established between threats to law and order and the presence of specific groups of ('coloured') immigrants.

Increasingly, discussions and decisions did relate to the migration issue. In 1951, however, official statements concluded that migration control was not necessary. This was justified by reference to the small scale of the migration in question, namely that from former colonies. However, the path for future policy making with respect to this migration, and indirectly to racist violence, had been laid. This was obvious when this specific type of migration to Britain did increase after 1952.[2]

The Conservative government was beginning to consider the possible consequences of this migration on the structure of British society. These assumed consequences were closely linked with perceived prospects about 'race riots', colour-bar incidents and the emergence of a pattern of politics cutting across the 'ordinary' political issues (Pilkington, 1988: 70). In 1953, the Cabinet present this perception explicitly:

How far trouble between white and black people can be avoided in future if the coloured community continues to increase is a matter of speculation.

Against this background the question whether it would be desirable to legislate to restrict the right of British subjects to enter the United Kingdom has to be considered.[3]

This statement explicitly emphasised the dominant perception that although they were British subjects, their perceived different 'racial character' constituted the main reason for expected problems. This resolves clearly too from the fact that the entry of a mere 3,000 (black) people from the colonies was of such concern whereas the entry of 60,000 post-war Irish immigrants was much less so (Layton-Henry, 1992: 33).

Economic motivation

Migration control increasingly was regarded as the solution to supposed threats to law and order. A mild recession in the mid-1950s contributed to increasing pressure for migration restrictions. 'Had this pressure been mainly politically motivated before, now the economy provided an excuse for politics' (Sivanandan, 1987: 9). This pressure was established by actors outside as well as within state institutions. At their annual conference in 1955, the Transport and General Workers' Union (TGWU) accepted a resolution in favour of legislative migration control as well as an increase in capital investments in the West Indies to reduce the need for migration (Pilkington, 1988: 69). This was an example of efforts by external actors (i.e. those outside the state) to bring the migration issue on to the public and formal agenda and show the direction in which solutions could be found (outside initiative).

An example of internal actors seeking to achieve the inclusion of this issue on these agendas is provided by the work of the Conservative MP Cyril Osbourne, one of the initiators of an increasingly influential anti-migration campaign. This campaign was established on three levels: first, by directing parliamentary questions at the government about alleged diseases in, and crime by, black communities; second, by campaigning within the Conservative Party to increase support for migration restrictions; and third, by activities organised to attract maximum media attention to this campaign (Layton-Henry, 1984: 31–2). These activities represent a case of the mobilisation model of agenda building (see Chapter 1).

This national debate, and the increasing pressure in favour of migration control, were highly relevant to racist violence and responses to this violence. They helped to shape an environment in which violent attacks against specific minority communities occurred and determined the content of future state responses to these attacks.

Local situation and local responses

Public responses to the arrival of migrants from former colonies were more or less limited to those cities and areas in which these migrants settled, such as London, the main cities in the Midlands, and the North of England. Some local union groups pleaded for restrictions and even for a total ban on migration. A majority of the migrants frequently met hostility to their presence in the neighbourhoods in which they were more or less forced to settle down, due to socioeconomic conditions. In 1954, serious clashes occurred in Camden Town, London, where migrants were attacked for two days by a white mob using bottles and axes who finally threw a petrol bomb into the house of a West Indian (Sivanandan, 1987: 9; Fryer, 1991: 38).

The mid-1950s saw the emergence of a youth sub-culture movement which contributed greatly to the feelings of insecurity among minority communities, the so-called Teddy Boys. Many of these white youths, dressed in Edwardian style, often acted very violently, especially towards individual black people. At the weekend in particular, gangs of Teddy Boys would cruise the streets looking for West Indians, Africans and Asians. Despite the increasing occurrence and severity of these attacks, the police in general took little notice (Fryer, 1991: 378).

The decline and deprivation of inner cities increasingly received public, media and political attention during the second half of the 1950s, with the media frequently linking the decline to the presence of certain minority communities. Solomos explained the development of this media coverage along two lines.

Firstly, there were articles reporting on the arrival of groups of immigrants, on specific localities, and on confrontations between blacks and whites. Second, feature articles were written which considered the prospects for 'race relations' and conflicts more generally within British society.

(Solomos, 1988: 57)

The media played a significant role in establishing a link between social and economic deprivation and threats to law and order on the one hand, and the presence of black migrant communities on the other. Often this causal connection was established implicitly in newspaper articles, while sometimes statements made this explicitly clear, as in the Sunday newspaper, the *People*, on 25 May 1958, where an article was headed 'For Their Own Sakes Stop Them Now!' The article continued: 'With the greatest possible urgency *The People* now asks the government to put a bar against the free admission of coloured immigrants in Britain. We are not yielding to colour prejudices. But the wave of immigrants rolling all over our shores has now risen to threatening proportions'.[4] The 'threatening proportions' in connection with the headline 'For Their Own Sakes' clearly indicated a threat of racist violence against these specific immigrants. In itself, this could be perceived as an example of the 'excluding recognition' of racist violence by the *People*.

Attempts to introduce anti-discrimination legislation

At the end of the 1950s, the dominant public and political discourse became fixated on the migration issue. In this situation, any attempt to challenge discrimination practices and racism in British society was destined to fail. Every now and then, discrimination attracted the attention of Parliament through initiatives by internal actors. In 1956, Labour MP Fenner Brockway introduced an anti-discrimination Bill with respect to dance halls, pubs, and other public places. The Conservative MPs Bell and Braine, however, were successful in preventing the Bill going to a second reading. Until 1964, Labour MP Fenner Brockway made eight similar attempts to introduce anti-discrimination legislation, all of which failed to overcome the Conservative opposition (Layton-Henry, 1984: 123).

The Conservatives especially were not convinced of the need to challenge discriminatory practices by law. Opinions were expressed that anti-discrimination legislation would even encourage, rather than reduce, its occurrence. The Conservatives were afraid, with no evident reason, that such legislation would be very difficult if not impossible to implement, and oversee.

Three different arguments on which these opinions were partly based have been identified (Pilkington, 1988: 48). First of all, there were those who argued that there was no discrimination at all in Britain. Therefore, legislation to exclude something viewed as being non-existent did not make sense. A second line of argument, by those who recognised the existence of discriminatory practices, consisted of the argument that prejudice constituted the basis of these practices, and the best way to combat or prevent this prejudice was assumed to be through educating public opinion, not through legislative measures. A third line of argument stated that anti-discrimination legislation would remove the individual rights of house-owners and employers. The leading opinion here was opposed, by definition, to any state involvement in private conflicts.

The Far Right

In the second half of the 1950s, extreme-rightist groups received increasing support for their anti-migration propaganda, directed at concerns portrayed in the media. One of these groups was the White Defence League with its headquarters in Notting Hill, London, where a large swastika hung from the top of the building, and from which martial music could be heard playing at high volume. Organisations such as these were allowed to express their arguments and propaganda openly. They did not have to fear legal reprisal, partly because the law at that time stated that the offence of defamation could involve the protection only of individuals, rather than groups. In this way, overt verbal and printed abuse of people was legally sanctioned. Although these organisations did perhaps not create racist hatred, they certainly exploited and encouraged it. 'By providing an organised forum and by urging white people to take action, the fascists helped to translate racial hatred from its passive to its active voice – from pub gossip to street violence' (Pilkington, 1988: 98–9).

Immediate responses to the 1958 riots

In the 1950s, debates about the need for (black) migration control became increasingly politicised. Within these debates the view that migration caused inner-city problems was central. The popular and political discussions about migration from the former colonies and the priority of migration on the formal agenda intensified in the aftermath of rioting in 1958. 'By the time of the 1958 riots, . . . the mobilization of opinion in and out of Parliament in favour of controls was well advanced' (Solomos, 1989: 48). This was used by the anti-migration lobby to support demands for banning migration from former colonies and to support their argument that black immigration constituted a threat to law and order and to the English way of life.

There was little response from the majority of politicians during, and in the direct aftermath of, the 1958 riots, partly due to the summer recess. But MPs representing the districts involved in the riots, who already had reputations as supporters of migration restrictions, gave an immediate response. Maurice Edelman, MP for Coventry North, stated in the *Daily Mail* (2 September 1958), that if 'blacks' are to continue being attacked, it will be in their own interest to be kept out of Britain (Pilkington, 1988: 129). Notting Hill (Labour) MP, George Rogers, argued in the *Manchester Guardian* (4 September 1958) that the riots were not caused by Teddy Boy hooligans, but had to be viewed as 'the legitimate reaction of the local community to undesirable sections of the black population. Violence had been provoked by Blacks refusing to adopt the British way of life' (as cited by Pilkington, 1988: 133). Both statements were clear examples of the 'excluding recognition' of racist violence.

Occasionally other opinions were heard, showing the diversity among state authorities. The well-known Labour Party chairman Tom Driberg, argued at the Trades Union Congress (TUC) that prejudice constituted the problem, rather than black skin.[5] However, this line of the 'including recognition' argument was rather rare in those days.

Besides internal actors, responses by external actors were also reported. For example, the violence was condemned by the TUC at its annual conference during the rioting. Another example was the responses of West Indian politicians who visited Britain at the time. And Fascist organisations also sought to exploit the situation – especially in Notting Hill.

Local authorities outside the government responded too. For instance, the Reverend C.W. Harrington, the Vicar of Woodborough and former Minister in the Orange Free State, South Africa, argued that he was opposed to any form of 'racial' discrimination, having seen the consequences of Apartheid. He said, however, that acceptance of immigration control was necessary because Britain was 'over-crowded', although this had to be viewed on the basis of educational or cultural characteristics rather than 'racial' ones. In the *Nottingham Evening News* (25 August 1958) he argued that 'Black people are human beings. They are not animals, although they sometimes behave like it because they have not our cultural or educational background' (as cited by Pilkington, 1988: 111).

Solutions to perceived problems

Four possible solutions were identified which took account of the circumstances in which the 1958 disorders were perceived to have taken place (Miles, 1984). First, there was the supposed solution of the strict maintenance of law and order. The second solution consisted of stricter migration control – or the complete cessation of migration to Britain. As shown, this plea was articulated long before the disorders occurred. The activities of the anti-migration lobby expanded and intensified after the disorders. Of particular importance here is the fact that these activities received a lot of attention.

Integration was the third solution. According to this position, the disorders were caused by ignorance and lack of knowledge, and this problem had to be tackled by mutual understanding. The fourth perceived solution was to combat racism in Britain. Supporters of this solution argued that an explanation for the disorders could not be found among the immigrants, nor in their alleged 'race', but in the images of and attitudes towards them.

These so-called solutions were not articulated and introduced at the same point in time, nor were they all afforded a similar degree of attention by the media and politicians. The migration control solution was dominant, and conditioned all other reactions. This was for two reasons. First, because the demands for migration control were expressed immediately and constituted the first response to which everyone else responded. Secondly, this solution – as shown – cohered with the political and ideological developments within the mainstream political and public discourse at the time.

Concrete national state responses

The dominance of the mainstream discourses was reflected in the judicial procedures against perpetrators of the violent attacks during the 1958 riots. Layton-Henry (1984: 111; 1992: 38–9) argued that harsh punishment, along with 'widespread disapproval of the riots', could be seen as preventing the re-occurrence of these riots. Some reports of court cases, however, showed the nonconformity among state actors because legal attention to the rioters' actions was directed towards their violent methods, rather than to their racist motives. With the separation of the racist and the violent elements of these acts, an image was established in which the first seemed to be tolerable and only the latter was met with condemnation and sanction by the state.

Talking about the motives for his violent behaviour, an arrested man stated that 'we must get rid of those niggers'. The judge responded to this argument saying 'if you have an object at heart like the one you spoke of, you can't try to get it by breaking the law. If you want to get something done, do it by attending public meetings and in other proper ways. Be a man who helps and not a man who hinders' (Pilkington, 1988: 128). The notion that it was possible to express racist views in 'proper ways' and the notion that only the violent methods used during the 1958 riots were illegal, prevailed in the dominant discourses and the atmosphere in Britain at the end of the 1950s.

The Conservative government did not wish to respond over-hastily to this situation, but preferred rather to wait and include all responses in their own considerations. The Labour Party did not reject the 'migration control solution' explicitly before 11 September. The responses, or the lack of them, could be viewed as examples of state responses in which delaying tactics were used to try and avoid panic. These responses, however, implicitly acknowledged the legitimacy of the demands concerning migration restrictions as the solution. But debates and discussions had already started – with or without governmental statements and decisions.

By the time the government and the opposition responded officially, the formal agenda had already largely been set. The dominant political and media responses included interpretations of the events in terms of the 'race/immigration' dualism. The focus on acts of aggression and violence against the West Indian migrants shifted towards the phenotypical characteristics of those who were victimised, and the legitimacy of their presence was questioned (Miles, 1984). The dominance of the mainstream political and public discourses was so overwhelming that the fourth solution mentioned, combating racism in British society, was totally subordinated. In this respect, state responses to racist violence developed in the direction of the 'excluding recognition' of this violence.

The concrete realisation of the 'excluding recognition' consisted of the introduction and implementation of the Commonwealth Immigrants Act. Within the Conservative government, the group supporting restrictions on migration had gained the upper hand and introduced the Bill in 1961. This Bill divided Commonwealth citizens into three groups with the proposed migration restrictions mainly aimed at the group of black migrants. The Bill 'can be seen as the climax of the campaign for the control of black immigration which was launched from both within and outside government during the 1950s' (Solomos, 1989: 52).

The Commonwealth Immigrants Act was of immense importance due to the absolute distinction it made between British citizens in general and those who originated from the Caribbean and the Indian sub-continent and were the victims of racist violence. The latter were denied the right of entry into Britain. This was a clear example of the 'excluding recognition' of racist violence by the state authorities. The 1958 disorders contributed to a climate which enabled politicians to racialise British politics in a new way (Miles, 1984).

The argument for the Bill was based on the supposed limited ability of British society to absorb 'coloured' immigrants. In and outside Parliament, the Bill was considered directly opposed to black migration. At first, the parliamentary debates concerning the Bill included strong opposition by the Labour Party. Within this party, as well as within some sections of the media, the Bill was condemned as a cave-in to racist pressure. Partly due to this opposition, some minor changes were implemented, but there were no fundamental changes. In the end a considerable number of Labour MPs abstained from the final vote due to pressure from their constituencies. As a result, the Commonwealth Immigrants Act was implemented on 1 July 1962.

By the early 1950s, the idea that too many black immigrants constituted a potential problem had already become institutionalised (Solomos, 1988: 33). With the Commonwealth Immigrants Act immigration was racialised (Solomos, 1989: 50), and with its implementation in 1962, racism was institutionalised, legitimised and nationalised (Sivanandan, 1987: 12). The mainstream discourse emphasised that 'the problem was not white racism, but the black presence' (Fryer, 1991: 381). In other words, one might speak of the 'excluding recognition' of racist violence by British state authorities in these years.

Another consequence of the 1958 disorders was an increased feeling of distrust of the British State among minority communities. This situation had its influence on the development of the West Indian identity. In the aftermath of the riots, West Indian organisations were founded, and some joined together, like the West Indian Standing Conference in Greater London. 'From then on, much of the West Indian political energy was channelled into these organisations, and not into the major British political parties' (Hiro, 1992: 41).

Not only did migrants from the former colonies organise themselves as a result of the increased feeling of insecurity, but also the Warsaw Ghetto Memorial Committee was founded by members of the Jewish community alarmed by racism in general, and racist violence in particular. Partly in response to a 'swastika epidemic' in Europe during 1959 and 1960, but also in response to racist violence in Britain against New Commonwealth migrants, the Memorial Committee promoted activities 'to lessen racial tension, to condemn racial discrimination, and to work with others doing likewise'. However, in a climate in which state responses to racist violence were dominated by the 'excluding recognition' of this violence, these were difficult to promote (Kushner, 1994: 250).

The 1960s: racist violence as an individual problem

This second period might be characterised by the fact that racist violence did not constitute a topic on the public or the formal agenda. In 1962, the Commonwealth Immigrants Act was implemented by the Conservative government with the intention of ending the furious debates in and outside British state institutions. The phenomenon of racist violence had played its role by providing proof of the necessity for migration control and disappeared from the formal agenda.

The migration issue, however, did not. And the prevalence of this issue – implicitly as well as explicitly – had its influence on the living conditions of minority communities in Britain, including the situation with respect to racist violence. Responses by state authorities to racist incidents have to be looked for at local levels.

Migration and 'race relations'

In the 1960s, the focus turned to the connection between migration and 'race relations'. Between 1962 and 1965, the Labour Party moved away from its opposition to immigration controls and began to articulate a dual strategy of maintaining and strengthening controls while at the same time promoting the 'integration' of immigrants already settled in Britain (Solomos, 1988: 38). It was here that Labour MP Roy Hattersley made his famous statement: 'Integration without limitation [of migration] is impossible; limitation without integration is indefensible.'[6]

Two main problems were foreseen and perceived as demanding immediate state response: (1) the negative response by a majority of the population towards migrant workers because of the real or alleged competition in housing and labour markets; and (2) the frustration of migrant workers, who felt excluded from equal opportunities in British society by a 'colour bar' in both markets in relation to the process of discrimination practices (Solomos, 1989: 71).

A resulting state response to these two assumed problems included two Race Relations Acts to improve relations in Britain and a second Commonwealth Immigrants Act to implement further restrictions on migration. Labour's intention with this dual strategy was to remove the migration issue from the formal agenda and to achieve a consensus between the two main parties on this matter. This intention led to Labour statements, during the 1964 elections, that the Commonwealth Immigrants Act 1962 should remain in force.

Smethwick

Another event which took place during the 1964 elections was regarded as shocking and strengthened Labour's opinion. In the Smethwick district of Birmingham, the Conservative candidate Peter Griffiths won the election against one of the representatives of the new Labour leadership, Patrick Gordon-Walker, who had been a minister in the previous Shadow Cabinet. The shock was caused by the fact that Griffiths' victory was partly due to an openly anti-immigrant campaign. Gordon-Walker was not known for being a 'liberal' with respect to the migration issue (Tompson, 1988: 66–7). However, his opponent campaigned by using the slogan 'If you want a nigger for a neighbour, vote Labour' (Solomos, 1989: 53–4).

This campaign slogan constituted the first occasion in which racism was openly used in a political campaign and it proved successful. Other anti-immigration candidates also had done well in the elections in Southall and Birmingham. Fenner Brockway, campaigner for anti-discrimination legislation, lost his seat in these elections (Layton-Henry, 1992: 78). The 'race' and migration issues were brought to the centre of the political spectrum and this contributed to a further alienation of minority communities in British society (Hiro, 1992: 44).

Race Relations Act

Having won the overall election (1964), Labour responded to these developments by proposing intensified control of the implementation of the Commonwealth Immigrants Act 1962 and by introducing policy measures to improve the integration of immigrants in Britain, including legislative sanction against discriminatory practices. In November 1965, the Race Relations Act was implemented, its main aim being to achieve a reconciliation in Britain between minority and majority communities. The 1965 Act challenged discriminatory 'colour bars' in public places and the incitement of racial hatred. The housing and labour markets, however, were not included. This absence was criticised both inside and outside Parliament. The only consolation consisted of the classification of the practice of racial discrimination as a criminal offence (Hiro, 1992: 210–11). After parliamentary debates, punitive measures were omitted once the Act was implemented. The irony is that only fifteen cases reached the courts concerning incitement to racial hatred between 1965 and 1969. Five of them involved prosecutions of members of the 'black power' movement, including Michael X (Michael de Freitas), founder of the Racial Adjustment Action Society in 1965 (Fryer, 1991: 383).

A special junior minister was appointed at the Department of Economic Affairs who would be responsible for coordinating the government's policies with respect to integration and 'race relations'. For the same purpose, welfare organisations were set up. However, their work was soon frustrated by the increasing pressure from the government to further migration restrictions including an increasingly negative perception of migrants (Layton-Henry, 1984: 127).

In February 1966, the Race Relations Board was set up as a consequence of the Race Relations Act 1965. One of its tasks consisted of the organisation of local discrimination reporting centres. The Board was soon checked by the limitations of the Act. For instance, the Act prohibited discrimination in certain public places, although a number of other places were excluded from this ban. Also excluded from this Act was discrimination against religious groups, such as Sikhs and Jews.

A White Paper by the Labour government in August 1965 linked further restrictions on migration with policy measures to improve the integration of migrants in Britain. A National Committee for Commonwealth Immigrants was created to coordinate and improve the local activities in favour of tolerance and to combat prejudice. There were, however, few concrete measures to improve daily life within migrant communities, except some support in the field of education. The White Paper obviously perceived immigration, in essence, as a 'race' issue. This was in tune with the dominant perception that an increasing number of black citizens in Britain could be a real or potential source of social problems and conflicts (Solomos, 1989: 72).

For Home Secretary Roy Jenkins the integration side of Labour's dual strategy needed to be emphasised, because of the social tensions and violence which were regarded as increasingly threatening. Jenkins argued that integration should not be viewed as a process of assimilation, but as offering the possibility of equal opportunities in relation to cultural diversity in a mutually tolerant atmosphere. This integration could be successful, according to Jenkins, only with the support of political institutions in solving the social problems of immigrants and of the areas where they were settled.

Measures against racist violence were not included in the Race Relations Act which was directed at the improvement of the life of migrants in Britain. The leading argument was to prevent circumstances which were believed to have led to tensions and violence in the United States, i.e. the inner-city riots of major US cities in 1965. As shown, violence in this dominant political discourse was perceived as 'racial', i.e. between people of different 'races'. Violent behaviour had always been perceived as a characteristic of the lower classes residing in the inner cities, whereas 'fairness' and 'negotiation' were perceived characteristic of the higher, more educated and political classes. Tension and the threat of violence in the inner cities were met by measures to regulate, adjust and improve relations between perceived distinct communities there. In this period, however, racist violence was not a specific topic of the discourse not in measures proposed. Certainly discrimination was such a topic (in phase D), yet its most violent extreme expression was not (and was positioned in phase A).

Changing climate in the late 1960s

In 1967, two reports argued that the level of discrimination was much higher than had been hitherto assumed (Layton-Henry, 1984: 66; Hiro, 1992: 218).[7] According to these reports voluntary reconciliation was not enough to eliminate discrimination, and legislative measures were needed. Home Secretary Jenkins put the case for revision of the Race Relations Act, and in May 1967 the Labour government announced the preparation of new proposals in line with these findings. The political climate at the end of 1967, however, contributed to an increasing emphasis on the migration issue and temporarily lessened the attention given to these revisions.

The political and popular climate was increasingly dominated by 'panic' concerning the possible arrival in Britain of Kenyan Asians, holding British passports. Such an event was perceived and represented in the mass media as a crisis for Britain and British people rather than for the Asians themselves. The *Daily Express* report was headed: 'A Million Chinese Can Arrive Here Next Week If They Want To'.[8] On 1 March 1968, during this 'Kenyan Asian Crisis', the Labour government introduced a new Commonwealth Immigrants Act, regarded as one of the instances in which British policies were racialised with respect to migration and migrant populations (Solomos, 1989: 54). The Act's implementation is also perceived as the logical outcome of Labour's dual strategy and eagerness for consensus. In fact, it was unlikely that the Conservative would have even dared to introduce this far-reaching Act (Layton-Henry, 1984: 69).[9]

It was six months after the introduction of the new Commonwealth Immigrants Act that a new Race Relations Act was implemented. The Race Relations Act 1968 extended the tasks and authorities of the Race Relations Board and prohibited discrimination on the grounds of skin colour, 'race', ethnicity, or national origin in the areas of employment, housing and commercial and other services. The emphasis of the 1968 Act – like the 1965 Act – lay on reconciliation, with legislative means seen as the last solution. The Community Relations Commission (CRC) was created to promote 'harmonious community relations' and to work as an advisory commission to the Home Office. It served as a statutory body to implement the duties and functions which previously had been carried out by the National Committee for Commonwealth Immigrants.

Two goals were set out in both Race Relations Acts (Solomos, 1989: 73): (1) the establishment of special bodies to deal with the social problems of minority communities; and (2) education of the population as a whole with a view to improving 'race relations'. The basic assumption behind these policy targets was the perceived threat of 'racial' conflicts caused by the number of migrants from former colonies. Many were motivated by the fear that Britain might develop a situation of conflict and lawlessness similar to that thought to exist in certain parts of the United States.

The dual strategy of the Labour Party and government was successful in the sense that some state attention and state action were directed against discrimination in British society. Besides the Race Relations Acts mentioned, measures were introduced to extend the degree of influence by the central state with respect to the response of local authorities to 'race' issues. The Local Government Act 1966 and the Local Government Grants (Social Needs) Act 1969 originated in the debates on 'race' and immigration. Yet, these first measures at the local level were merely symbolic rather than national action programmes.

One of the activities of the CRC was to establish a network of local Community Relations Councils. An important point to be made here is that local authorities themselves showed little interest in developing policies in this field during the 1960s. At best, there was some limited support for the local Community Relations Councils (Solomos, 1989: 90–2). It should be noted that participation of local authorities was a precondition for grant aid from the Community Relations Commission (Layton-Henry, 1992: 55).

The Race Relations Acts can be perceived as an important development in relation to the mobilisation model of agenda building because these Acts were an appeal by state authorities (Labour government) for fair and equal treatment. In other words, it was an issue on the formal agenda and thereafter action was taken to mobilise the public (to put it on to the public agenda). The Commonwealth Immigrants Act was a response to a situation resembling that of the outside initiative model of agenda setting (Studlar, 1986: 161–2), mobilising public opinion and gaining entry on to the public agenda in order to place the issue on the formal agenda.

Police and criminalisation

In the dominant discourses, black immigrants and their descendants were perceived as potential sources of social problems and instability. Since the 1950s, the police had been actively involved in establishing this view. Crime and related problems were increasingly represented in 'racial' terms. Solomos (1988) makes clear the dominant view during the 1950s and 1960s that there was a causal connection between the level of concentration of migrant population in certain areas and problems of law and order.

Attention by the state and especially by the police to the alleged connection between 'race' and crime, consequently leading to the criminalisation of black youths, originated and developed during the 1960s. Joseph A. Hunte's report, *Nigger Hunting in England?* (1966) was the first report concerned with the relations between the police and minority communities. Hunte's study was carried out following a spate of anti-black operations by the Brixton police – called 'nigger hunting' by the police themselves. The report examined a series of complaints against the police of attacks and other kinds of misconduct in the first half of the 1960s. One observation in this report referred to an increasing distrust and aversion within minority communities towards the police.

After interviewing police officers, Hunte reported several motives for police (mis)conduct with respect to 'immigrants'. First, it was quite puzzling to the police, indeed to most members of the host community, how an immigrant – having lived in Britain for only a few years – could own a car and a home. According to interviewees, there had to be some dishonesty involved. Secondly, West Indians were perceived as being argumentative and nearly always willing to take up the issue of compensation when they won a case against a police officer. Thirdly, West Indians were considered to be impudent; they needed to be put in their place, 'after all [they] had come from the jungle'. Fourthly, West Indians were infamous for living on immoral earnings. This alleged type of life, where 'coloured' men used white women as prostitutes for monetary gain, had always been regarded as particularly loathsome and disgusting by members of the host community. This habit was believed to be a way of life inherent to 'the West Indian'. Fifthly, West Indians were seen as boisterous creatures, who did not conform to the conservative standards of their English counterparts. They were untrained and alien to the niceties of life, and hence they were despised (Hunte, 1966: 8). Hunte's report criticised police failure to protect black people, and at the same time, accused the police themselves of attacking and harassing them.[10]

Another study, in Leamington Spa by the Runnymede Trust (Jenkins and Randall, 1970), characterised the mid-1960s as a very tense period, in which a series of violent racist incidents took place. In general, the police response consisted of playing down the incidents and representing the perpetrators as 'hooligans from outside'. In the same period in London, the Pakistani Workers' Union complained about police failure to protect Asian workers going home from work in London's West End (Gordon, 1990: 1–2).

The Runnymede study stated that the police began taking racist attacks seriously only when black people started to defend themselves (Gordon, 1993: 167). Neither Hunte's report nor the Runnymede report attracted much public or political attention. They are worth mentioning, however, because they showed examples of the worsening relations between police and minority communities as well as of the misconduct and racist violence by the police towards these communities. These issues would become increasingly important in Britain in the years to come.

Both the Hunte and the Runnymede Trust reports can be perceived as cases of the specification of matters concerning racist violence which was positioned in phase B, and therefore as outside initiatives in relation to agenda setting.

Powellism

The lack of attention to the reports by Hunte and the Runnymede Trust (or failure of expansion of the issue) was due to the dominant popular and political discourses in the late 1960s. Discrimination practices in everyday life, portrayed by the two reports and the dominant discourses, provided a strong political and popular anti-migration climate in Britain at the end of this decade which was fertile ground for any new or strengthened agitation and rhetoric (Holmes, 1981: 58). This agitation and rhetoric was then personalised in the figure of Enoch Powell – the personalisation of particular issues around public figures was one of the means by which periodic national 'panics' were manufactured in the media (Joshua, Wallace and Booth, 1983: 96).

The Conservative MP Enoch Powell, who had welcomed West Indian nurses to Britain as a Conservative Health Minister in the 1950s (Fryer, 1991: 373), played an important role in the further sharpening of the situation. In several speeches, in 1967 and 1968, he warned of the alleged dangers presumed to be caused by immigration. These speeches attracted enormous media and public attention and even forced the Labour government on the defensive. These speeches can be perceived as examples of the mobilisation model of agenda setting.

In October 1967 in Deal, Kent, Powell delivered a speech opposing the Commonwealth Immigrants Act 1962: 'It is monstrous that a loophole in legislation should be able to add another quarter of a million to that score [of Commonwealth immigrants].'[11] This speech was made during the so-called 'Kenyan Asians Crisis' and was a major contribution to the 'moral panic' at the time. The media paid extensive attention to Powell's statement in a way which fuelled the panic even more. In a front-page editorial, the mass circulation *Daily Mirror* warned that 'the country now faces the prospect of an uncontrolled flood of Asian immigration from Kenya'.[12]

One year later, in April 1968, Powell made a speech in Birmingham which also received enormous media attention and became known as the Rivers of Blood speech. In this speech Powell argued that immigration would lead to 'a total transformation unknown in a thousand years of British history'. He warned of the alleged danger of increasing 'racial' tensions, at which point he referred to the tensions in the US and predicted that with unchanged policies, Britain had to expect the same:

His rabble-rousing speech at Birmingham in April, with its images of foaming blood, and shit pushed through letter-boxes, and overcrowded maternity wards, and impending national disaster – soon to be followed by unaffectionate and icily calculated references to 'grinning piccaninnies' – mobilized and inspired popular racism all over the country.

(Fryer, 1991: 384)

Powell delivered his Rivers of Blood speech just two days before Parliament started to deliberate upon the Race Relations Bill (Layton-Henry, 1992: 80; Smith, A.M., 1994: 152).

Powell and other anti-immigration lobbyists no longer limited themselves to demands for restrictions, but started to plead, in and outside Parliament, in favour of repatriation. Powell took the popular and political perception of concern about immigration to its logical conclusion. The number of migrants from former colonies was perceived as too large, and migration control was presented as no longer sufficient. Thus, he argued for sending 'back' people who had once entered the country (Kettle and Hodges, 1982: 52).

The importance of this period in the context of state responses to racist violence, in which racist violence did not constitute a topic on the formal agenda, is clarified by Cook (1993):

The final solution to the 'problem' (as defined by Powell) involved the total exclusion of black people through repatriation. Twenty-five years on, these conceptions of race and immigration have not disappeared, but have been transformed both into the language of racial abuse and into the expression of racial violence.

(Cook, 1993: 141)

Powell's speech was not just a major expression of anti-immigrant resentment, but challenged the bipartisan consensus so carefully constructed by the Labour government with the Conservative Party leadership (see for further details Layton-Henry, 1992: 79–85; Smith, A.M., 1994: 129–82). Consequently, Powell was removed from the Conservative Shadow Cabinet after the Rivers of Blood speech, but the support for him was obvious. Pro-Powell demonstrations were organised – for instance, by London dock workers who marched to the House of Commons in his support (Fryer, 1991: 384) and thirty-nine immigration officers at London Airport publicly announced their support for Powell (Kettle and Hodges, 1982: 48). In the first week after the speech, Powell received 105,000 letters of support and in a May 1968 poll 74 per cent stated that they agreed with the speech (Smith, A.M., 1994: 161). No longer did the initiative with respect to the 'immigration race' issue lie in the hands of the Cabinet, but with Powell and his allies. The bipartisan consensus with respect to migration and 'integration' seemed from now on to be history.

The pattern of racialisation through the evocation of fear, resulting in increasing violence against the assumed cause of the fear, seemed to be quite obvious in the 1960s. The number of violent attacks on blacks increased dramatically directly after Powell's speech (Smith, A.M., 1994: 162). Racist violence, however, was not an issue at all on the public and formal agendas. The violence itself was perceived as just more 'proof' of the deplorable state of the inner cities due to the scale of immigration.

In Powell's speeches, the threat of violence was closely linked with the presence of specific minority communities. These speeches may have legitimised racist violence by implying that 'black people were attacking the white English by taking over their areas, frightening them out of their houses and by the use of phrases like "unparalleled invasion" and "the transformation of whole areas into alien territory" ' (Layton-Henry, 1992: 139). Implicitly these communities were perceived and represented to be potential sources of violence, rather than the victims. Only a few reports by external actors showed instances of this violence and the increasing worsening of the relations between the police and the black communities. Violence against groups or individuals because of their real or alleged membership in minority communities based in phenotypical characteristics, or religious, cultural, or national origin, did not constitute a topic on the public and formal agendas. In the late 1960s, racist violence as such was 'stuck' within phase A of a phenomenon only perceived and experienced problematic by individuals (see Chapter 1).

The 1970s: racist violence increasingly a social problem, but not a major issue

The 1970s were characterised by an increasing awareness of the phenomenon of racist violence by several sections of British society. Increasing pressure in and outside the establishment to bring the issue of racist violence on to the public and formal agendas was partly due to this increasing awareness. Besides the criminalisation of black communities in general and of black youths in particular, discussed later, the 1970s showed an increase of reported racist incidents and of media coverage. Racist incidents and the resulting casualties started to be registered, and several delegations visited Parliament and the Prime Minister's residence in Downing Street demanding state action (Gordon, 1993: 165). In retrospect, the start of a process of increasing attention to, and awareness of, racist attacks in British society was noticeable. The reported violence and the media attention did not, however, bring the topic immediately onto the public and formal agendas. At first, the early 1970s were dominated by the introduction of a new Immigration Bill and a process of criminalisation of minority communities.

'Paki-bashing'

In the late 1960s, a new phenomenon increasingly attracted media attention: groups of white youths attacking and harassing people of migrant origin, labelled as Paki-bashing by the media after the murder of Tausir Ali in April 1970 (Joshua, Wallace and Booth, 1983: 42 and 97). Causes of this racist group violence were perceived to be competition for jobs and girls, or hooliganism, without any reference to a possible racist nature of the violence. An underlying cause – migrants were increasingly targeted as scape-goats for the deplorable economic situation in the textile industry – was not given attention at all. After Powell's famous speeches, an increase in racist incidents of this kind and the increasing number of statements that specific minority communities were now facing this violence on a daily basis, were reported (Fryer, 1991: 385). The media and public attention to the phenomenon of Paki-bashing reached its climax and became national news during the spring of 1970 (Hiro, 1992: 161).

The emergence of the skinhead 'gangs' in the early 1970s, regarded as responsible for many violent racist attacks, increasingly attracted media attention too. In the East End of London alone, 150 people were reported to have been attacked from March to May 1970. In other places, such as Wolverhampton, Luton, Birmingham, Coventry, and West Bromwich, similar developments were registered. Paki-bashing increasingly became newsworthy, and when Tausiz Ali, an East Pakistani, was stabbed to death near his home in Bow, East London, the Pakistani Workers' Union demanded an inquiry into the failure of the police to act. A statement by the Metropolitan Police, however, denied the existence of any evidence to suggest that black people were attacked any more frequently than whites (Gordon, 1990: 2).

A new Immigration Bill as the answer?

The enormous pressure of Powell's popularity forced the Conservative Party to include promises for a new Immigration Act in its election manifesto (Layton-Henry, 1992: 83). And with the actual introduction of a new Immigration Bill in 1971, the newly elected Conservative government expected, once again, to end all discussions about immigration policies and thus withdraw the topic from the formal agenda. One year later, however, this expectation was shattered by the so-called Ugandan Asians Crisis.

In August 1972, President Idi Amin of Uganda decided that all Asians had to leave the country. Most of the 50,000 Asians were British passport-holders, and for most Britons, it was obvious that the main responsibility lay with Britain. The possibility of these people coming to Britain created an enormous shock and 'moral panic' in the media and among some politicians, with Powell in the foreground. In the end, 27,000 Ugandan Asians were permitted entry. This crisis was followed by a huge revival of anti-immigration organisations – within the Conservative Party (e.g. the Monday Club, an extremely conservative, intellectual society) as well as more far right organisations, such as the British Movement and the National Front.

Internal tensions within the Conservative Party with regard to the migration issue reached a peak during the annual party conference. A liberal amendment by the Young Conservatives against Powell's resolution to condemn the government's action in respect to the Ugandan Asians Crisis was accepted at the end of the conference presenting Powell with clear defeat. In the aftermath, many extreme-right Conservatives turned their back on the party and a considerable number of them joined the National Front. Enoch Powell remained for some time as a Conservative Party member, until he finally left the party in February 1974 following disagreements over other issues. The importance of Powellism was, as Mercer (1990) argues, that 'Powell did not make racism respectable: he transformed the moral threshold of legitimacy itself' (cited by Smith, A.M., 1994: 173).

The Labour opposition found itself trapped in a peculiar double role concerning the proposed Immigration Bill. On the one hand, Labour opposed the new Bill and emphasised the need for policy measures focusing on integration. On the other hand, the Bill was a clear continuation of the 1968 Act, implemented by the previous Labour government. 'The Ugandan Asians Crisis in 1972 also provided comparisons with the Kenyan Asians Crisis in 1968 and the relatively positive response of the [Conservative] Heath administration compared well with the negative treatment of the Kenyan Asians by the previous Labour Government' (Layton-Henry, 1984: 85). The new Immigration Act was implemented on 1 January 1973.

'Mugging' and the criminalisation of black youth

In 1971, an investigation into police–immigrant relations by the House of Commons Select Committee on Race Relations and Immigration showed a low rate of crime among black immigrants. But the study also showed that police officers often believed that black people were more often involved in crime (Layton-Henry, 1992: 126). Despite the outcome of this study, minority communities – especially black youth – were increasingly linked with crime and problems of law and order in popular and political discourses in the early 1970s. This process of criminalisation had already started to become common during the 1960s. However, 'it was during the 1970s that these images reached full maturity' (Solomos, 1988: 88). The broader process of racialisation through debates on immigration and 'race' increased the influence of policy debates about the alleged link between crime and 'race'. This perceived link underlined the statements and warnings made by Powell about the presumed dangers of immigration for the 'British way of life' and about the catastrophes predicted with regard to life in the inner cities. 'The imagery of black involvement in criminal activities and in public order offences helped to fuel and give a new direction to the increasingly volatile public debate about "race relations" ' (Solomos, 1988: 92).

An important influence on the process of criminalisation was the 'moral panic' about mugging in 1972–73. The history and influence of this panic was well documented in *Policing the Crisis: Mugging, the State, and Law and Order* by Stuart Hall *et al.* (1978). This study shows the ideological process by which minority communities were increasingly regarded as social problems, which laid the foundation for the criminalisation process. The word 'mugging' was imported from the United States, and referred to violent street robberies, perpetrated by black youths. One of the consequences of the introduction of this racist term was the perception of a new, 'black' kind of crime. Also the notion of 'mugging' established a link, with American circumstances, construed as the British future. Within discussions in Britain, the situation in the United States with regard to 'race relations' always constituted a threatening example:

The underlying image of the United States . . . is central . . . for it played a major part in the three stages of the transfer of the 'mugging' label from the United States to Britain. First, the idea of a 'special relationship' legitimised the transfer of an American term to the British situation. Second, this transfer allowed the designation of British events as incipiently 'American' in character. Third, the vision of the United States as the 'potential future' could then be used to legitimise the measures being demanded and taken to control 'mugging'. . . . The ultimate effectiveness of the American imagery is the almost routine way in which it came to provide a basis for the justification of extreme reaction (social, judicial, political) to the crime problem.

(Hall *et al.*, 1978: 26)

The introduction of the term 'mugging' made this threat extremely concrete within popular and political discourse. The moral panic over mugging in the early 1970s was caused by an excess of publicity and a series of exaggerated responses. Mugging as a 'black juvenile crime' was perceived by the public as constituting a major social problem. This was not very different from the situation within political circles, as seen by the terminology used in statements of police officers and politicians, such as the 'war on muggers', and 'mugging as a disease of the community' (Hall *et al.*, 1978: 8).

A number of issues were identified which preoccupied state institutions and the police and which contributed to the politicisation of the mugging issue (Solomos, 1988: 101). The main issues were (1) a breakdown of consent to provide policing in certain areas; (2) confrontations between the police and young blacks; and (3) concern that Britain was becoming a 'violent society'. In 1973, the linking of arguments about 'black crime' to wider concerns in parliamentary debates occurred at the height of the public debate on mugging. MPs talked about 'the crisis in the cities' and 'linked the growth of violence to the issue of immigration and their impact on urban localities' (Solomos, 1988: 105).

The breakdown of relations between young blacks and the police was one of the main consequences of this process of criminalisation. Young people from 'imagined minority communities' were perceived as 'potentially criminal' and therefore the areas in which they lived were regarded as 'potential trouble-spots'. The minority communities who were at the centre of the immigration control debates were increasingly subject to special police control, too (Kettle and Hodges, 1982: 54). Special police squads were established to crack down on mugging and these squads, according to minority community leaders, were harassing and intimidating black youngsters suspected of being potential muggers.[13]

The phenomenon of street crime, particularly mugging, was a symbol of a broader process through which young blacks were constructed both in policy and popular discourse as caught up in a vicious circle of unemployment, poverty, homelessness, crime and conflict with the police. This was encapsulated in Enoch Powell's statement in 1976 that mugging was a 'racial crime', with black youths as the main actors.

(Solomos, 1988: 117–18)

Under those conditions, racist violence hardly received public or political attention, although signs of protest were becoming increasingly louder.

Rising protest against racist violence

In the first half of the 1970s, protest against racist violence and harassment increased. Activities, mainly by minority organisations, were
directed towards racist violence in general and to the role of the police
in particular. The police were criticised on two counts. On the one
hand, criticism was directed at the perceived failure by the police to
protect minority communities. On the other hand, criticism was increasingly levelled at the police as perpetrators of racist violence. Maureen
Cain (1973) reported that racism became a key element in the oc-
cupational culture of the police.[14] This culture was riddled by the
dominant discourse explained above, which regarded certain minority
communities as areas of threat to law and order and potentially criminal
by definition.

An example of external actors trying to attract attention to the
phenomenon of racist violence in the 1970s (i.e. the specification and
expansion of the issue), consisted of the West Indian Standing Conference complaining to a Select Parliamentary Committee on relations
between black people and the police in 1972 about police racism.
Another example was presented by the Standing Conference of Pakistani
Organisations and the Asian Action Group, which called for an inquiry
into the rising level of racist incidents in 1976.[15] No inquiry followed
these demands. An example of an internal actor (i.e. within the state),
trying to attract more attention to the phenomenon of racist violence
was the Labour MP Paul Rose. In 1975, he began recording violent
incidents by the extreme right and claimed to have found a thousand
such incidents after just twelve months.

There is an interesting distinction here between the subjects on which
the external actors focused their attention and those which Rose, an
internal actor, focused on. External actors such as the Standing Conferences talked about 'racist violence and harassment', while Rose paid
attention to 'extreme right incidents'. Although no detailed information
is available on the exact definitions used, this distinction marked a
difference in the perception of the phenomenon. 'Racist violence' in
general includes racist motives, while 'extreme right violence' points at
perpetrators involved in an extreme right organisation and/or ideology.

This distinction is important because the notion of racist violence
places the phenomenon within a social, ideological (racist) context,
whereas the notion of extreme right violence places the phenomenon
within a political (right wing–left wing) context. The context in which
a phenomenon in general, and this specific form of violence in
particular, is placed, is of course of major importance when ways of
combating it have to be defined and implemented. In a political context,
the violence could be viewed as merely the work of a few, crazy
political extremists ('the lunatic fringe'). Solutions would then be found
in the legal system or in ordinary political debate and education. In a
social, ideological context, the violence is regarded as a pervasive
problem in society and solutions of a much more fundamental nature

would need to be found, addressing the social and ideological fabric of society as a whole.

Blood on the Streets

Due to the lack of concrete responses by local and national authorities, inquiries were started and findings were published by minority and anti racism organisations themselves. In 1978, the Bethnal Green and Stepney Trades Council (BG&STC) published a report called *Blood on the Streets* and gave it to the government in September that same year. The report recorded 110 incidents (including two murders) during the period of 1976 to August 1978 – with a peak during the autumn of 1977. 'The barrage of harassment, insult, intimidation, week in week out, fundamentally determines how the immigrant community here lives and works. . . . The experience of life in East London has led many Bengalese families to accept racial abuse and attack as a constant factor of everyday existence in Britain' (BG&STC, 1978: 2–3).

Beside the intensity and the scale on which racist violence was shown to occur, the report also reinforced earlier criticisms of police responses – or rather the lack of them. Many situations were recorded in which the police tried to avoid pressing charges when they arrived at the scene of a racist attack, if they arrived at all. Victims were asked to drop the case for the sake of 'good community relations'. Police officers suggested that the victims should take out their own private summons against the assailants and take them to court for common assault (BG&STC, 1978: 8).

As a matter of course, the racist elements of an attack were negated by the police – explicitly or implicitly. In such instances, the police took no action, occasionally they even undertook action against the victims themselves. In many cases, the first and sometimes only police response consisted of investigating the status of the victim(s) and the witnesses by asking them for proof of identity and their legal status. 'Nowhere has the lack of police responsiveness and lack of police sensitivity been more emotively exposed than over the question of attacks on black people and their property' (Kettle and Hodges, 1982: 68).

Response by victimised communities

On more than one occasion, the police took a racist incident seriously only when victimised people started to defend themselves. The 1970 report by the Runnymede Trust (see p. 41) reported on a situation in which the police reacted only after rumours had spread about Asians buying guns to defend themselves against racist attacks (Gordon, 1993: 171). Several instances showed the arrest and criminalisation of people who had decided to defend themselves.

In April 1977, one of the best known and publicised examples of

this police conduct occurred in the East End of London. While working on their car, four Asians, the Virk brothers, were attacked by a
gang of white youths. One brother went to call the police while the
others defended themselves as best they could. When the police arrived, it was the Virk brothers who found themselves under arrest.
Their attackers were not arrested (Fryer, 1991: 396). In fact, the attackers turned up in court as the chief prosecution witnesses. Attempts
by the lawyers of the Virk brothers to point out the racist nature of the
attack, by questioning the attackers on their alleged membership in the
National Front, were ruled out by Judge Argyle (Newham Monitoring
Project/CARF (Campaign Against Racism and Fascism), 1991: 36).
The Virk brothers were convicted and received heavy prison sentences.
Although some of the sentences were reduced on appeal, their convic-
tions have not been reversed (Gordon, 1993: 172).

More than once, individual racist incidents and/or the police responses
were followed by demonstrations and even strikes to attract public and
media attention. The murder of Altab Ali in the Brick Lane area of
London on 4 May 1978, for instance, led to several strikes and
demonstrations in the following months. The arrest of two Bengalese
youths, after an incident in which they were attacked, led to a
demonstration and a sit-down by some 3,000 people outside Bethnal
Green Police Station on 17 July, that same year.

Such experiences prevented people from reporting racist attacks,
and it surely contributed to the increasing isolation of the victimised
minority communities. 'Disillusionment with the police had caused
Bengalis to give up complaining and to tolerate attacks as a fact of
life which they could do little to prevent except by retreating further
into their own ghetto for protection and security by living close to
members of their own community' (Layton-Henry, 1984: 113). It should
be noted, however, that this situation also led to an increasing process
of self- and group-identification and organisation within the victimised
communities.

The National Front

Another factor which contributed to increasing isolation – besides
racist violence and the criminalisation of these communities – was the
increasing support for the extreme-right National Front (NF), one of
the major beneficiaries of Enoch Powell's anti-immigration campaign
(Layton-Henry, 1992: 89). In West Bromwich by-elections in May
1973 the National Front candidate, Martin Webster, gained 16.3 per
cent of the vote. During the second half of the 1970s, a shock wave
went through Britain when the National Front appeared to have
extensive support. In 1977, efforts were made to establish an organisation
to combat xenophobia and discrimination in general and against the
National Front in particular. A proposal to invite both main political
parties to fill the position of chairman, seemed at first to be accepted

by both the Conservative and Labour parties. Finally, however, Conservative participation was vetoed by party leader Margaret Thatcher, who was highly alarmed at the idea of possible cooperation with Labour and perhaps even groups from the extreme Left (Layton-Henry, 1984: 149).

The National Front was regarded as constituting an important background determinant of many racist attacks and harassment. The party organised street corner meetings in which racism was propagated openly. Their distribution of racist pamphlets at the weekly market in Brick Lane, London – an area in which many Bengali migrants and their descendants live – was well known. In 1978, the leader of the National Party (a split off from the NF), John Kingsley Read, commented after the racist murder of 18-year-old Sikh, Gurdip Singh Chaggur: 'One down – a million to go.' This statement caused a media and public fury. However, prosecution under incitement to racial hatred against Read was unsuccessful (Layton-Henry, 1992: 92).

The direct involvement of the National Front in racist incidents turned out to be difficult to expose, as was shown in a study by the Commission for Racial Equality (CRE) in 1979.[16] The Bethnal Green and Stepney Trades Council report, however, stated that there was no doubt that many members of the NF and the British Movement were taking part in racist attacks. The continuing provocation and the unending stream of obscene racist propaganda on the streets of the East End contributed largely, according to the Council, to a tense atmosphere and offered legitimation to perpetrators of racist attacks. Of course such attacks had occurred in the East End long before the National Front turned up, but the number of incidents was seen to coincide with the increasing support for the Front locally (BG&STC, 1978: 48). One of the major points of the *Blood on the Streets* report was that the Asian population accused the police of protecting the National Front (BG&STC, 1978: 46).

Southall

On 23 April 1979, unrest broke out in Southall, London, that would be regarded by the victimised communities as 'proof' of the alleged protection of the National Front by the police (i.e. the state). It was at the time of an election campaign and the National Front planned to meet that night in Southall Town Hall. The NF had no support whatsoever in Southall and the meeting was viewed as an obvious provocation of the relatively large local minority community, who responded with massive protests against the planned meeting and against the decision to let it take place in the Town Hall. Five thousand people had marched on the previous day and on the day itself local businesses, factories and transport were closed down from 1 p.m. for a half-day strike (CARF/Southall Rights, 1981: 1). Police officers, 2,756 in number, poured into the area to protect a handful of NF supporters. The paramilitary Special Patrol Group (SPG) was called in, as were horses, dogs, vans, and a helicopter.[17] In the resulting clash, a black meeting centre was vandalised, 342 people were arrested, hundreds injured and one demonstrator, Blair Peach, was killed (Fryer, 1991: 397).

Discussions and debates linked the NF meeting to civil liberties, such as the right to assemble and to demonstrate. The same discussions appeared every now and then with respect to the right to print and publish racist propaganda. 'In each case, however, the chosen solution creates the impression that the police appeared to be protecting, or even supporting, the National Front in its hostility to black people' (Kettle and Hodges, 1982: 76–7).

Police Against Black People

In 1979, the Institute of Race Relations (IRR) submitted a report, *Police Against Black People*, to the Royal Commission on Criminal Procedure. The report argued that police misconduct towards black citizens had become 'an everyday occurrence, a matter of routine'. It identified seven elements of police misconduct: stop and search without reason; unnecessary violence during arrest; particular harassment of juveniles; danger of arrest when suspects asserted their rights; risks to witnesses and bystanders; repeated arrest of individuals; and entering black homes and premises at will (Haro, 1992: 80).[18]

The IRR study examined the breakdown of police–minority communities relations. On the one hand, the report focused on the use of police powers against black people over a period of time and the ways in which criminal procedures were being used to harass minority communities. On the other hand, it reported on the failure, the refusal even, of the police to protect communities under attack (IRR, 1979: 2).

State response to this increasing awareness

State responses at the national level to the increasing pressure and demands for recognition of the existence of the phenomenon of racist violence as a social problem which had to be confronted by state action were hardly concrete at first. A new Race Relations Act in 1976 improved possibilities for combating discrimination, including indirect discrimination. Individuals received the right to take their complaints to the courts in all cases except employment, for which they had to turn to industrial tribunals. The Commission for Racial Equality was set up, and given better means and more powers than the Race Relations Board to execute their work against discrimination. The migration issue however was still prominent on the formal agenda and migration control was still perceived as a major solution to domestic problems and conflicts in the mid 1970s. Reports by external actors, such as the Bethnal Green and Stepney Trades Council and the Institute of Race Relations, met with little response from internal actors, which seemed to confirm the suggestion that these reports were regarded as politically motivated and therefore not taken seriously by the state.

At the annual conference of the Conservative Party, the Shadow Home Secretary William Whitelaw stated that the Conservatives supported the 'two way policy', with immigration restrictions on the one hand, and stimulation of equal opportunities and treatment in Britain on the other. Whitelaw also emphatically supported the anti-National Front campaign. The Conservative contribution to this campaign, however, was partly vetoed by Margaret Thatcher (as mentioned on p. 51).

During the debates on the Race Relations Bill and in an attempt to achieve parliamentary consensus, Labour Home Secretary Jenkins stated that there was a definite limit to the number of migrants that could be absorbed by a country, and that it was in 'their own interest' for the state to maintain strict controls on immigration.

In 1976, the Conservative Minister on Immigration, who was considered to be a 'liberal', was replaced; one year later the newly elected Labour government introduced new restrictive measures. This was merely another expression of the dominant discourses of the time.

In September 1976, a campaign was started mainly due to pressure by external actors, especially the unions, emphasising the need for the education of Labour and union members about the dangers of racism and about the consequences of the neo-fascist policies propagated by the National Front and other extremist parties. At the Labour Party annual conference in 1976, a resolution was accepted which pleaded for the repeal of the 1968 and 1971 Immigration Acts. The election manifesto of Labour in 1979, however, hardly contained extensive material on 'race relations', although Labour did call for the strengthening of legislation to protect minorities against discrimination and racism (Layton-Henry, 1984: 155–6). The Labour Party was not, however, the only example of an institution affiliated with the state in which several, contradictory opinions existed.

In the early 1970s, differences within the Conservative Party led to the resignation of several Conservative members, some of whom turned to the National Front. Election polls during the 1970s showed that supporters of the Conservative Party increasingly defected to the National Front and in the late 1970s, the Conservative Party was increasingly concerned about these developments (Layton-Henry, 1992: 91–5).

'This country might be swamped'

That is an awful lot, and I think it means that people are really rather afraid that this country might be swamped by people of different cultures. The British character has done so much for democracy, for law, done so much throughout the world that if there is any fear that it might be swamped, then people are going to be rather hostile to those coming in.[19]

After some initiatives to attract immigrant votes in the mid-1970s, the Conservative Party returned to tightening its position on immigration and called for stricter controls.[20] On 30 January 1978, party leader Thatcher appeared on television expressing her fear that Britain and its character might be 'swamped' by people from other cultures. She pointed out that with the present scale of immigration, 4 million people from the New Commonwealth or Pakistan would be settling in Britain before the end of the century.

In that same interview, Thatcher stated that she saw the success of the National Front as follows: 'We are a British nation with British characteristics. Every nation can take some minorities, and in many ways they add to the richness and variety of this country. But the moment a minority threatens to become a big one, people get frightened.'[21] By these statements, Thatcher more or less condoned aggressive and violent expressions of racism towards those communities, which were viewed as representing this 'different culture' as 'natural human responses'.

Thatcher announced that it was the intention of the Conservatives to limit all immigration, except for 'the extreme cases'. To ignore the migration issue, according to Thatcher, would cause people to join the National Front. Thatcher wanted to regain the supporters of the National Front, who had previously voted Conservative. 'Mrs. Thatcher was . . . determined to impress the electorate that she was responsive to popular anxieties over immigration and that the Conservative Party would bring New Commonwealth immigration to an end' (Layton-Henry, 1984: 150).

Thatcher's statements attracted enormous publicity and were generally regarded as contributing to the increase in support for the Conservative Party in the election polls. Other polls in this period showed a sharp increase in the percentage of people who saw migration as one of the most important issues. In this period the Conservative Party (i.e. Thatcher) seemed to regain the political initiative previously in the hands of Labour, by exploiting the migration issue.

At times of increasing attention to racist violence and increasing pressure to effectively combat this violence, the state at the national level responded mainly to the increasing support for the National Front. This meant that state responses consisted of an increasingly harsh position on migration and on issues perceived in relation to minority communities, and failed to establish a broad anti racism platform. The 1979 general elections turned out to be a total disaster for the National Front, and the major reason for its electoral reverse clearly was 'Mrs. Thatcher's public identification of the Conservative Party with a hard line on immigration' (Layton-Henry, 1992: 96). Mainly because of activities of external actors in the late 1970s, the phenomenon of racist violence increasingly started to be perceived by certain sections of British society as constituting a social problem which had to be dealt with by the state. However, it did not reach the formal agenda, where the migration issue was still attracting prominent attention. Other events had to occur before racist violence entered the formal agenda. It was not until the beginning of the 1980s that it developed into an official party issue, leading to the publication of the 1981 Home Office report on *Racial Attacks* (Bowling and Saulsbury, 1993: 222).

The year 1981: 'a matter of fact, and not of opinion'

In November 1981, the Home Office published the report on racist violence in Britain which will be discussed in this section. The study found that there were 'a significantly high number of racially motivated attacks on persons and property by one ethnic group on another' and that 'both blacks and Asians suffer disproportionately from racially motivated attacks' (Home Office, 1981: 28, nos. 65–6). The report concluded that 'the incidence of racial attacks presents a significant problem. The frequency of such attacks, . . . are a matter of fact and not of opinion' (1981: 35, no. 82). The report also recorded that there had been a tendency on the part of the police to underestimate the significance of these attacks (1981: 32, no. 76).

The 1981 report constituted the first official 'including recognition' of racist violence by British state authorities. Because of the significance of the report to the subject of this study, separate attention is given to it here. The key feature of the following section is the state's attitude of 'including recognition' by the 1981 report. Why the inquiry leading to this report was executed, and why the phenomenon of racist violence was recognised to be 'a fact' in 1981, will be analysed and discussed.

Prior to the report

In the 1970s, anti-racism organisations were founded, such as the Anti-Nazi League, Rock Against Racism and the Campaign Against Racism and Fascism (CARF) – organisations and movements which increased in the second half of the 1970s in size and the attention paid to them. At the end of the 1970s and the early 1980s, incidents of racist violence and harassment were increasingly reported by these and minority organisations. Over and over again, these organisations requested and demanded state action, for instance with regard to public inquiries into specific incidents. The latter were always turned down.

As we have seen in 1978 and 1979, two reports, by the Bethnal Green and Stepney Trades Council and the Institute of Race Relations, were published and presented to the state agencies. These two reports provided evidence about the scale and the intensity of racist violence by groups and individuals – outside and inside the state. At first, hardly any official government response to these reports and to this violence was heard. This lack of state response probably was partly due to the fact that this violence contradicted the prevailing emphasis by the government and the police on the criminal activities by black youths and to the image of 'black crime' presented in the popular press (the process of criminalisation).

In April 1980, riots broke out in Bristol after the police raided a pub in the St Paul's area. This pub was one of the few meeting places left for black youths after years of police harassment. The resistance to the raid was tough, and the police were even forced to withdraw for some hours. 'In fact, they ran away, and for four hours St Paul's was a "no go" area. Bristol became a symbol of resistance' (Fryer, 1991: 398; see for detailed report: Joshua, Wallace and Booth, 1983).

The Bristol riots came as a complete surprise to most people in Britain and at first were seen as a one-off event, 'a strange aberration in social behaviour' (Benyon and Solomos, 1987: 3). At the same time, it also gave rise to public and political debates about 'racial' violence, 'race riots', and the emergence of 'ghetto violence' along American lines (Solomos, 1988: 180). This perception was furthered by the mass media reports headlining articles with Black Riots, War on the Streets, Riot Zone and Mob Fury (see Joshua *et al.*, 1983: 99–119). Throughout the late 1960s and 1970s, public and political debates about black youths resonated with images of violence and riots. The intermingling of discourses of 'race', youth, and violence had a long history in Britain, as shown. But the Bristol events in April 1980 awakened popular opinion to the alleged dangers, and strengthened and underlined these fears around the specific form of street disturbances involving violent confrontations with the police (Solomos, 1988: 179).

In the summer of 1980, this situation led to discussions in both the Executive and the Council of the Joint Committee Against Racialism (JCAR). Launched officially in December 1978 (Bowling, 1993b: 23), the JCAR included representatives of the main political parties, churches, youth organisations and of some minority community organisations.[22] Every year, the committee reported racist incidents to the Home Office, but nothing seemed to be done with the information.

The Home Office

Internal affairs and developments within the Home Office appear to be important with regard to a changing evaluation of the JCAR reports by the state. Initially, as a matter of course, incidents of racist violence and harassment were regarded and treated as a matter of law and order, and therefore of policing. Thus the JCAR reports on racist incidents were always transmitted to the Home Office Police Department and did not get any further than a desk drawer or, at best, the incidents reported were treated as individual instances.

At the end of the 1970s and the early 1980s, the Home Office Race Relations Division increasingly argued that racist violence and harassment had to be dealt with within the context of 'race relations' policies and not treated as a matter of policing. Any attempt to explain this change must be speculative. Undoubtedly there were conflicting views of racist violence. The Race Relations Division perceived it as a reflection of present 'race relations' which had to be dealt with in the context of improving relations. The Police Department, as we have seen, took little notice of this kind of violence, considering it as 'normal' crime.

However, an important factor with respect to the increasing pressure exerted by the Race Relations Division was the desire to expand or defend their territory – not uncommon within bureaucratic systems. As a matter of fact, the staffing of the Race Relations Division had been severely cut by the Conservative government (Layton-Henry, 1982: 13) and in its bureaucratic struggle for survival the division claimed the issue belonged to them. Here, then, was a political battle within the Home Office between different internal agencies, their interests and their perceptions, which crystallised around the specific phenomenon of racist violence. Perhaps the important point is, that it seemed worthwhile for the Division to capitalise on this specific issue.

In 1980, the JCAR decided to seek an urgent meeting with the Home Secretary to put forward their findings and to discuss the seriousness of the situation, which also was demonstrated by an increasing number of media reports on the matter. For instance, in October 1980, the London Weekend Television programme *Skin* reported over 200 instances of serious violence against black people in London (Klug, 1982: 7). The goals of the JCAR coincided with and paralleled the demands and claims by the Home Office Race Relations Division. In fact, the situation supported this division's views on the racist violence issue in contrast to that of the Police Department.

On 4 February 1981, Home Secretary Whitelaw met with representatives of the JCAR. They presented their report which expounded their view that the scale, intensity and impact of racist violence and harassment was underestimated both within and outside British state apparatus. One of the major concerns of the JCAR was directed at the attitude of the police, who denied that attackers had any racist motives. This was undermining the confidence of minority communities in the police. The JCAR also warned that this attitude created the wrong picture of what was actually going on. And the JCAR concluded that this, in turn, actually encouraged these attacks (JCAR, 1981: 1).

Home Office inquiry into racist violence instigated

The next day, the Home Secretary reported to the House of Commons his decision to initiate an inquiry into the incidence of 'racial' attacks, and the activities of the 'racialist' organisations alleged to be responsible.[23] In comparison to the JCAR report, the reports by the Bethnal Green and Stepney Trades Council and the Institute of Race Relations gave a much broader and more thorough picture of the situation on racist violence (and police response). Yet, it was the former which functioned as the real trigger for the 1981 Home Office study. Why?

The JCAR represented all the main political parties as well as several other sections in British society, such as the churches. The

JCAR, therefore, was perceived not only as being of importance (i.e. influential within the state), but, even more importantly, as being non-political. The Bethnal Green and Stepney Trades Council and the Institute of Race Relations, on the other hand, were considered politically extreme by state authorities in general and by the Conservative government in particular. They were alleged to be extreme left wing, and both were dismissed or ignored by the state establishment. Later, this fact was underlined in the 1981 report which stated that 'against all the evidence that had been published over the years, the government's failure to appreciate the seriousness of the problem had been largely due to a lack of *reliable* information about it' (Gordon, 1993: 169; my italics). So, the failure was represented as not due to a lack of state action or interest, but due to the reliability of those who had reported evidence!

Four other reasons were distinguished for setting up the Home Office inquiry in 1981 (Gordon, 1993: 168–9): (1) the riots were often sparked off by particular instances of racist policing; (2) the seriousness of the situation with respect to racist violence; (3) victimised people were increasingly turning to measures of self-defence; and (4) the JCAR report. Racist violence no longer appeared to be a marginal issue that could be ignored.

With respect to the third point made by Gordon, racist violence and harassment and the responses to this phenomenon increasingly isolated victimised communities. At the start of the 1980s, it was increasingly the case that at least some sections of these communities, especially the youth, were no longer prepared to sit back and let things take their course. Self-defence was well known in the history of racist violence, but at the end of the 1970s it became ever more prevalent in Britain.

This development, which will be elaborated upon later, was considered as threatening by the state, which had a monopoly on the right to use violence to maintain law and order. The response by means of self-defence occurred in different forms, such as demonstrations, but also actual physical defence and counter-attacks, sometimes leading to major disturbances of law and order. This perceived threat obviously contributed to the decision by the Home Office to establish an inquiry on racist violence and harassment. However, before the Home Office inquiry started to collect and publish its findings, tensions increased even more.

Increasing tensions in 1981

In February, thirteen black youths were killed in a fire in a house in New Cross, Deptford, where they were having a party. Deptford was known as an area of south London where homes of black people were attacked and a black community centre had been burned down before. The entire community was convinced that this New Cross fire was the result of a racist attack. The inability of the police to find the cause of this disaster, police statements denying the fire had been caused by a racist attack, as well as the rising anger towards the police concerning their attitude and (lack of) action towards the increasing number of racist incidents, led to an enormous increase in local tension.

In March 1981, 15,000 people marched from New Cross to central London to protest against the failure of the police to find those responsible for the fire and deaths. The demonstrators also protested against the indifference of the mass media to the racist killing (Fryer, 1991: 398). Some argued that this indifference was partly due to the fact that young blacks were not normally featured as victims, which had led to a degree of uncertainty concerning its initial press treatment. The march, however, did attract massive media attention and was covered as a 'race' riot. Headlines such as 'Confrontation' and 'When the Black Tide met the Blue Line' reflected a treatment by the press which would become the norm throughout the rest of the decade.[24]

The aftermath of the New Cross fire confirmed what had become apparent during the previous ten to fifteen years, that is, a rising protest within minority communities as well as a deep crisis in the relationship between these communities and the state, especially the police (Kettle and Hodges, 1982: 63). The dominant discourses represented instances of protest and resistance by victimized communities as threats to law and order themselves.

The bad relations and increasing tensions led to a situation classified as 'an undoubted watershed in British race relations' (Gordon, 1993: 168). In this very tense atmosphere, the Brixton police launched 'Swamp 81' in April 1981. The purpose of the operation was to detect and arrest burglars and thieves on the streets of Lambeth, London.[25] 'A crowd rescued a black youth from a police car, then stood up to police reinforcements and forced them to withdraw. Next day, Brixton exploded' (Fryer, 1991: 398).

The rioting was brought home 'live' to millions of people by television and they witnessed the 'unleashed fury' (Benyon and Solomos, 1987: 3). Lord Scarman, who carried out an official inquiry into the resulting Brixton riots, concluded: 'Operation Swamp was a serious mistake given the tension which existed between the police and the local community in the early months of this year' (Lord Scarman, 1981: para. 4.76).

The Brixton riots were the first in a year of unrest and rioting. There were clashes in April too between the police and youths at Finsbury Park, Ealing Common and Wanstead in London. In July, riots occurred in Toxteth, Liverpool (District 8) on Merseyside. These riots were particularly violent. 'For the first time ever in Britain, CS gas was fired at rioters by the police' (Solomos and Rackett, 1991: 46).

In that same July, riots were reported in Moss Side, Manchester, and in at least twenty other places, such as Handsworth (Birmingham), Sheffield, Nottingham, Hull, Slough, Leeds, Bradford, Leicester, Derby,

High Wycombe, Cirencester, and London. On 15 July, riots erupted in Brixton again, when the police raided eleven houses.

> The police had warrants to look for evidence of unlawful drinking and to search five houses for petrol bombs, although no evidence of either was found. During the operation the houses sustained very considerable damage. ... This raid and the resultant violence on the streets of Brixton convinced many people that the way policing is carried out is a vital factor in the context of urban unrest.
>
> (Solomos and Rackett, 1991: 46)

On 28 July, there were riots in Toxteth, Liverpool, resulting in many seriously injured and the death of one man, David Moore, who was hit by a police vehicle.

Responses to the 'hot summer of 1981'

The direct political response to these events included strong condemnation of the rioters and led to comments supporting police conduct. Prime Minister Thatcher stated that there was no justification for such riots in a democracy, and that her government would ensure that 'law and order' would be upheld.[26] The participants in the disorders were both black and white, despite media assertions to the contrary. In July 1981, almost 4,000 people were arrested of whom about 67 per cent were white (Benyon, 1986: 14). These figures did of course vary from area to area. The 1981 riots, however, were commonly portrayed and believed to have involved black rioters against the police.

'The further outbreaks of violence in Brixton (10–13 April 1981) and nation-wide (July 1981) provided the spur for a fundamental rethinking of the inner-relationship between "race", youth and street disturbances' (Solomos, 1988: 179). The imagery of an 'alien disease'[27] spreading through the towns and cities of the whole country and 'undermining the social and moral fabric resonated through the pages of official reports, the press, the coverage on television and the debates in Parliament' (Solomos, 1988: 182).

One of the central themes in the responses to these disorders was the emphasis on family responsibility as a way of keeping children 'under control'. The arguments 'resonated in important ways the symbolic use of racial symbols to explain violent disorder, particularly in relation to the supposed pathology of the West Indian family and the social "alienation" of young blacks' (Solomos, 1988: 186). Prime Minister Thatcher, Home Secretary Whitelaw, and also Chief Constable Kenneth Oxford of Merseyside, referred to these opinions explicitly.

Special inquiries into the 1981 riots, such as the report by Lord Scarman on the Brixton riots, referred to the discriminatory situation in the cities and criticised the performance of the police. The responses by the government and the police to the recommendations made by Scarman were rather ambiguous (see Solomos, 1989: 214–20; Solomos and Rackett, 1991: 51–6).

Four explanatory frameworks were identified in the responses relating to the core issue: 'race', violence and disorders; the breakdown of law and order; social deprivation and youth unemployment; and political marginality (Solomos, 1989: 103). The relation between black youths and street violence was clearly established within the popular press, with headlines such as 'Mobs Of Black Youths Roaming The Streets' (*Daily Mail*, 5 April 1980).[28] This period between April and July of 1981 has been characterised as a crucial phase in the racialisation of discourses about violent protest (Solomos, 1989: 105).

Enoch Powell and some of his supporters, both in Parliament and in the media, claimed the riots proved their arguments, namely that the number of black migrants in Britain inevitably would cause tension and bloodshed. After the Bristol riots of 1980, the main discussions were about the question of whether these were 'race riots'. In July 1981, this discussion was transformed to the representation of the riots as being 'racial' or at least the result of bad relations between the police and black youths.

This transformation was important, because mainstream explanations of and responses to these riots as a threatening element in British society in the 1980s were implicit in the symbolic political language used. The notion of 'race riots' in 1980 had specific references to 'the American model' (read: the American-like future) and had established a link between black youth and street violence. The notion of 'racial riots' creates an image of riots in which 'race' somehow was a central variable or even the main one (Solomos, 1989: 106). Racism hardly constituted an issue in the debate.

The fear of Britain sliding towards a violent society had attracted much attention. According to many commentators, lawlessness and violence were threatening to undermine traditional British values and institutions. In several parliamentary meetings, these supposed threats were discussed at length, and the maintenance of law and order received high priority on the formal agenda. 'Law and order' as a central issue, the perceived threat of street violence to the English 'way of life' and the alleged links with 'black youth' highlighted 'the symbolic evocation of the re-establishment of order as the main concern of official language during this period' (Solomos, 1989: 109).

A number of responses related the riots to social factors. In parliamentary debates, the Labour opposition referred to a correlation between social and economic deprivation. According to this point of view, bad housing, a lack of social, cultural and welfare services, poor educational opportunities, high (youth) unemployment and social disarray were perceived to be the most important causes of the riots. In response, Home Secretary Whitelaw and Prime Minister Thatcher admitted that the circumstances in many inner cities were bad. They both, however, denied any assertion that these circumstances were the cause of the riots. Therefore, the main government response consisted of reinforcing the police and improving training facilities so that the police were better prepared.

Another important consequence of the 1980–81 riots was a major shift from national to local approaches. Local authorities increasingly began to develop anti-discrimination policies. Three important policy changes are mentioned in this respect (Solomos, 1989: 93): First, local authorities directed their attention to the realisation of equal treatment in different areas, such as housing. Secondly, they formulated policies to employ more migrants within their own institutions. Thirdly, a number of measures were taken to improve communication with and awareness of the difficulties faced by 'black and ethnic minorities'. This situation shaped the popular and political context in which the Home Office published its report *Racial Attacks* in 1981.

The Home Office report, 1981

An incident, or alleged offence by a person or persons of one racial group against a person or persons or property of another racial group, where there are indication of a racial motive.

This definition of a 'racial' incident was adopted by the Home Office inquiry in 1981 (Home Office, 1981: 7). The impressions stated by the Joint Commission Against Racialism were confirmed by this Home Office report. 'With the results of our survey in mind we estimate that at the present rate about 7,000 or so racially motivated incidents falling within our Groups A and B [strong evidence or some indications of a racial motive] will be reported in England and Wales in a year' (Home Office, 1981: 14). The report confirmed that their estimate with respect to the crime rate would, almost certainly, be on 'the low side'. Minorities, and particularly Asians, were reported to suffer disproportionately from 'racial' attacks. The rapidly growing lack of trust between the minorities and the police was stressed in this report and the number of 'racial' attacks appeared to be on the increase.

Although it proved difficult to confirm direct involvement by extremist organisations, the report concluded that far right racist groups did play a major role in establishing tension within the community through their propaganda and influence which encouraged the expression of 'racialist feeling' (Home Office, 1981: 35).

The 1981 report constituted an official state recognition of racist violence and harassment as a significant problem in British society. The Home Secretary stated his intention of pursuing the following lines of action: (1) collection of details of 'racial' attacks by the police; (2) arrangements for liaison between police, local authorities, and minority communities; (3) training police officers to develop greater sensitivity; (4) improving assistance to the police by minority groups; and (5) ways of combating 'racialist' activity and propaganda among young people (Home Office, 1981: iv). The action proposed was directed against the occurrence of the violence as well as against circumstances favourable to this occurrence. Therefore, this 1981 report constituted the first example of the 'including recognition' of racist violence by the state. This, however, did not mean that no criticism was heard – on the contrary.

Responses to the 1981 report

The Home Office report was widely welcomed because of its confirmation that racist violence was widespread and it was 'the first to suggest that systematic racial attacks were taking place against members of the ethnic minorities' (Layton-Henry, 1982: 3). 'In many ways it goes beyond what any government has said' (*Searchlight*, no. 79, 1982: 17). However, many criticisms were also raised. First of all, of course, there was discussion about the definitions used. The Home Office included attacks on whites by non-whites. The report stated that the victimisation of minority people was reported to be much higher, particularly among the Asian community, than for the indigenous white community. The report claimed the rate for Asians to be fifty times that for white people and the rate for blacks to be over thirty-six times that for white people (Home Office, 1981: 10–11).

The use of the term 'racial' attacks including attacks on white people by non-whites, however, was criticised for ignoring the racism in society and for reducing it to a law and order problem, that is a police problem (*Searchlight*, no. 79, 1982: 17). 'The government was not prepared to recognise that racially motivated attacks on black people are different from others because the phenomenon of racism underlies such attacks, or that the racist attacks act as both a reflection and a reinforcement of the racism institutionalised in society' (Gordon, 1983: 55).

In a situation in which disagreement existed between the victim and the police on the 'racialist' motive of the incident, according to the Home Office, 'the victim rather than the police officer . . . was reluctant to ascribe a racial motive' (Home Office, 1981: 14). This was hard to reconcile with yet another finding regarding the police tendency to underestimate the significance of 'racialist' incidents for those attacked or threatened (Home Office, 1981: 32). Criticism was also directed at what was considered to be the report's ignorance of the failures of the legal system, the police service, prosecuting authorities and the courts, to accord black people equal protection (Bridges, 1982: 9).

The police, on the other hand, criticised the report for allegedly excluding certain types of crime and for solely focusing on 'racial' violence committed against minority communities. The police argued that the Home Office report 'highlights the impact of racial attacks on the ethnic minority communities, [but] it should be remembered that racial attacks affect all parts of the community and the impact of street crime committed by black youths on elderly white women cannot be passed over lightly'.[29] These comments by the police precisely fit the criticisms by Gordon and *Searchlight* above.

Another reaction was that the report threw back, at least in part, the responsibility for action against racist violence on to the victims

(Gordon, 1983: 54). The report was criticised because of its assumption that black people did not understand the basic requirements of evidence, that they lacked an adequate understanding of police procedures, and that they did not join the police force. Bridges (1982: 10) called it a classic example of transferring the blame.

Criticism also pointed at the report's conclusion that direct involvement of the political extreme right in organising racist violence was hard to prove. Layton-Henry (1982: 10) argued that 'its inadequate coverage of the role of extremist organisations in instigating and encouraging racial violence and harassment' constituted a major weakness of the report. He pointed at the fact that ultra right-wing organisations 'foster a climate of violence and approve certain forms of violence' (Layton-Henry, 1992: 11).

A last criticism to be mentioned involved the Home Office's view of community organisations. The report suggested that Community Relations Officers constituted an important link in reporting 'racial' attacks to the police. Misunderstandings, however, could arise with some sections of minority communities regarding the Community Relations Commission (CRC) as unrepresentative and wishing to create their own groups and associations to outflank the CRC. The reaction of the Home Office was that 'such groups have a tendency to stoke up the temperature in order to justify their own existence' (Home Office, 1981: 22). It was this notion of community representation that was criticised, for it implicitly claimed that communities could be represented only by organisations which were recognised as such by the state rather than by the community itself.

Why did the Thatcher government recognise racist violence?

The four factors identified by Gordon (see p. 58) surely played a role in the ultimate recognition of 'racist' violence by the report. But other factors have to be mentioned to fully understand this recognition and its publication by a right-wing Conservative government.

One of the reasons for its recognition was the internal struggle within the Home Office already mentioned. As in most struggles there were no real winners or losers. The Race Relations Division surely had contributed to the entrance of racist violence on to the formal agenda, as well as to the changing perception of racist violence within the Home Office, and the top priority given to this phenomenon. But the issue of racist violence remained under the responsibility of the Police Department.

Recognition by the Thatcher government was partly made possible by 'keeping the matter under police supervision'. In this way, recognition of racist violence as a social problem which needed to be dealt with by the state matched the Conservative notion of racist violence predominantly as a matter of law and order and therefore of policing. It fitted the dominant Conservative discourse on criminalisation and the politicisation of law and order (see Solomos, 1989: 99–121). The definition of 'racial' violence used was important, because it emphasised the law and order concept instead of a more political and ideological one like 'racist' violence. These grounds for the recognition of racist violence by British state authorities also explained the crucial role the police were perceived to have and were to take in the near future with respect to tackling racist violence.

The 1980s to the early 1990s: two-faced state responses

One of the consequences of the 1981 report by the Home Office was a whole series of reports, both governmental and non-governmental, on racist violence in Britain which were published during the 1980s. These made clear that racist violence was viewed as widespread in Britain and needed to be combated. In fact, it was seen as constituting a part of everyday British life. The last period under observation, therefore, might be typified as a period of extensive study and experimentation to combat this phenomenon ('including recognition'). However, this view is rather one-sided because at the same time, measures and policies were introduced and implemented which presented a contrasting picture including restrictive policies with respect to migration (examples of 'excluding recognition'). For that reason, this last period might be characterised by the two-faced state responses to racist violence involving examples of the 'including' and 'excluding recognition' of this phenomenon.

The impact of the 1981 report within the state

The Home Office report did not have the same impact everywhere. One year after the Home Office publication, a survey by the Runnymede Trust (Klug, 1982) recorded no changes in police conduct and police responses to racist violence. Even members of those police forces which had taken part in the Home Office inquiry did not know of the existence nor the findings and recommendations of the 1981 report (Gordon, 1993: 169).

In April 1982, the Metropolitan Police of London introduced a new system to register 'racial' incidents as such, based on a new definition of 'racial' incident. Previously, in 1978, the Metropolitan Police had defined a 'racial' incident as:

(a) an incident involving premises, individuals or organisations associated with the furtherance of community relations; or
(b) an incident involving political movements which arose from their involvement in community relations; or
(c) an incident where there was some indication that the offender was in some way motivated by racial prejudice; or
(d) an incident involving concerted action by or against members of an ethnic group. This will include such action which was directed against the police.[30]

This definition has been operational since 1978 for the purpose of reporting serious incidents and disturbances to local senior officers, the Community Relations Branch, Public Order Branch and Special Branch (Bowling, 1993b: 31). In 1982, a 'racial' incident was redefined by the Metropolitan Police as involving:

any incident, whether concerning crime or not which was alleged by any person to include an element of racial motivation or which appeared to the reporting or investigating officer to include such an element.[31]

The main changes from the previous system for recording racial incidents were a new emphasis on recording *all* incidents, whether or not a criminal offence was committed; a widening of the definition of a racial motive, to include the victim's as well as the police officer's views; and the responsibility for the collection of figures placed in the hands of the district community liaison officer (Greater London Council Police Committee, 1984: 4).

As a result, a sharp increase in the number of reported incidents was shown (see Table 1).

Table 1   Number of reported racial incidents 1980–89

1980	277 incidents
1981[a]	727 incidents
1982[b]	1,293 incidents
1983	1,277 incidents
1984	1,515 incidents
1985	1,937 incidents
1986	1,733 incidents
1987	2,179 incidents
1988	2,214 incidents
1989	2,697 incidents

Notes: [a]Until December 1981
[b]May–December 1982: after the introduction of the new system
Source: Figures until 1982 from Greater London Council Police Committee (1984: 4); and for the period 1983–89 from the annual reports by the Commissioner of the Metropolitan Police.

In 1984, the Greater London Council (GLC) Police Committee concluded that 'racial' harassment posed an increasingly serious problem in London. It should be noted that the GLC did not speak of 'racial' attacks or incidents, but of harassment. The GLC brought racist behaviour by the police themselves within the definition of 'racial' harassment (Bowling, 1993b: 37). The role of the police was criticised by the GLC report:

It was clear from the strength of the criticisms of police response and the variety of quarters from which those criticisms came, that police failure could not just be put down to the attitudes of a few individual police officers or to general inefficiency. Rather it is necessary to tackle the institutional racism within the police force. This encompasses both the racist behaviour of individual police officers and their refusal to pursue incidents reported to them.

(GLC, 1984: 2)

The GLC report included a long list of recommendations, adopted by the Council on 25 October 1984, with respect to: police policies;[32] the registration of incidents; prosecution; 'racial' harassment by the police; housing policies;[33] and action against perpetrators (special clause on 'racial' harassment in its tenancy agreement) (GLC, 1984: 53–5).

A report by the Policy Studies Institute (Brown, 1984) revealed that the figures on 'racial' violence found in the 1981 Home Office study would probably need to be multiplied as a factor of ten, in order to match reality. The PSI also reported on 'an alarmingly low level of confidence' among Asians in the ability of the police to protect them from 'racial' violence and considerable support, from about half the black people questioned, for the creation of self-defence groups where necessary (Gordon, 1990: 29). The PSI study showed that West Indians were more vulnerable than whites to assault, burglary and vandalism (Mayhew, Elliot and Dowds, 1989: 43).

Several reports at that time proposed the formation of so-called racial incident prevention panels. The Metropolitan Police did set up five experimental panels in London. The idea was that such panels would bring together police, local authorities, teachers, Community Relations Officers, minority community groups, and others. Later, this approach became known as the multi-agency approach (discussed on pp. 72–74). The request, for instance by the JCAR in 1981, for the introduction of special police units to deal specifically with the 'racial' violence and harassment was turned down by the 1981 Home Office report.

The British context in the 1980s

In 1981, racist violence had been officially recognised by the state as constituting a social problem in Britain. However, daily problems directly and indirectly connected with racist violence did not undergo an immediate change. For instance, it would be wrong to conclude that the rest of the 1980s were peaceful after the 1980–81 disorders. The defeat of the National Front in 1979 seemed to have driven at least some of their supporters from the political battleground into street violence. The involvement of extreme right groups in racist incidents sometimes was extremely obvious. And so was the contribution of the general political climate in Britain to the perceived increase of this violence.

An example of the elements contributing to this climate was the implementation of the Nationality Act in 1981, the same year as the publication of the *Racial Attacks* report. This Act brought the rules on nationality into line with British immigration legislation. 'In practice, however, the purpose of the Act was to surround blacks with a maze of nationality definitions complex enough both for them to feel insecure about their status and for harassers to have carte blanche to act against them' (Tompson, 1988: 75). 'Given the prevalence of racialised political discourse, and the emphasis of the new-right on the need to reassert the importance of patriotism and nationalism in British political culture, it is perhaps not surprising that it is during the 1980s that the issue of racial attacks has become such a major issue' (Solomos, 1989: 134).

Social unrest was evident throughout the 1980s. In 1982, some disturbances occurred but these were overshadowed completely by the war in the Falklands. In 1983–84, riots took place in London and Liverpool (Benyon and Solomos, 1987: 5). In the summer of 1985, serious riots occurred in areas such as Handsworth in Birmingham and Tottenham in London; in September and October 1985, there was rioting throughout Britain (see Benyon and Solomos, 1987; Rose, 1992, and others). These disturbances were mainly triggered by police stop and search operations. These stop and search operations were still prominent in the police tactics designed to prevent crime, even after strong criticism was expressed in the aftermath of the 1981 riots. At a Monday Club meeting in October 1982, Inspector Basil Griffiths, Deputy Chairman of the Police Federation, stated that 'There is in our inner cities a very large minority of people who are not fit for salvage ... the only way in which the police can protect society is quite simply by harassing these people and frightening them so they are afraid to commit crimes'.[34]

The Cabinet decided against complying with demands for a public inquiry. Home Secretary Douglas Hurd claimed the riots to be 'not a social phenomenon but crimes: not a cry for help, but a cry for loot'. Labour MP Roy Hattersley condemned the riots as criminal and as 'an act of pure wickedness' (Layton-Henry, 1992: 136). The Asian members of the Birmingham Community Relations Council resigned, protesting against the insufficient condemnation of the violence in Handsworth. On 20 September, Powell delivered a speech which was widely condemned and which seemed to call for a policy of repatriation (Benyon, 1986: 95).

Conservative politicians, newspapers, and police officers 'ascribed the riots to criminality and subversives, imitation, base impulses in human nature and general evil, or to a failure in education and a breakdown in family life and proper values' (Benyon, 1987a: 32). Conservative Party Chairman Norman Tebbit stated the riots to be the result of 'wickedness' and suggested that this moral degeneration was a legacy of the permissive society of the 1960s. Police officers stated that the riots were planned by political extremists or by drug dealers. The *Daily Express* newspaper (8 October 1985) published an article about a 'death squad' trained in Moscow and Libya.

Some police officers, however, pointed to social disadvantage and unemployment as important factors, and the Labour and Alliance parties, churches and community leaders adopted the view that poverty, deprivation, political exclusion and marginalisation, and alienation and discrimination were the main causes. Black community leaders blamed police harassment and abuse as well as 'racial' discrimination and disadvantage.

'The immediate precipitant or trigger events in each one of the disorders consisted of an incident involving police officers and black people, and each occurred in areas in which there is widespread antagonism between some members of the ethnic minorities and the police' (Benyon, 1986: 3). Five characteristics were reported to be common to the areas where the rioting occurred: (1) 'racial' disadvantage and discrimination were major afflictions; (2) unemployment was high, and particularly affected youth and especially young black people; (3) deprivation was widespread; (4) political exclusion and powerlessness were evident; and (5) mistrust of and hostility towards the police was widespread among certain sections of the community, particularly the young (Benyon, 1987a: 33–5).

Lord Scarman's report on the 1981 riots showed unemployment, urban deprivation, 'racial' disadvantage, bad relations between young blacks and the police, the decline of civil consent and political exclusion to be key issues. Both the Labour and Conservative speakers in parliamentary debates about the riots accepted the need for supporting the police. Any substantial disagreement centred around the socioeconomic and social factors.

The public and state responses to the 1985 riots were different from those in 1981, at least in degree, and to the extent to which the riots were seen as a 'race' phenomenon. 'The racialisation of public debate about the 1985 riots went much further than 1980–1. In this context it was the externality of British Afro-Caribbeans and Asians which was highlighted rather than the racist institutions and processes which worked against blacks at all levels in society' (Solomos and Rackett, 1991: 56–7).

The 1985 riots marked another turning point in the mainstream discourses because the riots were mainly perceived as the work of a criminal and desocialised minority. Responses to the riots were dominated by the perception of youth alienated and violent towards the rest of society. In the aftermath of the 1985 riots a transformation was noticeable in which certain minority communities and especially black youth were now presented and perceived as 'the enemy within' (see Solomos, 1988: 204–5). This led to a notion of the riots being not social phenomena to be dealt with by social and socioeconomic policies, but 'pure crimes' which had to be confronted only by (tougher and more advanced) policing measures.

After the unrest in 1985 and particularly after the 1987 elections, the Conservative government announced a number of initiatives with respect to the inner cities. There was, however, a great discrepancy between government promises of action and the allocation of resources for their implementation. During the previous decade, the intent of the government had been to reduce the powers of local authorities rather than improve them in favour of fundamental changes in the social conditions of the inner cities (Solomos and Rackett, 1991: 62–3). This policy was highlighted by the dissolving of the Greater London Council. (One should remember that a number of major city councils were dominated by the Labour Party.)

Social resistance against racist violence in the 1980s

The 1980s showed an increasing number of demonstrations and other protest activities against racist violence and harassment. The demonstration in March 1981 which 15,000 people attended after the New Cross fire has already been mentioned (p. 59). In 1982, 1984 and 1985, similar demonstrations which also attracted a lot of publicity were organised after incidents of racist violence.

In the 1980s, an increase in the number of self-defence cases was noted. However, in practice, the right to self-defence recognised by law was denied by the police and by the courts. The example of the Virk brothers has been mentioned (p. 50). In 1981, twelve Asian youths in Bradford were arrested for making petrol bombs. They stated that they had done so in order to defend their community from an attack believed to be imminent. The jury accepted their argument and the 'Bradford 12' were acquitted.

In 1983, eight Asians in East London ('the Newham 8') were arrested after a fight with a number of men who turned out to be plain clothes police officers. The Asian youths had created a self-defence group after a series of attacks on school pupils. The jury finally acquitted four of them on all charges, and four others were convicted of affray. The threat of the emergence and expansion of self-defence groups played an important part in securing the place of racist violence and harassment on the formal agenda. The phenomenon of self-defence was seen as threatening public order and taken very seriously by the state authorities (Gordon, 1993: 169), but it also ensured that racist violence was perceived as a recognised cause.

Several monitoring groups were created and met much resistance, especially from the police and other state agencies. For instance, after three police monitoring groups had published a dossier on 'racial' attacks and criticised police inaction, the Metropolitan Police Commissioner responded by saying that the groups' involvement was often motivated by political activism and posed 'practical complications for the police'.[35] Implicitly, this made clear the police's belief that monitoring groups themselves were responsible, at least in part, for the failure of the police to deal with racist violence (Gordon, 1990: 30–1).

Responses since the mid-1980s: more reports

Every now and then, the 'racial' attacks issue attracted attention in Parliament. In 1985, a Racial Harassment Bill was introduced by MP Harry Cohen, but did not proceed because of lack of parliamentary time. This Bill did not introduce anything new, as everything mentioned by Cohen was already included in existing legislation. The problem was not that the law could not deal with racist violence, but rather that the state authorities did not want to deal with it. There were no measures to change this situation (Gordon, 1993: 23). Another Racial Harassment Bill was put before Parliament in 1986;[36] this also failed in the House of Commons, and 'its chances of success in the immediate future are unlikely' (Commission for Racial Equality, 1987: 29).

In the mid-1980s, a large number of studies on racist violence were published in relation to local housing policies. These studies concluded that tenants were increasingly faced with 'racial' violence. The studies also made clear that only a few housing associations were registering racist incidents at all. The 1987 CRE report *Living in Terror* made clear that racist violence was widespread and common and still on the increase. The definition used by the CRE in this study involved:

Racial harassment is violence which may be verbal or physical and which includes attacks on property as well as on the person, suffered by individuals or groups because of their colour, race, nationality or ethnic or national origins, when the victim believes that the perpetrator was acting on racial ground and/or there is evidence of racism.

(Commission for Racial Equality, 1987: 8)

There was an important change here in defining racist violence in comparison with, for instance, the Home Office report. The victim's perception became one of decisive influence. Besides this, there were more grounds on which an incident was perceived to be an incident of 'racial' harassment. Not only 'race', but colour, nationality, ethnic and national origin were now included. Partly due to the CRE report as well as to others, a few, mainly local, policy changes were implemented. For instance, many local authorities amended their tenancy clauses to include 'racial' harassment as a specific reason for eviction (CRE, 1987: 26).

Many more studies and reports were published during these years. Racist violence and harassment were reported to occur on all levels of everyday life and each level was studied.[37] The reports themselves were taken as growing evidence that racist violence and harassment constituted a part of everyday life in Britain for minority communities.

Studies of local areas and annual reports by monitoring groups/projects also provided evidence of the nature and extent of the problem. These studies showed that racist violence was not limited to London. A 1987 report from Leeds, for instance, described what it called a 'daily barrage of violence and harassment' experienced by black people in the city. The report claimed that nearly half of the black people interviewed claimed to have been forced to change their lives in some way because of racist attacks (Gordon, 1990: 43).

The answer: the multi-agency approach

In July 1986, the parliamentary Home Affairs Sub-Committee on Race Relations and Immigration claimed the incidence of 'racial' attacks and harassment to be the most shameful and dispiriting aspect of 'race relations' in Britain.[38] The sub-committee noted that the violence and harassment was not only concentrated in parts of London and other major cities, but also appeared to occur in areas where visible minorities were smaller in number and therefore perceived to be more vulnerable. The sub-committee raised the possibility that, away from the major cities, 'racial' incidents were more, rather than less, numerous in proportion to the minority population (1986: iv).

The report presented a number of recommendations. One of these was 'that all police forces covering areas with appreciable ethnic minorities [should] make clear that tackling racial incidents is regarded as one of their priority tasks' (1986: vii). Another recommendation asserted 'that all police forces and local authorities whose areas contain an appreciable ethnic minority population [should] give serious consideration to the establishment of a multi-agency approach to racial incidents, and that the Home Office ensure that knowledge acquired as to the best ways of organising a multi-agency approach is disseminated' (1986: xv).

The multi-agency approach might be compared with the racial incident prevention panel (see p. 67). This approach shaped the future answer to the problem according to the official state point of view. The government decided to set up an Inter-Departmental Working Group on Racial Attacks and Harassment, which would report to the Ministerial Group on Crime Prevention. This would give further impulse to the development of a multi-agency approach (Gordon, 1990: 45).

In 1989, the so-called Inter-Departmental Racial Attacks Group (RAG) published its report and intended to give guidance to the statutory agencies with regard to the response to racial attacks and harassment. The report recommended the definition for incidents of racial attacks and harassment adopted by the Association of Chief Police Officers (ACPO) in England and Wales (1985):

any incident in which it appears to the reporting or investigating officer that the complaint involves an element of racial motivation, or any incident which includes an allegation of racial motivation made by any person.
                    (Inter-Department Racial Attacks Group, 1989: para. 14)

The Racial Attacks Group argued that 'it is best for any agency with a responsibility for responding to racial incidents to use as wide a definition as possible' (1989: para. 14). The report drew attention to the responsibility of 'all those with an influence on public opinion . . . to ensure that nothing they do or say might encourage feeling of racial antipathy' (1989: para. 28). RAG examined all the different sectors which were involved such as the police, the education agencies, social services, housing agencies, and minority groups, and presented recommendations as to how the problem should be handled.

Combating 'racial' attacks and harassment was regarded as one of the major goals of the multi-agency approach. RAG claimed 'racial' harassment to be a complex social problem to which there was no single solution (1989: para. 185). Therefore it needed 'to be addressed in a variety of social contexts, from a variety of angles, and by staff from a variety of disciplines if it is to be tackled effectively' (1989: para. 186).

According to RAG, the multi-agency approach aimed at the cooperation of several statutory agencies, and such a multi-agency group should:

• develop and sustain a coordinated response
• share information
• improve response of individual agencies
• improve mutual understanding
• provide greater reassurance to the minority ethnic communities that racial harassment is being taken seriously and dealt with in a comprehensive way.

One of the recommendations by RAG was that 'for practical reasons one of the statutory agencies will almost certainly need to take the lead in establishing multi-agency working. We recommend that . . . the police should take on this responsibility' (1989: para. 281). Although the report also argued that the multi-agency groups should not be led or dominated by the police once they were established, this turned out to be one of the main points of criticism towards the approach.

The report of the Inter-Departmental Group firmly came out in favour of the multi-agency approach to the problem of 'racial' attacks. A report by the Home Affairs Committee on Racial Attacks and Harassment that same year agreed on the definition used by RAG (similar to that used by the CRE and the ACPO). The report stated that despite 'the progress made, racism and its most ugly manifestation, racial attacks and harassment, are still frightening realities for many British citizens. An effective response to this problem by all of us, but particularly by the Home Office, police and statutory agencies is a prerequisite of a civilised multi-racial society in the United Kingdom' (1989: xiv, para. 33). The report also recommended that the Home Office should monitor the development of multi-agency cooperation, and the appropriate support and encouragement should be provided for such multi-agency approaches (1989: xvi). At the same time, the Department of the Environment (1989) published guidance on how to tackle 'racial' violence and harassment in local authority housing. It emphasised the need for liaison with other agencies, which was regarded as vital to an effective multi-agency approach.

The second report by the Inter-Departmental Racial Attacks Group in 1991 indicated that 'in over half of police force areas (27 out of 43) there is a multi-agency initiative, and this does not take into account the multi-agency work carried out within local authorities without police involvement' (1991: 28). There were several types of multi-agency initiatives recorded: crime prevention; joint action; information sharing; information transfer; evidence gathering; and victim support. Home Secretary Kenneth Baker argued in the foreword that nothing 'casts a greater blot on our civilised society than people's lives being ruined because of who they are – black, Asian, white or whatever group. Nothing demands greater commitment, energy and co-ordination in resolving it' (1991: 1).

This RAG report, as well as the report of the pilot multi-agency project funded by the Home Office, in Newham, East London (Saulsbury and Bowling, 1991), indicated that there were a lot of problems to overcome concerning this multi-agency approach such as a lack of financial resources, differences in perspectives of the different agencies and groups involved, apparent inequality of commitment, and constraints on data-gathering.

Criticism

Criticism was directed at the role of the police. Although it was generally recognised that the police should be involved, the criticism spoke of too much involvement. This was mentioned in relation to the leading role of the police in the discussion on who should participate in the multi-agency group. Self-organised, independent community groups were sometimes excluded from participation.

Debates on 'who represents whom?' were numerous and common. 'Once again we can see that, although the police and government continuously emphasise that tackling racial harassment is not just the responsibility of the police, it is they alone who determine the action to be taken by all' (Newham Monitoring Project, 1988: 29). The multi-agency approach was often questioned as to whether it allowed individual agencies to shirk their individual responsibilities and whether it obscured the fact that 'racial' attacks and harassment were criminal acts, often serious ones (Gordon, 1990: 45).

Racist violence in the late 1980s and early 1990s

At the end of the 1980s and in the early 1990s, racist violence definitely constituted a topic on the formal agenda. But the gap between theory and policy intentions on the one hand, and the practice and policy outcomes and implementations on the other, was still tremendous and obvious. The level of racist incidents reported by the police, which had risen from 4,383 in 1988 to 6,359 in 1990 and to 7,780 in 1991 (Smith, A.M., 1994: 61), did not fully indicate the scale of the problem, as the Home Secretary stated (Inter-Department Racial Attacks Group, 1991: 1). Everyone was convinced it was a matter of under-reporting, but in spite of this the figures did indicate an increase in violence and harassment.

The Salman Rushdie affair (when a fatwa or death sentence was issued against the novelist Salman Rushdie for his allegedly blasphemous book the Satanic Verses) and the Gulf War in the 1990s showed that even international developments could easily lead to an enormous increase in the number of incidents of racist violence.

What is most apparent about the Rushdie affair is the way in which the British establishment and media have exacerbated it, giving further respectability to racist ideas and actions. As a result, there has been increased racial polarization, racist violence, criminalisation of black people, as well as a fascist resurgence.

(Newham Monitoring Project, 1989: 49)

In the early 1990s, there were no signs that the problem of racist violence and harassment had diminished. In 1992, eight people were killed in racist incidents.[39] Paul Gordon mentions three reasons for this: (1) the straightforward failure by agencies to recognise the existence of the problem, to take it seriously and to implement the numerous recommendations; (2) many treated the problem as one of management and responded by seeking improved bureaucratic procedures; and (3) it had to do with the nature of 'racial' violence and its context. 'Racial violence and harassment do not occur in a vacuum but in a social and political context which can be either more or less favourable' (Gordon, 1990: 48–9).

An increase of 300 per cent in the number of racist incidents was reported after Derek Beackon of the British National Party (BNP) won a seat in by-elections in the London Borough of Tower Hamlets. In January and February 1994, an unprecedented wave of racist violence was reported in the East End of London (MacEwan, 1994: 368).

State responses in the early 1990s

In January 1989, Home Secretary Hurd stated that 'racial discrimination is not only wrong but hostile to any sense of common nationhood or hope of social peace'. He also said that strict migration control remained necessary. 'The two go together. I am certain that the creation and maintenance of [immigration] restrictions were indispensable in helping to drain the poison from discussions about immigration and race relations' (cited by Smith, A.M., 1994: 99). This is a clear linking of the 'including' and the 'excluding recognition' of racist violence by a state authority, and is a good example of a two-faced state response to racist violence.

In December 1992, MP David Winnick introduced a Bill to include racist violence as a separate criminal offence in the British Penal Code. Although this Bill was not approved by Parliament, it opened up a debate on the matter. The Commission for Racial Equality demanded such a separate status and this opinion was also heard within the Labour Party (Bindman, 1994: 526).

In 1994, a discussion paper (Bhiku Parekh, 1994) was published by the All-Party Parliamentary Group on Race and Community. This paper discussed the question of whether 'racial' violence should be included in the British Penal Code as a separate offence or that the 'racial' element of this violence should be categorised as an aggravating circumstance. In fact, this question constituted one of the major discussions on racist violence and harassment in the late 1980s and early 1990s in Britain. The discussion paper showed that the issue had entered the formal agenda. A final answer had not been given at the end of 1994.

Conclusion

In the history of Britain since 1945, the phenomenon of racist violence reached the formal agenda (i.e. phase D) twice. In the late 1950s this situation coincided with the construction of specific migrations and migrant communities as the cause of inevitable social problems within popular and political discourses. International developments like those in the United States as well as domestic developments – such as economic recession, urban unrest and 'moral panics' in relation to the arrival of specific groups of migrants – contributed to this view.

The 1958 disorders constituted the trigger event, or accelerator, which provided for its entrance on to the formal agenda. Due to the dominant popular and political discourses at the time, state responses might be typified as the 'excluding recognition' of racist violence by the state. Violence against people as alleged representatives of 'imagined minority communities' based on skin colour or national, religious, or cultural origin, was recognised as constituting a major social problem which had to be dealt with by the state ('recognition'). The concrete state responses, however, were directed against the increasing presence of the victimised groups of people ('excluding') and this was underlined in the Commonwealth Immigrants Act 1962.

The issue of racist violence disappeared from the public and formal agenda in the early 1960s. There was growing support for the anti-migration campaign, Powellism, and a process of criminalisation of specific minority communities (especially black youth); in this context certain sections of British society began to organise resistance to racist violence. In the 1970s, they attracted much attention and publicity. In terms of agenda-setting, these activities were directed towards the specification and expansion of the issue (in phase B).

This led to the second occasion on which racist violence entered the formal agenda in the early 1980s. This entrance was partly due to the work of external actors (i.e. outside initiatives) such as minority and anti-racism organisations, and of internal actors (i.e. inside initiatives or mobilisation), especially the Joint Commission Against Racialism, and the struggles within the Home Office, as well as social unrest (perceived in connection with specific communities, 'race relations' and socioeconomic deprivation). The 1981 report could be typified as the 'including recognition' of racist violence by the state. The violence was recognised as constituting a social problem which the state had to deal with, and policy measures were formulated to combat the occurrence of this violence as well as circumstances that were favourable to its occurrence ('including').

Since 1981, racist violence has been an issue on the formal agenda resulting in many studies, reports, proposals and policy initiatives. The main state responses towards this phenomenon have been based on the notion of the multi-agency approach. Despite much criticism, this approach of 'including recognition' of racist violence by the state was still recognised as the key feature of state policy against racist violence. Besides the 'including recognition' of racist violence, instances of 'excluding recognition' by local as well as national state authorities have also occurred since the early 1980s. This period was not a phase of united state action against racist violence. A number of examples indicated that there were different perceptions and definitions of the issues surrounding racist violence even within a state machinery in which the view of racist violence as a matter of law and order and of policing was still dominant. Therefore, this period might be characterised as one of two-faced state responses to racist violence.

Notes

1 In this chapter, the term 'black' will generally refer to British citizens of both Afro-Caribbean and Asian origin.

2 This increase was a direct consequence of the implementation of the McCarren-Walter Act in the United States (Kettle and Hodges, 1982: 40; Layton-Henry, 1992: 31). This Act constituted a ban on West Indian migration to the USA, which until then was by and large more extensive than the migration to the United Kingdom. This US Act obviously 'boosted West Indian migration to Britain' (Hiro, 1992: 15).

3 PRO-CAB/142/1191, December 1953; as cited by Pilkington (1988: 70).

4 As cited by Pilkington (1988: 97; my italics).

5 Report of Proceedings at the 90th Annual Trades Union Congress (1958: 326; as cited by Fryer, 1991: 380).

6 Hansard, vol. 709, 1965: cols 378–85, as quoted by Solomos (1989: 73).

7 One report was by the Political and Economic Planning Ltd (PEP), 'Racial Discrimination', London, 1967. The other report was a national opinion poll, quoted by the *Sunday Times*, as cited by Hiro (1992: 218).

8 *Daily Express*, 1 March 1968; as cited by Joshua *et al.* (1983: 97).

9 For further detailed descriptions, see e.g. Layton-Henry (1984: 69); Solomos (1989: 54); Fryer (1991: 383–4); Hiro (1992: 212–15).

10 As quoted by Gordon (1993: 167).

11 As cited by Hiro (1992: 212).

12 As cited by Hiro (1992: 214).

13 *The Times*, 12 March 1973; as cited by S. Hall *et al.* (1978: 8).

14 M. Cain (1973) *Society and the Policeman's Role*, London: Routledge & Kegan Paul, pp. 117–19, as cited by Fryer (1991: 392).

15 This perceived peak of racist incidents coincided with intensifying debates

by the media and politicians with respect to the subject of so-called illegal immigration and immigrants in 1976.

16 This Commission (CRE) was established after the implementation of the third Race Relations Act in 1976 and might be perceived as the fusion between the Race Relations Board and the Community Relations Commission. The CRE had more authority in the field of research and more possibilities to use the right of 'public interest' in cases of discrimination practices.

17 The SPG was instigated in the aftermath and as a consequence of the moral panic about mugging.

18 For an impression of the living conditions meant here, see the television movie *Black and Blue* by D. Hayman, 1992.

19 The Granada Television programme *World in Action* (30 January 1978), see Solomos (1989: 129) as well as Fryer (1991: 397).

20 In the 1974 elections – which Labour won with a very narrow margin – the Conservative Party turned out to have attracted hardly any support from within the minority communities.

21 *Guardian*, 31 January 1978, as cited by Solomos (1989: 130).

22 The Joint Commission Against Racialism included the Conservative, Labour and Liberal Parties, the British Council of Churches, the Board of Deputies of British Jews, the National Union of Students, the British Youth Council and leading immigrant organisations (Bowling, 1993b: 23–4).

23 Hansard, 5 February 1981, col. 393, as cited by Home Office (1981: 1).

24 Simon Cottle, 'Race', Racialisation and the Media: A Review and Update of Research', an unpublished paper, p. 12.

25 This stop and search operation by the police between 6 and 11 April resulted in 943 stops, over two-thirds were aged under 21 and more than half were black. During the operation, 118 people were arrested and 75 charged, but these 'included only one for robbery, one for attempted burglary and twenty charges of theft or attempted theft' (Lord Scarman, 1981: para 4.40).

26 BBC, 3 May 1981; as cited by Layton-Henry (1984: 161).

27 *Financial Times*, July 1981, headed with 'Outbreak of an alien disease', as cited by Solomos (1988: 179).

28 As cited by Solomos (1989: 103).

29 House of Commons (1982: 17); as cited by Bowling (1993b: 35).

30 Metropolitan Police Force Order on Racial Incidents 1978, cited in House of Commons (1982: 17) as quoted by Bowling (1993b: 31).

31 Metropolitan Police Force Order 1982; as cited by Bowling (1993b: 36).

32 For instance, a central coordination and observation unit; improvement in responses to emergency calls, detailed instructions to police stations.

33 For instance crime prevention measures and fullest possible support to a Race and Housing Action Team.

34 *The Times*, 7 October 1982; as cited by Layton-Henry (1992: 128).

35 Report of the Commissioner of Police of the Metropolis for the Year 1983, June 1984: 47–8.

36 This Bill
   • declared that racial harassment was an offence
   • provided penalties against perpetrators
   • required that landlords take action against perpetrators in specific circumstances
   • placed duties upon local authorities to investigate complaints of racial harassment

- provided an appeals procedure for defendants who felt they might have been wronged
- gave power to the Commission for Racial Equality to investigate landlords who had failed to support tenants against racial harassment
- provided for individual redress against perpetrators
- placed duties on landlords to inform tenants of the possible consequences of racial harassment.

37 Examples were: *housing* (CRE, *Living in Terror*, 1987; Forbes, 1988; and Department of the Environment, 1989), *education* (CRE, *Learning in Terror*, 1988; MacDonald *et al.*, *Murder in the Playground*, 1989; and Newham Monitoring Project, *Racism and Racist Violence in Schools*, 1990), *the police* (the Institute of Race Relations, *Policing Against Black People*, 1987; and *Deadly Silence: Black Deaths in Custody*, 1991), and the *victimization of ethnic minority groups* (Mayhew *et al.*, 1988).

38 The third report by the Home Affairs Sub-Committee on Race Relations and Immigration, Racial Violence and Harassment (1986: iv).

39 *Manchester Weekly Guardian*, 28 February 1993: 3; as cited by Smith, A.M., (1994: 61).

CHAPTER 3

State responses to racist violence in France

Introduction

> The fight against this type of violence, and against the circumstances in which it flourishes in our cities, remains a priority within my actions.[1]

This statement by the French Prime Minister, Michel Rocard, was made after several racist incidents in the first months of 1990. The action he promised included an invitation to all political parties, except the extreme-right *Front National*, for a round table meeting concerning racism. The initiative was intended to elicit and enhance, state responses to racist violence in France, In early May 1990, the French Parliament had passed legislation which included stronger sanctions against racism and against the denial of the genocide of Jews during the Holocaust. However, it was another racist incident which brought this kind of violence really to the centre of the formal agenda.

The discovery of the desecration of a Jewish cemetery in Carpentras (10 May 1990) attracted enormous national and international attention. After this incident, state authorities were even more eager to develop measures in line with the 'including recognition' of racist violence in French society.

This was not the first time that racist violence constituted a topic on the French formal agenda. In the French history of state responses to racist violence since 1945, four periods can be distinguished: the 1950s and mid-1960s, the late 1960s to 1980, the early and mid-1980s, and the late 1980s to early 1990s. This periodisation is based on key features in the state responses to racist violence, as well as to the political, ideological and public discourses which were dominant at the time.

The 1950s to mid-1960s: the problem of 'political terrorism'

The 1950s and early 1960s were years of decolonisation – not least of all in France. This process had an impact on the ex-colonies involved, as well as on France itself. After the Second World War, France was a devastated country with respect to both human resources and material circumstances. The French economy had to be rebuilt, and the means to do so were urgently sought.

Post-war migration

The enormous need for helping hands led to a more or less spontaneous migration of European and non-European workers and their families for demographic and economic reasons. Labour migration was assumed to be the solution to post-war labour shortages. The French government set up a special office (*l'Office National d'Immigration*, ONI, 1945) to organise the recruitment of these migrants. Since 1945, France has seen a continuous migration of workers (see Freeman, 1979; Castles, Booth and Wallace, 1987; Wihtol de Wenden, 1988; Noriel, 1988, among others).

In the beginning, the majority of migrant workers arrived from Italy. Once the demand in western Europe for migrant labour increased, people from Spain, Portugal, Yugoslavia and Turkey were recruited. Up until 1954, the agricultural sector was the main employer of migrant workers in France (Salt, 1976: 84). Labour migrants recruited by the ONI originated from European countries. Figures in 1962 showed that a vast majority of the migrants entering France in this period originated from EC countries and Spain and Portugal (Freeman, 1979: 23).

Non-regulated migrations, however, included many people from the French colonies who held French nationality. In the first decades following the Second World War, focus turned towards the migration to France by people from Algeria. Many of them had served in the French and 'allied' forces liberating the European continent from fascist occupation. Although many returned to Algeria after the war, a number of them stayed and worked to rebuild France. In the years after the war, further groups of migrant workers came from Algeria where they found themselves in a complex situation, especially when the Algerian War of Independence started in 1954. Emphasis should be placed on the fact that these migrants were French subjects.

The defence of Algérie française

Resistance against the decolonisation process was organised both in the colonies and in France itself. In the mid-1950s, the opposition formed the *Union de Défense des Commerçants et Artisans* (UDCA) – better known through its leader Pierre Poujade. Through the years, the defence of *Algérie française* constituted the main issue of the Poujadist movement. This led to an influx of far right, extreme nationalistic, anti-Gaullist, and anti-communist militants into the party (Stouthuysen, 1993: 25).

Fascist and neo Nazi groups organised themselves outside the parliamentary political arena too. Many of those who had collaborated in the Second World War were pardoned in 1953. A number of these collaborators, and some of the so-called *pieds noirs* (French nationals born in, and repatriated from, the colonies), used the French wars in Indochina (Vietnam) and Algeria to mobilise popular support and recruit new followers amongst those who could not reconcile themselves to the loss of the colonies (Anne Frank Stichting, 1985: 51).

This resistance was directed not only against decolonisation, but also against their fellow French citizens living in France but originating from the (former) colonies. One of the well-known organisations, the *Organisation de l'Armée Secrète* (OAS), was active in both Algeria and France. After a failed military coup in Algeria (April 1961) the organisation took to terrorist activities. Apart from attempted attacks against popular and political figures, such as President de Gaulle (August 1962), many Algerian migrants were victimised and killed. The OAS was responsible for the death of thoudands of Algerians and Europeans and received active support from certain sections of the French security forces (Schmid and Jongman, 1988: 549).

Deplorable conditions in France

During the Algerian War (1954–62), the problems of migrant workers were publicly discussed for the first time. With the migrant workers from Algeria the main subject of these debates. A number of Deputies in the *Assemblée Nationale* (Parliament) demanded immediate steps be taken to improve the terrible living conditions of immigrant workers, which were partly a result of the spontaneous and chaotic character of the immigration. These conditions were 'the most reprehensible social conditions of any group of workers in Europe' (Freeman, 1979: 78). Often migrant workers and their families lived in and around industrial centres in *bidonvilles*: places built with tin cans and cardboard, without any facilities. These conditions were considered 'all too visible signs of the Third World in the metropolis' (Castles, Booth and Wallace, 1987: 52).

Their situation grew worse as hostility and violence towards them increased. During the Algerian war, an enormous increase in violence against French citizens of Algerian origin was reported. The war even introduced a specific word into the French language to describe attacks on North Africans: *ratonnades*, literally 'rat hunts'. Many *ratonnades* were said to be organised by the OAS and executed by off-duty police officers. These attacks were aimed against the *bidonvilles* (Lloyd, 1993: 211).

In these years, the connection between certain migrant groups and social problems was established due to the public debates and a growing awareness of migrants' living conditions. The influence of 1 million *colons* (former colonists) who had repatriated, as well as the emotional consequences (read: frustrations) of the Algerian War, impeded this – it was a situation in which demands for and efforts at improvement did not stand a chance (Freeman, 1979: 82).

At the end of the war in October 1961, the Paris Prefect of Police, Maurice Papon, announced a curfew on 'Algerian' French citizens.[2] The measure was introduced, according to the Minister of Interior Roger Frey, in order to protect 'honest French Muslims, and to be able to distinguish them from criminals.'[3] According to Frey, it was necessary to ban 'Algerian people' from the streets at night, and to close down the cafés they visited.

A demonstration was held on 17 October against this curfew, against terrorisation by the police and by the OAS, and for the independence of Algeria. The demonstration, attended by some 30,000 people, ended in a massacre. The police drove people into the River Seine to drown, clubbed people to death, and fired into the crowds. It was not until the early 1980s that the facts surrounding these events became widely known, discussed and studies. The newspaper *Le Monde* (10 February 1980) estimates that at least 200 people had been killed during the demonstration, while others report more than 400 deaths (van den Brink, Cuartes and Tanja, 1988: 18). Until the early 1980s this massacre constituted a remarkable example of national amnesia (Guidice, 1992: 337). At the time, media reports gave the police version – portraying the demonstrators as terrorists (Lloyd, 1993: 212). The casualties were also portrayed as the result of gang violence (see Guidice, 1992: 333–51; Woodall, 1993: 27).

State responses to 'political terrorism'

Racist violence during these years was not recognised as such. It seems reasonable to conclude that racist violence in the Algerian war period was perceived only within a context of the decolonisation process and not in a political, ideological, racist context. For instance, this was shown by the establishment of the *Service d'Action Civique* (SAC) in 1958 as an unofficial security arm of the Gaullist movement. SAC recruited former resistance people and underground figures, and fought a deadly, secret war against the OAS. The OAS opposed de Gaulle's policy of negotiation and final withdrawal from Algeria. SAC held the status of an extra legal security force in the early 1960s.[4]

Another response constituted the banning of organisations and continued to be a political response against organisations linked with extreme right racist terrorist activities throughout the years; the extreme right-wing *Occidence* was banned in 1968. In 1973, the *Ordre Nouveau* (New Order) which had been set up as the successor to *Occidence* in 1969, was also banned. The *Ordre Nouveau* looked up to military dictatorships in Greece, Spain and Portugal, and the system of Apartheid in South Africa. Their activities were directed against what they called 'the invasion of Europe by Arabs'. The organisation was banned because of its violent activities, links with neo Nazi and fascist groups in Europe, and the possession of an arms cache. By the time of its banning, many members of the *Ordre Nouveau* had joined the *Front National* (van den Brink *et al.*, 1988: 18). In 1980, the *Fédération d'Action Nationale et Europeénne* (FANE), set up in 1966 and 'specialised' in anti-semitism, which has had a long history in France (this will be elaborated upon later) was banned, FANE was involved in many racist attacks.

In this period, granting pardons constituted a regular part of official policy in France too. In 1953, as already mentioned, many Second World War collaborators were pardoned. In 1968 this happened to many officials of the OAS. Among them was Pierre Sergent, who had been the military commander of the OAS in France, and was responsible for numerous terrorist attacks. He was twice sentenced to death *in absentia* before he was fully pardoned. In 1988 he became a member of the *Assemblée Nationale* for the *Front National*.

In this period of decolonisation, racist violence as such did not constitute a subject on the formal agenda. Nor were there any reports which show it had been placed on the public agenda. Violence with obvious racist aspects and motives were perceived in the context of decolonisation and defined as 'political terrorism'. The violence was not recognised as a problem of violence motivated by racist ideologies and sentiments.

State responses showed the perception of this violence as a problem of state security. This was underlined by banning specific organisations, and establishing a special secret service. These responses made it implicitly clear that the assumed threat to state security was at the core of the issue.

The specific victimisation of 'Algerian communities' in France did not enter the dominant discourse. This is made emphatically clear by the deadly state response in October 1961 towards those demonstrating against their victimisation. The demonstrators themselves were portrayed in the dominant discourse as a threat to state security. This was also the reason for the curfew introduced against these specifically 'Algerian communities'.

The late 1960s to 1980: from non-issue to 'excluding recognition'

The problematisation of North African migrants

The 1968 revolt by students and workers marked a turning point in French immigration policy. It brought the de Gaulle government to the brink of resignation. Foreign students, for instance Daniel Cohn-Bendit, and workers were subsequently expelled. The Minister of Interior had summary powers to remove foreigners whose presence created a public security 'emergency' without the right of appeal (Freeman, 1979: 85).

In these years, immigration was increasingly perceived as a problem. This applied to immigrants in general, but especially to those who originated from the African continent with or without French nationality and to Algerians in particular. In 1969, various statements were made defining a new immigration policy. The most important consisted of a report by M. Corentin Calves, adopted by the Social and Economic Council in February 1969.

This report concluded that France needed a systematic, coordinated, thorough policy, and that the immigration issue should receive first priority. The increasing numbers of North African immigrants was assumed to be causing social problems. These people were regarded as unskilled, and not easy to assimilate into French society. The report estimated that some 2.5 million Algerians would be in France by the year 2000, and spoke of the creation of an 'unassimilable island' (Freeman, 1979: 88). Not one word was said about the fact that by the late 1960s most immigrants were Europeans. Implicitly the latter were not perceived to be 'unassimilable' nor as 'causing problems'. By 1970, over 3 million immigrants lived in France. More than 2 million people originated from European countries, including 592,000 Italians, 645,000 Spaniards and 607,000 Portuguese. From Northern Africa, some 900,000 people resided in France, including 650,000 Algerians (Freeman, 1979: 23).

Four months after the presentation of the report, the Minister of Social Affairs, Maurice Schumann, publicly supported its major conclusions. He did not call for an outright selection policy on the basis of 'race' or culture. However, he stated that large-scale immigration from countries with a lower level of economic development than France needed to be reduced substantially (Freeman, 1979: 89).

Racist violence in the early 1970s

In January 1970, French public opinion was shocked when five African workers were asphyxiated while sleeping in a five-room building which they shared with forty-five other colleagues. Prime Minister Pompidou paid a visit to the scene. In the same period, violence against immigrants was increasingly reported. 'Algerians' were over-represented among those victimised. The involvement of extreme-right paramilitary organisations was obvious (Freeman, 1979: 91), and reported racist attacks by unorganised, individual French people on North African migrants were on the increase (Castles, Booth and Wallace, 1984: 52).

After the murder of the 15-year-old Algerian Djilali Ben Ali in Paris (27 October 1971), the subsequent protest attracted media and public attention. On 7 November 1971, a demonstration was held. This demonstration was the first, since 1962, which protested against the murder of a North African by a Frenchmen, described as a *crime raciste* (Guidice, 1992: 61). In the aftermath of this event, a 'Djilali committee' was set up, and a declaration against the violence was signed by fifteen prominent figures, among them Claude Mauriac, Jean Genet, Michel Foucault, Jean-Paul Sartre, Yves Montand and Simone Signoret (Guidice, 1992: 75).

State response

On 1 July 1972, anti-discrimination legislation was passed in Parliament. The new legislation could be perceived as a legal update of the existing legislation of 1881 and of the 1939 Marchandeau Law with respect to the freedom of the press directed against racist propaganda

(Viard, 1984: 1942). The new law (no. 72-546) included three elements: (1) the 1939 injunction of the incitement to racist discrimination, hatred and violence; (2) measures against discrimination based on the adherence or non-adherence to a determined ethnic group, nation, race or religion; and (3) the possible banning of organisations because of activities inciting racist hatred (Freeman, 1979: 154). The 1972 Act also included an addition to the Act of 10 January 1936 '*sur les groupes de combat et milices privées*', which made it possible to ban armed groups and private militia. The 1936 Act was extended to ban organisations on the basis of racist activities and racist violence (van Donselaar, 1995).

The 1972 Act constituted a response to the French ratification of the (UN) International Convention on the Elimination of All Forms of Racial Discrimination (New York, 1965) in 1971, and to the increasing social tensions in French society. However, it would be wrong to interpret its implementation as a consequence of central government policy priorities (Freeman, 1979: 94). The implementation of this new legislation mainly originated from the work carried out by individual Deputies (MPs) and organisations striving for equal justice. In fact, the 1972 legislation was the result of the Campaign for Law against Racism which was organised throughout the 1960s by anti-racist organisations such as the *Mouvement Contre le Racisme et pour l'Amitié entre les Peuples* (MRAP).[5] The campaign involved small-scale discrimination testing, publicity stunts to draw attention to racism with respect to housing and social conditions, and test cases (Lloyd, 1991: 69).

In 1959, 1962, 1967 and 1969, anti-discrimination Bills were introduced by Deputies. The government, however, never allowed these initiatives to be debated in the *Assemblée Nationale* (Parliament). This rejection was motivated by two important elements in the dominant political discourse of these years. First of all, the French political and cultural discourse was dominated by the assumption that everyone is (already) equal by law. France was the country, after all, where human rights and equality had been established since 1789. Thus, the opinion prevailed that present legislation was sufficient (Freeman, 1979: 154). The second element consisted of the belief that people were responsible for their own circumstances (Freeman, 1979: 156).

The acceptance of the 1972 law was a classic example of the way in which 'external actors' (outside the state apparatus) organised activities in order to place an issue (here: discrimination) on the formal agenda. This resulted in the implementation of legislation with the help of some 'internal actors' (Deputies of the *Assemblée Nationale*), even though the main state actors were not particularly involved in this.

In 1972, the Pompidou government issued two *circulaires* introducing new steps in policies towards existing and future migrants. The alleged purpose of these Marcellin and Fontanet *circulaires* (named after the Ministers of Interior and Labor who issued them) was to ensure adequate housing for immigrants, and to simplify administrative procedures. In actual fact, however, they resulted in increasing insecurity for migrant workers. Migrants needed a labour contract for a year, and residence and working permits were linked. Besides these measures, the local police were authorised to make any decision concerning renewal and extension of these permits. In this way the burden of responsibility for poor living and working conditions was placed on the migrant workers themselves. The *circulaires* created a situation in which many were afraid of any changes during the year in case these might result in loss of approved status (Freeman, 1979: 93).

Protest and even hunger strikes against these two *circulaires* were organised by organisations such as the *Fédération des Associations de Solidarité avec les Travailleurs Immigrés* and by the churches. The latter gave shelter to the strikers, many of whom were of Tunisian or Pakistani origin. Other protests in these years, directed against the circumstances in which immigrants had to live and against the violence in particular, were organised by the *Movement des Travailleurs Arabes* (Movement of Arabic workers, MTA) and MRAP.

The year 1973: a wave of racist violence

In June 1973, the new Minister of Labour, M. Gorse, announced his decision to humanise the Fontanet *circulaire*, but warned that all irregular workers would be dealt with severely, and that all borders remained firmly closed to illegal immigration (Freeman, 1979: 95). In that same month, the extreme right-wing organisation *Ordre Nouveau* launched a new campaign. This campaign had two targets: to stop the 'uncontrolled immigration by Arabs' and to fight anti-fascism (Guidice, 1992: 126). In the context of increasing public and political attention to immigration (restrictions), France was confronted with a dramatic wave of reported racist violence in the second half of 1973.

On 25 August 1973, a youngster of Algerian origin suffering from mental depression stabbed a bus driver to death in Marseille. This event was the trigger for a whole series of racist killings. That same day, three 'Algerians' were killed in separate incidents in Marseille and another 'Algerian' in Perreux (Val du Marne). The next day, a local newspaper, *Le Méridionale*, called for stringent government measures to be taken against immigration, and threatened direct action (Lloyd, 1993: 212–13). The editor of this, M. Gabriel Domenech, argued that:

Racism is Arabic; after all there is no European racism, since we have already long accepted the abuses of the Arab world . . . With the good reason being oil. (. . .) We have had enough! Enough of the Algerian thieves, enough of the Algerian rowdies, enough of the Algerian braggarts, enough of the Algerian agitators, enough of the Algerian sufferers of syphilis, enough of the Algerian rapists, enough of the Algerian pimps, enough of the Algerian lunatics, enough of the Algerian killers.

(Tahar Ben Jelloun, 1984: 68)

In the following two weeks at least another five 'Algerians' were killed – three in the Marseille region, one in Metz, and one in Maubeuge (Viard, 1984: 1946). Some have reported that at least ten people were killed in the whole of France (Lloyd, 1993: 213). Besides these killings there were shootings and arson attacks on cafés, hotels, *bidonvilles*, and Sonacotra hostels. These hostels were set up especially to accommodate migrant workers, and many North Africans lived in them. In 1973, thirty-two 'Algerians' were reported killed, mainly in Marseille, Toulon and Nice (Castles, Booth and Wallace, 1987: 52). In total, an estimated fifty-two 'Algerians' were either killed or badly wounded (Guidice, 1992: 126).

Two things at least were very obvious. There had been an enormous increase of reported racist killings in France, and 'Algerians' (with or without French nationality) were the main targets of this violence in 1973). This wave of racist violence took place within a context of increasing public and political debate about migration controls, and problems perceived in connection with the presence of specific migrant communities in France, especially those originating from North Africa.

State responses to racist violence

Few of these homicides were ever solved by the police. Only one of the perpetrators was reported to be arrested. He killed an 'Algerian' man (28 August 1973), and was arrested on 26 October 1973. He stated that he had taken part in *une chasse aux Arabes* ('a hunt for Arabs'). The perpetrator was never brought to trial because he died in 1974 (Viard, 1984: 1945).

On more than one occasion, the racist character of an incident was explicitly denied. On 14 December 1973, a bomb exploded at the Algerian consulate in Marseille. Four people were killed and twenty wounded. That same day, the Chief of Police in Marseille announced that it was not a racist attack. The attack, however, was claimed by the *Club Charles Martel*, a rightist anti-immigrant group known to be involved in violence against North Africans in France.[6] It proclaimed that violence was necessary to speed up the departure of 'Algerians' from France.

There was little direct state response to these incidents indicating a reluctance to recognise the racist character of the violence. At a meeting of the Council of Ministers (31 August 1973), President Pompidou argued that France should not become entangled in the snare of racism. 'Sometimes, the simple fact of mentioning the word summons up the idea, and reality, unfortunately, often follows the idea.'[7] Minister of Interior Marcellin started a debate about whether or not to expel foreigners who 'disturbed civil order'. Many people perceived the government as taking this response to the violent incidents in order to expel the cadres of the immigrant organisations.[8]

There were some responses by authorities, however, explicitly condemning violent racist attacks. One of the most outspoken condemnations was made by Prime Minister Pierre Messner who stated, 'I have said and I will repeat that racism horrifies me. I spent a part of my life fighting it and not just with words. I think that France should be and remain a country where foreigners are welcomed, understood, and respected.'[9] This statement could be classified as an example of individual 'including recognition' of racist violence by a state authority.

On 19 September 1973, the Algerian government announced a halt to all emigration to France for as long as the security and dignity of Algerian citizens could not be guaranteed by the French authorities (Viard, 1984: 1946). This provided 'a breathing spell' for the French authorities, and removed the onus from them of suspending Algerian migration. This was a step the administration surely had considered, but which, under the circumstances, would have appeared to be a cowardly attempt to punish the victims rather than the aggressor (Freeman, 1979: 95). This was one of the very few examples where a government of the country from which the immigrants originated acted as an external pressure group.

Another response, also in 1973, was the banning of *Ordre Nouveau*, as mentioned earlier. This action was directed against outspoken, organised violence, and was in line with the previously mentioned state response to assumed threats of state security. On the whole, however, there were no signs whatsoever of the recognition of racist violence constituting a social problem in France, a problem which had to be dealt with by the French state. Immigration controls were not implemented immediately, because Algeria was implementing those itself.

Neither racism nor racist violence nor migration were 'hot issues' during the election campaigns held after the sudden death of President Pompidou. The newly elected President Giscard d'Estaing stated that immigrant workers as a part of the 'French national productive community' should have a dignified and humane place in society. This declaration was 'the first serious attempt by a French political leader to exert a decisive influence on public opinion and to take a principled stand against racism'.[10] The statement could be seen as an example of the 'including recognition' of racist violence by a state actor. After three months in office, however, the new Giscard d'Estaing government announced a temporary suspension of all further immigration except from European Community countries, due to the oil crisis, economic depression, and a general decrease of demand for unskilled labour (Ogden, 1991: 300). Thus, while the state emphasised its position against racism (in the statement by Giscard d'Estaing), the first concrete state action consisted of a 'new immigration policy'.

In May 1974, Paul Dijoud was appointed Secretary of State for Immigrant Workers. He announced tighter control on entries, deportation of 'illegals' and integration of those migrants legally in France through a long-term programme of naturalisation and assimilation. In

July 1974, government action went even further. Not only was the entry of non-European migrant workers prohibited, but also that of family members of those migrant workers already resident in France (Castles *et al.*, 1984: 52–3).

The discourse of seuil de tolérance

One of the important elements in the state discourse involving the immigrant population was the notion of the so-called *seuil de tolérance* (threshold of tolerance). The theory posed a 'natural law' that any given society could absorb no more than a certain maximum number of 'stangers'. Exceeding this threshold would lead to social conflict. The dominance of this idea among members of the policy-making elite (Freeman, 1979: 159) resulted in steps to control immigration, and in the assumption that migrants had to assimilate fully. It was a genuinely 'social' law in that it denied motives and responsibilities of the individual people involved.

One implication of this *seuil de tolérance* was the idea that racism and racist conflicts (i.e. racist violence) could be prevented only by (1) stopping immigration and (2) dispersal policies with respect to the immigrant population. Another implication of this *seuil de tolérance* was the perception that individual racist notions were not the core of the problem of racist violence. It was not a problem of racism, but a problem of numbers, especially of a concentration of the immigrant population. This *seuil de tolérance* functioned as a 'scientific alibi' to justify the assumed impossibility of a coexistence of cultures (Tahar Ben Jelloun, 1984: 62). The danger of this formula lay in the alleged scientific justification for rejecting foreigners (Tahar Ben Jelloun, 1984: 88), and implicitly a justification for the violent rejection of specific fellow citizens.

This threshold discourse was not a new phenomenon. In the nineteenth century, a similar discourse had been notable within the urban bourgeoisie with respect to the working class. It consisted of a widespread fear of working-class areas as zones of concentrated criminality, disease and unrest. The alleged threat posed by the *classes dangereux* was combated by the demolition of existing slums and reconstruction of new, separate neighbourhoods (MacMaster, 1991: 14–15).

The *seuil de tolérance* was regarded as a 'natural law' of social interaction. The 'discovery' of these laws of social behaviour was attributed to French ethnologists who specialised in studying 'primitive societies', like Claude Lévi-Strauss, Jean Sevier and Dominique Zahan (Freeman, 1979: 158). The reasons for its re-occurrence in the 1970s, and its application to migrant communities, were threefold. During these years, immigrant communities began to move significantly from private into public housing. In other words, perceived competition in the housing market started to increase with migrant communities playing a major part. Besides, communist and socialist-controlled municipalities saw a 'hidden hand' behind this intensified competition, engineered by capitalist and right-wing interests. In addition, the migrant communities without French citizenship did not have the right to vote, so therefore did not represent a political power (MacMaster, 1991: 17–21).

The traditional dominant discourse of French society as a nation with unlimited capacity to absorb others implied the necessity for any minority to assimilate. A minority not fully assimilated would activate a process of rejection. The 'logical' response to groups, especially from Northern Africa, who were perceived as not undergoing 'Francisation', was the rejection of any further admittance (Freeman, 1979: 159–60).

The second half of the 1970s

During the second half of the 1970s, racist violence continued to be a phenomenon frequently and persistently reported in France with North African immigrants and their descendants as the main targets. In 1976 in the city of Paris alone, thirty immigrants were reported killed, thirteen of them on 11 August. The August killing was claimed by the *Organisation Delta* (Guidice, 1992: 136). That same year, at least eight attacks were executed against organisation offices of North African labour migrants, as well as Sonacotra hostels. At a press conference in February 1979, the *Amicales des Algériens en Europe* claimed one hundred 'Algerians' had been killed in France from 1971 to 1978, including their own night porter (2 December 1977). Several of these killings were claimed by organisations, such as the *Organisation Delta*.

The *Amicales* and the *Association Henri-Curiel* claimed that the *Organisation Delta* was responsible for the killing of Henri Curiel, and had connections with the French secret service (Viard, 1984: 1947).[11] The *Organisation Delta* was also held responsible for a parcel bomb sent to the director of *Le Monde* (Schmid and Jongman, 1988: 544). In 1979, two people were killed in Orange in the South of France in an arson attack. The liberal leftist newspaper *Libération* described the incident as a 'mini-pogrom' (Guidice, 1992: 138). One year later, a similar incident occurred again in Orange, with two killed in a night-time arson attack on two buildings housing African people. Two other people were killed by arsonists in Carpentras (Viard, 1984: 1947–8).

The reports by the *Ligue Internationale Contre le Racisme et l'Antisémitisme* (LICRA) showed an increase in reported anti-semitic incidents during the period of 1975 to 1980, from 53 to 235 incidents. Figures of other racist incidents were not recorded. The reported number of incidents by LICRA from 1975 to 1980 were as follows:

1975: 53, of which 17 very severe
1976: 68, of which 33 very severe
1977: 112, of which 40 very severe

1978: 126, of which 40 very severe
1979: 175, of which 61 very severe
1980: 235, of which 75 very severe.

(Viard, 1984: 1945)

In 1980–81, at least two incidents showed that racist sentiments and activities were in no way restricted to the political extreme right. On 24 December 1980, the communist mayor of Vitry-sur-Seine, Paul Merceica, headed a demonstration against the transfer of 300 people from Mali to a workers' hostel in Vitry. During this brutal and violent demonstration a bulldozer was driven into the hostel. In February 1981, the communist mayor of Montigny-lès-Cormeilles, Robert Hué, accused a Moroccan family of trading drugs.[12] On 7 February, he organised a hate demonstration in front of the building where this family lived.

The perhaps surprising involvement of the Communist Party might be explained as an effort to raise the alleged problem of the coexistence of French and immigrant people, while at the same time trying to endorse the racist sentiments of the workers' electorate (Tahar Ben Jelloun, 1984: 58–9). These communist-led actions aroused furious responses from both sides of the political spectrum. These responses were based on anti-racist sentiments, as well as on traditional anti-communism.

State responses

The racist character of incidents was often denied by local or judicial authorities, even when perpetrators were convicted, though often no one was arrested at all. There were no signs that racist violence constituted a subject on the public or formal agenda during these years. Within the context of rising social tensions, increasingly perceived to be closely linked with the arrival and presence of non-European immigrants, the violence itself was perceived as emphasising the dominant *seuil de tolérance* discourse. It was the arrival and the presence of immigrants which seemed to receive top priority in official policies.

During this second half of the 1970s, government policies were mainly directed towards a further tightening of immigration controls. In April 1976 and November 1977, two decrees were introduced to restrict family reunification. The first prohibited family reunion of persons considered to be a threat to public order, and the second prohibited family members from taking up employment. The Secretary of State for Immigrant Workers, Lionel Stoleru, announced that no family members of immigrants would be allowed entry for three years. He justified this decision with reference to the massive extent of unemployment, and to the high crime rate among foreign youth. In December 1978, the *Conseil d'Etat* (the French High Court) ruled that these measures were illegal.

The same minister, Stoleru, argued that one of his objectives was to reduce the migration population to 1 million within five years. Different strategies were introduced to encourage the return of migrant workers to their countries of origin. This policy of *coopération à la carte* (free choice cooperation) was directed towards migrant workers from the so-called developing countries. In the mid-1970s, the deportation of workers without documents was countered by demonstrations and hunger strikes.

It should be emphasised that until 1974 mainstream immigration consisted of non-regulated immigration. Up to 85 per cent of the immigration was regulated only after people had arrived, lived and worked in France for some time. In the second half of the 1970s, the *immigration clandestine* became a political subject of top priority. In 1980, a law was introduced which combined work and residence permits, linking immigration with employment, and extending grounds for deportation. By 1980, several hundred people were deported every month, many of them young people born and raised in France. The main targets for deportation were North Africans and blacks. The most trifling offence was sufficient pretext for deportation. One notorious case was that of a 13-year-old boy who had stolen a pair of trousers. He was deported for this offence when he reached the age of 18.[13]

The early and mid-1980s: racist violence increasingly perceived as a social problem

The year 1981: L'autre France?

In June 1981, the French Socialist Party won the presidential and parliamentary elections. Many changes were introduced. The *politique d'amélioration* (policy of improvement) was implemented immediately after the Mitterrand government was installed. Three laws on migration went into effect in October 1981 concerning (1) the right to associate; (2) the improvement of working conditions; and (3) the entrance and residence of 'strangers' (Wihtol de Wenden, 1988: 280; 1991: 321). The 1980 law (by Stoleru) was abolished and replaced by an immigration law designed to stop further entries, but permitting family reunification. The number of deportations was reduced considerably, although the threat remained. A general pardon was announced for 'illegal aliens'. This was directed towards people without working or residence permits who could show that they had a one year working contract. This arrangement concerned around 300,000 persons, of whom some 140,000 registered for this amnesty (Castles *et al.*, 1984: 56).

The victory of the Socialists in 1981 was perceived by many as a kind of liberation. For the first time since the constitution of the Fifth Republic (September 1958), the Socialists won the direct presidential elections.[14] Together with the parliamentary election victory by the

Socialists, this led many supporters to believe that France would no longer be the same. It was hoped that this '*autre France*' under the Socialists become a reality in the near future not only by many French people in general, but especially by members of immigrant communities. 'The hope is obvious: away with the arbitrariness of deportations, away with restrictive policies, away with the laxity of justice and with the lack of information!' (Tahar Ben Jelloun, 1984: 75).

This euphoria, however, did not last long. On the contrary, 1982 was a year of turmoil. Worsening economic conditions were not improved by the Socialist government, and strikes were organised in large numbers. As elsewhere in Western Europe, the economic crisis was particularly felt within labour-intensive industries. In France, this especially affected the automobile and building sectors. As in other West European countries, migrants and their descendants were over-represented in these industries. Immigrants therefore, played an important role in the strikes (see Castles and Miller, 1993: 182–8). The most notable of these took place in 1982 at the Citroën factories, followed eight months later by those at Renault.

In the election campaigns of 1983, the increasing feelings of social and economic insecurity were an important factor and were particularly exploited by the extreme-right *Front National* and its leader Jean-Marie Le Pen. The immigrant population had no active part (i.e. vote) in these elections. Although the right to vote was promised by the Socialist Party in the 1981 elections, it still had not been introduced by law. In the 1983 elections, the *Front National* had its first success.

The success of the Front National

Nationwide, the election results for the *Front National* (FN) were poor (0.2 per cent). In some cities, however, they were very successful – especially in the city of Dreux: 16.7 per cent in the first round of the election (see Elbers and Fennema, 1993: 50; Singer, 1991: 372–4). The FN had been campaigning in local elections in Dreux since the mid-1970s, and had shown slowly increasing election returns ever since. This party, and its increasing electoral success, contributed to raising local tensions in 'French-immigrant relations' over housing.[15] In the second round, the FN entered a coalition with the established centre-right parties – the *Rassemblement pour la République* (RPR) and the *Union pour la Démocratie Française* (UDF). The importance of this success was twofold: first, from now on the FN had to be taken seriously by the other parties. Secondly, the election results received enormous attention in the mass media, particularly with regard to the 'migration/migrant issue' (Stouthuysen, 1993: 35).

The outcome of these elections was very significant with respect to the dominant political discourse, which showed the impact of racism and other extreme right opinions. Fear of the growth of the extreme right has curtailed political life in France since 1984 (Lloyd, 1991: 69). In 1991, the *Commission Nationale Consultative des Droits de l'Homme* (CNCDH) noted a general increase of racist violence since 1982, assumed to be closely connected with the rise of populist nationalism (of the FN), and the presentation of immigration as the scape-goat for all social ills, such as unemployment and insecurity. The CNCDH report argued that the Maghrebien population constituted the main target for racist violence (Lloyd, 1993: 215).

Violent racist outburst

In 1982–83, an outburst of racist violence was reported. Eleven people were reported killed in racist incidents in 1982; eighteen people were killed and many more severely wounded in 1983 (Bouzid, 1984). The murder of Habib Grimzi caused an uproar. On 15 November 1983 he was insulted and brutally beaten and finally thrown out of a moving train by three youngsters, who had just signed up for the Foreign Legion (Viard, 1984: 1950). In previous years, racist incidents were more or less concentrated within the region around Marseille – Les Bouches du Rhône – in the south-east of France, and in Paris. In the early 1980s, racist violence was increasingly reported in the whole of France, although the regions mentioned remained over-represented.[16]

Another significant aspect of racist violence in the early 1980s was that there seemed to be a new target for the violence: young people with immigrant parents (*les beurs*). Some examples were (Bouzid, 1984):

- On 27 June 1983, 15-year-old Abd Nabi Zigh was shot in the abdoment in Argenteuil.
- On 9 July 1983, 9-year-old Taoufik Ouannes was shot to death by a guard in La Courneuve.
- In that same month, 15-year-old Kamel was shot at from a window in Tourcoing.
- 11-year-old Mohamed Rebachi was wounded in Nancy.
- 12-year-old Massamba Badaine was wounded by a bullet in Aulnay.
- On 28 July 1983, 9-year-old Salah Djennane was wounded by an unknown person in Saint-Denis.
- In the same city two more children were wounded two days later.

One difference between the racist violence reported in the late 1950s and early 1960s and that reported in the 1980s was the unpremeditated and individual character of the latter violence. Often the perpetrator – if known at all – turned out to be a neighbour or other local residents showing up with a shotgn, or a group of youngsters 'hunting foreigners'.

State responses

Within this context of emerging extreme-right racist support, and increasing racist violence all over France, the Mitterrand administration showed uneasiness about its own proposed policies. On

13 September 1983, Mitterrand himself stated that France had to remember the way in which immigrants had been brought to France in airplanes and on trucks to help with economic reconstruction. These immigrants should enjoy all the rights equal to French workers, and should not be subjected constantly to police investigations. However, Mitterrand also argued that he had 'to protect the employment of the French' when he spoke of the alleged need of a harsh policy against 'illegal workers'.

In neighbourhoods with relatively large immigrant communities, raids took place, which affected the daily life of all residents – whether legal or illegal. This contributed to increasing feelings of insecurity and isolation among minority communities (Tahar Ben Jelloun, 1984: 47). Trade unions also contributed to these feelings. For example, the large, communist trade union *Confédération Générale du Travail* (CGT) organised a strike to protest against the employment of a Moroccan man in a weaving factory. The CGT argued that priority within employment should be first with local (i.e. French) people.[17]

In the aftermath of the racist killing of Habib Grimzi on 15 November 1983, the official spokesman of the Mitterrand government, Max Gallo, spoke of his indignation over this barbaric act. The government expressed its determination to combat all forms of racism and Gallo announced the preparation of a law to combat racist activities more effectively (Viard, 1984: 1943).

At the end of 1983, however, the only concrete measures taken by the Socialist government were a reversal of some of the measures implemented in 1981, such as the amendment which made it impossible to expel people without a judicial decision. These changes were partly due to depressed economic circumstances which were placing the Socialist government under enormous political pressure, and resulted in a very weak showing in the opinion polls. It was clear that Le Pen's success had an enormous influence on the formal agenda. 'Surely, after 1974, immigration had been an election issue of strong debates and political effort. But with Jean-Marie Le Pen, the electoral importance of the migration problem received another dimension incomparable to the past' (Wihtol de Wenden, 1988: 333).

During this period, racist violence never really constituted a specific topic. Violence in general was integrated into debates about law and order. These debates were particularly exploited by the extreme right. Although state authorities, including ministers, promised to take initiatives to combat the violence, no serious action was taken. The only concrete move was to enable existing voluntary associations to take action against racism through the law courts, thereby passing on responsibility (Lloyd, 1993: 214).

Two concrete state responses

In the actual state actions taken, however, two simultaneous responses were noticeable. On the one hand, racist violence seemed to be recognised as constituting a social problem rather than a criminal act, and combating it was not perceived to be a priority of the state. Rather, approaching the violence as a structural issue was seen to be the responsibility of anti-racism and migrant organisations. This was obvious too in changes implemented in 1985 in relation to the Anti-Discrimination Law 1972, which allowed anti-racism organisations to take legal action as civil parties in cases where a racist dimension was present (Oakley, 1992: 24–5, no. 2.3). The uneasiness of the Socialist government in relation to the success of the *Front National* was emphasised by the withdrawal by the Mitterrand government of a pamphlet in early 1983. This pamphlet – called *Vivre ensemble: les immigrés parmi nous* (Living together: the immigrants among us) – was meant to counter-attack Le Pen's demagogic statements. Two and a half million pamphlets had already been printed when the government decided not to distribute it, shortly before the 1983 local elections (van den Brink *et al.*, 1988: 46–7).

On the other hand, the only official measures taken by the state consisted of debates, and restrictions on immigration. In the political context of the time, which included increasing support for the extreme right, this response constituted an example of the 'excluding recognition' of racist violence by the state. This type of response was obvious in a statement issued by the mayor of Paris, Jacques Chirac,[18] after the racist killings of July 1983: 'The threshold of tolerance has been crossed, especially in certain neighbourhoods, and there is the danger that this will provoke racist responses. Therefore we have to follow a clear and courageous policy to try to limit the influx of those arriving, among whom there are certain criminal elements.'[19] In Chirac's perception, the way to combat racism was obvious: more effective control of the places of residence of migrant workers, because they were over-crowded and sources of tension and trouble (Tahar Ben Jelloun, 1984: 41).

This policy included measures which were proposed and implemented by the Chirac government after the right won the 1986 parliamentary elections. The new Minister of Interior, Charles Pasqua, introduced two Bills to reduce 'illegal immigration', and to extend the legal means to take action against foreigners who constituted an alleged threat to public order. From now on, a visa and sufficient financial resources were needed to enter the country. The *préfets* (Chiefs of Police) – instead of the judiciary – were empowered to give orders to escort 'illegal' residents to the border. These changes, and a new Nationality Bill, caused turmoil; many demonstrations and protests were organised against them.

In 1985, the existing majority system had been changed by the Socialist government into a proportional representation system. This change was meant to keep the political right divided. In the 1985 elections, this resulted in thirty-five parliamentary seats for the *Front National*, and the centre right parties still won the majority of the parliamentary seats. In 1988, the proportional representation system was changed again into a majority system by the centre-right government. Although their support in the 1988 elections was as large as in 1985 (9.8 per cent), the *Front National* was left with only one parliamentary seat (Stouthuysen, 1993: 37 and 46–7).

The new youth response against racist violence in France

Anti-racism organisations have existed in France for a long time, such as the above mentioned MRAP and LICRA (pp. 86 and 91). These older organisations played a significant role during the late 1960s and 1970s, for instance, in relation to the implementation of the anti-discrimination legislation in 1972. In addition, MRAP was often involved in judicial procedures on behalf of clients who had been discriminated against.

In the 1980s, France saw the rise of the 'young anti-racism movement' of which *SOS Racisme* and *France Plus* were the main representatives. Youth groups were active in organising hunger strikes in response to specific racist incidents and deportations, such as the group of the Minguettes estate (Lyon) or the *Jeunes Arabes de Lyon et sa banlieu* (JALB). On occasion, local defence committees were set up after an incident had occurred. These committees directed their activities at specific problems on the local scene, such as racist violence, housing conditions or racist police behaviour.

In October–December 1983, a three-month March for Equality and against Racism, organised by youth groups, took place (see Hargreaves, 1991: 356–61). The motivation for organising this march was the terrifying increase in reported incidents of racist violence, and the organisers took with them a list of more than fifty violent acts that had occurred since early 1982 (van den Brink *et al.*, 1988: 70). The demands of the march were to modify legislation to combat racist violence more effectively (Guidice, 1992: 183). The march had started in October 1983 in Marseille with thirty participants, but attracted a hundred thousand people by the time it arrived in Paris. In Paris a reception for the marchers was held by President Mitterrand (Lloyd, 1993: 218). In the next two years, similar marches (*Convergence 84* and *Convergence 85*) were organised.

In October 1984, *SOS Racisme* was set up, and had enormous success with its badge *Touche pas à mon pote*, that is, Do Not Touch My Friend (see Desir, 1985; Hargreaves, 1991: 362). Their campaign consisted of practical action and immediate responses to any incident. *SOS Racisme* presented one of the first opportunities for the *beurs* to organise themselves. Since 1981, *étrangers* ('foreigners') have been allowed to organise themselves in France, something which had been prohibited since 1939.

Although many members were involved in mainstream political parties, especially the Socialist Party, *SOS Racisme* was not, at first, directly linked with established parties. *France Plus* was set up with assistance of the Socialist Party and other organisations (Hargreaves, 1991: 362). The activities of these organisations were 'colourful, joyful, self-assured and ingenious' (van den Brink *et al.*, 1988: 72). The initial impetus for organising activities were local experiences, particularly with racist violence. For instance in Le Havre, Marimas and Menton, demonstrations were organised after violent racist incidents in the spring of 1985. Other activities, in direct response to racist violence in those years, were the Rock-against-Police concert (in the Paris region) and the *Zaama d'Banlieu* demonstration (in the Lyon region), following conflicts between the police and young people (Lloyd, 1993: 217). None of these demonstrations were gatherings with long speeches, but were more like rock concerts with films, pamphlets, etcetera. On 15–16 August 1985, *SOS Racisme* organised an anti-racism concert in the middle of Paris (Place de la Concorde) that lasted for twelve hours, and which was attended by more than 400,000 people. The whole concert was broadcast live on television. National newspapers, like *Libération* and *Le Matin,* released special editions (van den Brink *et al.*, 1988: 74).

Of course there were differences among the anti-racism organisations. *SOS Racisme*, for instance, claimed *le droit à la difference* (the right to be different). This slogan was challenging to the assimilation discourse which was still very dominant in France. *France Plus* defended *le droit à l'indifference* (the right of indifference).[20] These two organisations also had different points of view concerning participation in elections. *SOS Racisme* strove for voting rights for immigrants who did not have French nationality, whereas *France Plus* strove for the nationalisation of immigrants in order to have as many French people of immigrant origin as possible on the lists of candidates.

The impact of these new anti-racism organisations was important and manifold. They drew attention to racism in general, and racist violence in particular. They showed, contrary to common belief, that youngsters were politically interested, although not in the way the 'old' political parties were used to. Precisely one of the problems here was the trouble these 'new' organisations had in keeping out, and staying out of, established party politics.

The extreme right, personified by Le Pen, continued to have its successes, but these new organisations at least showed the existence of an enormous potential for anti-racist action in France. They also showed new ways of organising activities, such as music and film festivals. They were more oriented towards concrete, practical events and results, rather than changing the whole system – as for instance the earlier generation of the late 1960s had been. At the end of the 1980s, these organisations increasingly turned their attention towards the more institutional forms of racism and discrimination and their products, like unemployment, poor housing conditions and education, and so on.

The late 1980s to the early 1990s: the hectic years

In 1986–87, public and political attention was drawn to the Klaus Barbie trial, and Le Pen's statement in September 1987 that the massacre of the Jews during the Second World War was just a detail in the history of that war (Elbers and Fennema, 1993: 56).[21] Another discussion which influenced the political climate in these years involved debates about the alleged association between immigration and AIDS.

The Chirac government, installed in 1986, introduced new Bills to tighten up (particularly 'illegal') immigration and to restrict the opportunities for naturalisation. Many demonstrations were organised in 1987 against these proposed legislative changes. Several diverse sections of French society were involved in these protests, from the 'young' and 'old' anti-racism organisations to the churches.

A commission was set up by the Chirac government to develop new legislation. This commission concluded that naturalisation should be encouraged, and that the naturalisation procedures needed to be improved. The report by the commission, however, more or less sank without trace in the wake of the 1988 presidential elections. In April 1988, these elections brought a major success for the extreme right. The *Front National* leader, Le Pen, gained 14.4 per cent of the vote (4.4 million votes). This success shocked many people in and outside France. One month later, new parliamentary elections showed a level of support of 9.8 per cent for the *Front National* (similar to that in 1986). Due to the re-introduction of the majority election system, the *Front National* gained only one seat in Parliament and did not get the key position it had hoped for.

A statement by Le Pen in August 1988, that the gas chambers in the death camps had been no more than four crematoria, did considerable damage to the *Front National*. It looked as if the end of the success of this party and its leader was near (Singer, 1991: 369). Within four months, public and political attention moved away from surprised shock to the feeling that it had all blown over.

In the same year, reports of racist incidents increased in number again, and the bombing of an immigrant hostel in Nice in December 1988 (with one killed and twelve injured) attracted enormous attention. Although there had been other racist incidents in the same year and in the same region, this incident was the trigger event ('accelerator') which 'led the [newly elected] Socialist Prime Minister, Rocard, to set up the first initiative specifically devoted to racial violence' (Oakley, 1992: 25, no. 3.3). One of the reasons for this was the viciousness of this particular incident. People running away from a first bomb explosion were then caught by a second one (van Donselaar, 1995).

Responses to racist violence

On 2 August 1989, the Joxe Act, named after the Minister of Interior, was introduced. This Act included the proviso that discrimination could constitute an aggravating circumstance in the French Penal Code. However, it should be noted that it 'is a fundamental principle of French criminal law that the motive of an act is not indictable: to constitute specific offences, racism and discrimination must be expressed explicitly, and not only result from the origin or appearance of the victim' (Costa-Lascoux, 1994: 376).

An Inter-Departmental working group was set up to coordinate, and to organise, a campaign against racist violence. In addition, the *Commission Nationale Consultative des Droits de l'Homme* (CNCDH) started to report on an annual basis on the nature and scale of the violence in France, and on the responses to this phenomenon. The CNCDH was set up in 1984 to advise the government on matters of human rights. The Commission includes internal actors, such as the Ministries of Interior, Social Affairs, Education and Justice, as well as external actors, such as anti-racism and migrant organisations (for instance CIMADE and MRAP), Amnesty International, the Red Cross, and church organisations. CNCDH submitted its 1989 report to Prime Minister Rocard, and reported a substantial increase of racist incidents from 1979 to 1989. Since 1982, a general increase of racist incidents had been reported – between 46 and 70 recorded instances each year. In the mid-1980s, according to the report, there had been a stabilisation of the number of instances – around 100 each year. Since 1987, racist violence had risen dramatically, to 135 incidents in 1988 and 237 in 1989. Between 1987 and 1989, 6 persons were killed and 120 injured by such violence (Oakley, 1992: 23–4, no. 2. 6–7). These figures were presented to the Commission by the French Ministry of Interior. The Commission distinguishes between 'acts and threats', and between 'racist and anti-semitic violence'. Racist violence for its part is divided between 'racist violence against people of Maghrebian origin' and 'racist violence against others'. Anti-semitic violence is divided between 'extreme right-wing actions', 'extreme left-wing actions' and 'actions linked with international terrorism or arabic milieu' (see CNCDH, 1994; 1995).

L'affaire du foulard

In 1989, a two months-long national public and political debate took place in France, in what would come to be known as the *affaire du foulard* (headscarf affair). Three muslim girls in Creil in northern France refused to take off their traditional headscarves in school, and for this reason were expelled. Without going into detail, it should be noted that in 'a split second' the whole of France started to discuss this 'affair', (the threat of) Islamic fundamentalism, and (the threat to) the French 'way of life' and culture (Wihtol de Wenden, 1991: 328; see for a comparison between France, Britain and the Netherlands in this respect: Coppes, 1994). The debate about the 'headscarf' has never really ended and still comes to the surface every now and then.

This debate reflected the emergence of anti-Islam sentiments, as well as the assimilationist elements in dominant French discourse. For this study, the importance of this event was the 'moral panic' it engendered, accompanied by a new, sharp increase of reported racist incidents throughout France (see Ford, 1990; Oakley, 1992; Lloyd, 1993). The moral panic and the debates also had their influence on the political arena. In the end, only the *Front National* profited from this panic. The *Front National*, thought to be past its peak of success, returned to the centre of politics at the end of 1989. This party gained 61.3 per cent of the vote in the local elections in the city of Dreux, and 47.2 per cent in Marseille (Stouthuysen, 1993: 49).

A survey, held at the voting bureau in Dreux, showed 66 per cent of the FN voters claimed to have been influenced by the 'headscarf affair'.[22] The sharp increase in extreme right support led many politicians, whether they were aware of it or not, to relate their position on immigration isues to the opinion of the *Front National*. President Mitterrand himself caused a certain feeling of uneasiness by stating that France had reached its *seuil de tolérance* (threshold of tolerance) during the 1970s.[23] At the same time, the French centre right parties used their party conferences in early 1990 to adjust certain policy proposals in line with those proposed by the *Front National*. Some examples of this were: a referendum to be held on nationality legislation, fewer social security rights for foreign inhabitants, and restrictions on the opportunities for family reunification (Ford, 1990: no. 3.7.15).

The year 1990: a turning point in state responses to racist violence?

The history of state responses show that French authorities were actively involved in problematising specific (migrant) minorities. With the emphasis on assimilation and the prevalence of the *seuil de tolérance* discourse, as well as with policies to restrict migration, specifically those of (North African) origin, state authorities directly and indirectly contributed to, and emphasised, popular racist discourse. Racist violence was perceived to cross a boundary as soon as it was transformed into a state security problem (i.e. a problem of law and order). Racist violence therefore had never really been an issue except in relation to law and order. French state responses in this post-war period became manifest in law and order policies and measures implicitly 'blaming the victim'. Several instances showed elements of 'excluding recognition' of racist violence by state authorities, as described.

In early 1990, this situation seemed to change. This is explained by the threat of the *Front National* as a political power, and the rise in the reported level of violence, as well as the increasing protest and resistance to such occurrences. The pressure on state authorities to act increased enormously. Because of that pressure, attempts were made to construct responses which could be typified as 'including recognition' of racist violence.

In March 1990, three people were killed and two severely injured (all were of Moroccan origin) in one week. The Moroccan government sent a letter of protest to the French authorities, thus giving another example of how state reactions were bound also to international presure, as in the case of the action by the Algerian government in 1973. President Mitterrand expressed his condemnation of violent racist incidents in France. He stated that the racist killings were 'paradigms of senselessness, brutality and intolerance'. Even the hard-liner Gaullist and former Minister of Interior, Pasqua, proposed that the government and the opposition should investigate the situation in order to come up with concrete measures to combat the violence.[24]

Prime Minister Rocard invited all political parties, except the *Front National*, to attend a 'round table meeting' to discuss the above mentioned CNCDH report (p. 101) and the steps to be taken.[25] He also stated that 'the fight against this type of violence, and against the situations in which it flourishes in our cities, remains a priority within my actions.'[26] On 4 April 1990, Rocard announced an anti-racism plan including three elements: (1) transformation of existing legislation; (2) introduction of the denial of *crimes contre l'humanité* as a criminal act; and (3) the creation of an office to coordinate the fight against racism and anti-semitism.[27]

At first, the right-wing parties decided to boycott this round table meeting. They argued that they could not discuss anti-racist measures when immigration restrictions were not included in the debate. Chirac argued that 'to deal with racism, without dealing with immigration, boils down to dealing with the problem in the opposite direction'.[28]

After the first meeting, the right feared that Rocard would walk off with all the honours. This clearly indicates the increasing influence of the anti-racist discourse and movement in France in this period. The perceived fear of the right indicated that support for the anti-racist position was something to take into consideration. Rocard was expected to gain authority and power when his proposals were put into effect. The right demanded some preconditions from the Socialists. For instance, they demanded the abandonment of proposals for voting rights for foreigners at local elections.[29]

Anti-racism initiatives

After the killing of the three French youngsters of North African origin in March 1990, new anti-racist Bills and measures were introduced (Ford, 1990 no. 3.7.5).[30] This new legislation meant that people convicted of serious forms of racism would in addition to the established penal code, be deprived of their civil right to be elected for a maximum period of five years and prohibited from carrying out any state duties. The Bill also made revisionism and denial of the genocide of Jews during the Second World War punishable. Next to these legal proposals, a major programme of urban regeneration was announced. Its proclaimed aims were to promote a more effective integration of immigrants into French society, and to introduce a preventive approach to 'racial' tensions and racist violence (Oakley, 1992: 25, no. 3.6).

This anti-racist legislation was introduced as an initiative of the *Parti Communiste Française* (PCF) after an uneasy attempt to reach a consensus between the political parties. This led to the involvement of all kinds of political aspects within the debate on the initiatives. In spite of the agreement between the leaders of the parties (apart from the *Front National*) about the content of the proposed legislation, only the Socialists and Communists supported the Bill at the first reading. The centre-right parties – the RPR and the UDF – and the *Centre des démocratis sociaux* (CDS) voted against the proposals on 3 May 1990 after a ten hour debate.[31] These centre-right parties argued that Prime Minister Rocard was guilty of 'pure demagogy', and of 'political manoeuvring', by supporting a Communist Bill. The *Front National*'s Le Pen spoke of an 'attack on the principles of democracy which cannot be tolerated'. He argued that 'they want the civil and political death of citizens who are guilty of resistance against the immigration policies, and who defend the identity of France'.[32]

Carpentras

Seven days later (10 May 1990), a racist incident shattered French and international public and political opinion. In Carpentras, the cradle of Judaism in France, the Jewish cemetery was desecrated. Thirty-four gravestones were damaged and the corpse of a man buried two weeks before was removed from its coffin and mutilated.[33] The anti-semitic nature of the incident most definitely contributed to its enormous impact. French history with respect to anti-semitism, from the Dreyfus affair (1894) to the Holocaust, and the active role of the Vichy regime, was important in ensuring that this incident in particular was a trigger event. This will be elaborated upon in more detail in Chapter 5.

The next day, the French Parliament interrupted its debates to honour the dead of Carpentras.[34] Three days later almost the entire French Cabinet attended a massive demonstration in Paris. The Minister of Finance claimed, 'Tonight, we [the French] are all Jews'.[35] Totally unexpectedly, President Mitterrand also joined the demonstration, which meant that for the first time since the Second World War, a French President took part in such a 'silent demonstration' attended by 200,000 people (Ford, 1990: no. 3.7.18).

At the same time, thousands of people demonstrated in other French cities, such as Marseille, Nantes, Dijon and Rouen. On the night of the demonstrations, all six television channels broadcast the same Alain Renais movie, *Nuit et Brouillard*, about the death camps in the Second World War. Another response, directly linked to the Carpentras incident, was noticed within the academic community. The Council of the Jean Moulin University of Lyon took the unanimous decision to dismiss two extreme-right professors. One of them, B. Notin, lecturer in

Economics, was known to have written a revisionist and anti-semitic article (Ford 1990: no. 3.7.21).

Between 10 and 18 May 1990, there were some fifty demonstrations. Common features of these demonstrations were (1) they had an official character and were all headed by local authorities; (2) the demonstrations were supported by a broad popular coalition; and (3) the demonstrations were directed against racism and anti-semitism in general, and against the *Front National* and its leader, Le Pen, in particular (Mayer, 1992: 50).

The *Commission Nationale Consultative des Droits de l'Homme* (CNCDH) later reported an enormous increase of violent incidents in 1990 (372 compared to 149 in 1989). Half of these 372 incidents took place within the first two weeks after the Carpentras incident (Hansson, 1991; Mayer, 1992).

State responses in the aftermath of Carpentras

One set of official responses to Carpentras was directed against the *Front National*. The night before the desecration of the cemetery became known, FN leader Le Pen had appeared on television. On one of the major channels, the anniversary of the Second World War had been marked with a documentary on Nazi Germany and its anti-semitism. On the same channel, Le Pen 'had comfirmed the anti-Jewish orientation of his party by asserting that there were indeed "many Jews in the media" in France' (Hansson, 1991: 33). This was interpreted at the time as a reference to the anti-semitic slogans concerning their ideas about the existence of a 'Jewish world conspiracy'. One day later, after the discovery of the desecrated graves in Carpentras, the link between this desecration and Le Pen's remarks was easily made. However, whether the desecration had been executed before or after Le Pen's television appearance continued to be a matter of discussion.

In the immediate aftermath of Carpentras, the Minister of Interior, Pierre Joxe, argued that 'There is no need for a police investigation in order to know who the criminals are. . . . The criminals have a name. They are called racism, antisemitism, intolerance' (Hansson, 1991: 34). The reference to the FN was very obvious. In the weeks following the Carpentras incident, many meetings of the FN were banned by local authorities, and discussions were held as to whether the *Front National* should be banned.

The FN itself and the extreme right-wing press responded with suggestions that the Carpentras desecration had been perpetrated by the police, the KGB, Mossad, the Arabs, the Jews, and that racism and anti-semitism were inventions of the press (see Hansson, 1991; Mayer, 1992).

Besides the immediate response by the *Assemblée Nationale*, members of the Socialist Cabinet and the President, the Carpentras incident also seemed to lead to a change in the approach to racism by the other mainstream parties. The centre-right parties revoked their decision to boycott the so-called round table conference on combating racism instigated by the Rocard government.

The Carpentras incident presented hope for a renewed policy directed against racism and racist violence in France. The phenomenon of racist violence was a topic of high priority on the formal agenda (phase D). In spite of political differences, it seemed possible to come up with an anti-racism programme in France which would be broadly supported by the mainstream political parties. However, such hopes soon vanished. Within days, mainstream politicians were arguing and fighting with each other with no chance of agreement. Prime Minister Rocard postponed the round table meeting, set for 16 May 1990, until 29 May. Immediately after Carpentras, the centre-right parties regarded it as inappropriate to talk about immigration as planned. To bring in the immigration issue was in itself already a concession on the part of the Prime Minister, because his first intention had been to only include the issue of racist violence.

The Executive Committee of the Socialist Party announced its intention to abandon its earlier stance of giving voting rights to foreign residents. The parties of the right had demanded this before they would attend any round table meeting. The committee argued that the French population was not yet ready for such a measure, and it did not want to 'push the matter'.[36] In Parliament, Prime Minister Rocard stated that he would make a list of subjects of agreement between the government and the opposition, of subjects on which agreement could be achieved, and of subjects on which no agreement had been reached. This action might be perceived as an attempt to depoliticise the racism issue.

On 23 May 1990, former President and opposition leader of the time Giscard d'Estaing claimed that a charter had to confirm at least two principles: France was not a country of immigration and foreigners living in France had the guaranteed right of their dignity and respect and protection by French laws.[37] Two days later, Rocard introduced a charter 'for immigration and integration'. The charter was based on three principles: (1) knowledge before treatment (emphasis on education instead of repression); (2) prevention before control (emphasis on prevention instead of repression); and (3) a contract of integration.[38] Three subjects of agreement between the socialists and the opposition were mentioned by Rocard: (1) closing the borders to further immigration, (2) integration of legal immigrants present in France; and (3) encouraging the return of immigrants to home countries. The Socialist MP, Philippe Marchand, said that 'France was, and always would be, a country of immigration', while his political leader Rocard argued that 'France no longer was a country of immigration'.

No sign of agreement on any of these measures with regard to anti-racist violence was foreseen. Despite all the concessions by the Socialist government, the second round table meeting failed to achieve an agreement or 'minimum charter', as Rocard had wished for. Chirac argued that the government denied the fact that the *seuil de tolérance* had been crossed. This made it useless for the Gaullist Chirac to sign any charter, and he did not want to contribute to a popular gesture by Rocard and his government.[39]

The only concrete legislative state action in the aftermath of Carpentras was the adoption of the law (no. 90-615) on 13 July 1990. This Act ordered the CNCDH to report on an annual basis about initiatives taken against racism by state agencies. Their annual reports had to be published on 21 May (the International Day against all Forms of Racist Discrimination declared by the UN).[40] Two other aspects of this new Act included the proposals, above mentioned, concerning the possibility of depriving someone of certain civil rights after having been convicted of serious forms of racism, and making revisionism and the denial of the genocide of Jews during the Second World War criminal offences (Mayer, 1992; van Donselaar, 1995). On 21 March 1991, guidelines were distributed by the Minister of Interior, in which the attention of *préfets* was drawn to the large number of judicial means by which to conduct prosecutions on the basis of racism and racist violence (CNCDH, 1994; van Donselaar, 1995).

Debates on 'illegal immigration'

In early 1991, the Gulf War coincided with a reported new wave of racist violence in France.[41] Muslim people and buildings were among the main targets of this wave of violence. Le Pen was the only one during this war who did not support the Western allies. He even organised 'shuttle diplomacy' between Paris and Baghdad. He emphasised his nationalist position that every people had to take care of its own business (Iraq for the Iraqis, France for the French).

In the summer of 1991, a shift took place from Iraq to 'illegal immigrants' constituting the 'number-one-enemy' in French politics. The French Socialist Minister of Culture and government spokesman, Jack Lang, declared 'war on illegal immigrants'. Border controls would be strengthened, and methods were being worked out to speed up the deportation of 'illegal' people. The Prime Minister – Rocard's successor, Edith Cresson – took the opportunity of renting special charter aeroplanes to deport 'illegals' en masse.[42] These new measures seemed to be a response to the increasing pressure of the centre and extreme right, who accused the government of laxity with respect to 'illegal immigrants' and asylum-seekers.

Cresson's position was not shared by everyone within the Socialist Party. The party leader, Pierre Mauroy, argued against the use of charter flights. He called for all socialists to oppose these proposals.[43] But charter flights quietly left the Charles de Gaulle airport (Paris) regularly, with as little publicity as possible. The internal Socialist struggles and the statements made indicate the troubled and increasingly worsening position of this party in French politics in general, and with respect to the electorate in particular. This trend would continue throughout the next few years, leading to major defeats and loss of votes in the elections of 1992 and 1993. The proposed policies, however, were part of a toughening of the public and political debates with regard to immigration.

Disturbances in French cities

This toughening of opinion was partly a response to violent incidents in the suburbs of the big French cities. A policewoman was killed during one of the disturbances, when a 'joy-rider' with a stolen car drove into her police car. The perpetrators escaped, but when other joy-riders turned up at the scene, police officers opened fire and shot 23-year-old Youssef Khaïf, who was of Algerian origin (Guidice, 1992: 302). The death of the policewoman was used frequently to point to the 'need' to toughen up measures concerning immigration and migrant communities in France.

Other disturbances started after the death of another young French-man of migrant origin. In the Paris suburb Sartrouville riots broke out after Djamel Chettouh was shot by guards of a cafeteria in March (Guidice, 1992: 301). In Mantes-la-Jolie, another Paris suburb, riots broke out after the death in custody of Aïssa Ihich, of Moroccan origin, in May 1991. The official statement was that he died of a heart-attack. Some days later, it was announced that his death had been caused by the refusal of the police to give the youngster medicine, needed for his asthma, which had been brought to the prison by his father (Guidice, 1992: 301–2).

Responses

On 19 June 1991, Chirac argued that the immigrants were not the problem, but the fact that there was an 'over-dose of them present'. He argued that the 'smell' and the noise of 'them' drove French workers to madness.[44] Chirac argued that opportunities for reuniting immigrant families had to be stopped. He also called for a broad 'moral discussion' of 'the question (of) whether foreigners should profit – just like Frenchmen – from a social system to which they did not contribute anything, since they did not pay tax'.[45] He implicitly treated as one those residents of foreign nationality without legal permits (who did not pay tax) with all those foreign and French fellow citizens who were permitted to reside in France (and paid taxes). Although Chirac's statements caused a great deal of commotion, his popularity increased by several points.[46] The other centre-right party leader, Giscard d'Estaing, contributed to the toughening of the political debate by stating that France had to deal with an 'invasion' of immigrants.[47]

Response by the Front National

The leader of the *Front National*, Le Pen, responded to the 'adoption' of his issues like the experienced politician he is: 'The French people prefer to vote for the original rather than for a duplicate.' The *Front National* might be on the edge of the political arena, but nonetheless had a major impact on the formal agenda, and on the ways in which the debates were held and developed. 'It depends on the power positions created by the *Front National* the way political life mainly orients itself. . . . Surely one is not concerned with an ideological victory, but as everyone today knows, electoral victory is preceded by mayor points in the field of ideas', as FN ideologist Bruno Mégret stated in September 1991 (Stouthuysen, 1993: 53). Opinion polls showed him to be right: in 1988 16 per cent of the French agreed with the ideas of Le Pen, in 1991 it was 32 per cent.

In November 1991, the *Front National* introduced a '50 points programme'. Among these points were:

- the abandoning of all rights of family reunification
- the revision of all naturalisation since 1974
- the distinction of services specifically for Frenchmen from those for 'strangers'
- French nationality to be reserved for those with French parents
- foreign workers to pay extra taxes
- liberties of foreigners, like the right to associate, to be abandoned.

It was widely expected that the scales would now fall from the eyes of the FN voters.[48] In 1992 and 1993, however, electoral support for the *Front National* seemed to be increasing. The *Front* received 15.7 per cent in the city of Lille, for instance, making their support larger than that of the Socialist Party, the main loser in these elections.[49] In Nice, the *Front National* gained most of the votes in the first election round (38 per cent).[50] In the second round, the FN candidate was just beaten. In the 1993 parliamentary elections, the FN gained 12.4 per cent, which was their biggest success ever in these kinds of elections (Stouthuysen, 1993: 54) The Socialist Party was the main loser, and the centre-right parties won a majority in Parliament.

Increasing tensions between the state and youth

In September 1992, an Inter-Departmental working group on Integration published a report about the alleged tensions and difficulties concerning the integration of migrants originating from *Afrique noire*. An article in *Le Monde* (13–15 September 1992) about this report was headed: *L'intégration des immigrés d'Afrique noire se heurte a de serieux obstacles* (The integration of immigrants from Black Africa is confronted with serious obstacles). In the report, problems concerning the integration of 'Black African migrant communities', and especially of the so-called second generation, were blamed on 'wrong family values'. Alleged important elements in hindering integration were the role of the father and polygamy.

Tensions between state authorities and young people in general, and those whose parents originated from North Africa in particular, increased during 1992. In June 1992, many disturbances occurred again in France. Often those disturbances consisted of attacks targeted against the police, or they occurred after a violent incident believed to be racist. For instance in Argenteuil, according to the police, youngsters took to the streets after one of them was stabbed to death by a drug dealer. The youngsters claimed it was a racist killing.[51] In November, riots broke out in Reims after a woman was acquitted by the courts. She was believed to have killed a French boy of North African origin in February 1989, because she thought he wanted to steal bread. The jury, consisting of local residents, cleared the suspect, who became known as 'the Baker's Wife of Reims'. Friends of the victim had been accused and convicted earlier for stealing croissants.[52]

Conclusion

For a long time, racist violence was not constructed by state authorities as a serious problem in France. This seemed partly due to the prevailing discourse in which all residents in France were believed to be equal before the law. Violence against someone was perceived, and treated, as an 'ordinary' criminal act. Racist violence in the late 1950s and early 1960s was perceived in the context of the process of decolonisation, and state responses were closely linked with this perception. In this period of decolonisation and the Algerian War, the existence of violence against Algerian migrants was not denied, but was perceived as an act of political terrorism designed to threaten internal state security. The racist nature of the violence did not constitute an element in the responses of state authorities. Responses consisted of combating, and even banning, certain political organisations. The perception of racist violence as political terrorism was reflected in these responses, and waned in the aftermath of the Algerian War. According to the model of state responses to racist violence, the issue remained in phase A of the individual problem.

In the early 1970s, racist violence increasingly attracted public and media attention without ever entering the French formal agenda (phase B, and temporarily phase C). In the dominant discourse, the violence was regarded as proof of the prominent idea of *seuil de tolérance*. State responses to the situation, of which the violence was assumed to be a characteristic, might be typified by elements of the 'excluding recognition' of racist violence. Statements and responses by state authorities contributed to a racist discourse and violent expressions of that discourse.

In 1981, the mainstream political discourse seemed to be changing along with changing French political relations. Some signs and the hope of many communities that the 'including recognition' of racism and racist violence by state authorities would be translated into concrete measures, did not last long. Developments took a different direction. Increasing economic problems, rising social disturbances, and the growing support for the extreme-right *Front National* changed the political atmosphere dramatically.

The only concrete state response in those years seemed to be to devolve the direct combat of racist violence to organisations outside the state apparatus (phase B-C). Anti-discrimination legislation was changed to allow organisations to take legal action as civil parties in cases where a racist dimension was perceived to be present. This might be considered the result of increasing social pressure for action against racism, as well as a small 'left-over' of the earlier intentions of the Socialist government to improve living conditions for minority communities in France.

The second half of the 1980s also showed the emergence of new anti-racism organisations, especially organised by young people following racist incidents. These organisations were important because they contributed to an increasing public awareness of the subject. Their emergence was a clear consequence of the political climate of change in the early 1980s, the result of practical local initiatives against deplorable conditions, but also increasing support for racist ideologies and murderous violence, as well as the effect of enormous media exposure.

In the late 1980s and early 1990s, a mixture of 'two-faced' state responses to racist violence surfaced. Examples of 'including recognition' of racist violence were shown after several specific racist incidents. The desecration of Jewish graves in Carpentras, May 1990, looked like the accelerator for a real change in the responses by state authorities to racist violence. The number of alternatives in respect of the 'excluding recognition' of racist violence decreased, and awareness about the existence of racist violence, and pressure to act, increased. However, despite the implementation of new legislation in July 1990 to combat racism and racist violence, the former mainstream discourse was gradually re-established, and again immigration was the main issue tackled instead of racist violence. Since 1991, immigration restrictions, and control of the day-to-day life of minority communities have been extended. No longer is racist violence an issue on the formal agenda.

Notes

1 *Le Monde*, 14 March 1990.
2 During the Second World War, Maurice Papon was local Chief of Police in Bordeaux and responsible for 'Jewish Affairs', organising the arrest and

deportation of Jews to death camps. In the 1970s, he was Minister in the Giscard d'Estaing government (*de Volkskrant*, 16 September 1994).

3 *Assemblée Nationale Débats*, 13 October 1961: 2552; as cited by Freeman (1979: 81).

4 The SAC was banned in 1982, after taking the initiative to go fully underground in the aftermath of the left-wing victory in the 1981 presidential and parliamentary elections. Formally, the SAC was banned because its actions were based on violence and practices close to gangsterism (Schmid and Jongman, 1988: 542).

5 Previously MRAP stood for *Movement Contre le Racisme et l'Antisemitisme et pour le Paix.*

6 This group was named after the Frankish King who stopped the Arab advance into Europe during the battle of Poitiers in AD 732 (Schmid and Jongman, 1988: 542).

7 *Le Monde*, 1 September 1973; as cited by Freeman (1979: 109).

8 B. Granotier (1973) *Les Travailleurs immigrés en France* (revised edition), Paris: François Maspero, pp. 3–4; as cited by Freeman (1979: 109).

9 *Le Monde*, 1 October 1973; as cited by Freeman (1979: 109).

10 *Le Monde*, 1 March 1975; as cited by Freeman (1979: 98.10).

11 Henri Curiel was the founder of the Egyptian Communist Party (Schmid and Jongman, 1988: 544).

12 On 24 January 1994, Robert Hué was appointed leader of the French Communist Party (*Het Parool*, 31 January 1994).

13 'Immigration changes in France', in *Race and Immigration*, no. 147, September 1982; as cited by Castles *et al.* (1984: 54).

14 During the Fourth Republic of France (1946–58), the French President was elected by Parliament. With the implementations of the Constitution of the Fifth Republic (September 1958), the French President was elected by direct elections. Since 1958, the French Presidents have been: de Gaulle (8 January 1959 to 28 April 1969), Pompidou (20 June 1969 to 2 April 1974), Giscard d'Estaing (21 June 1974 to 21 May 1981), Mitterrand (21 May 1981 to May 1995) (see e.g. Wright, 1983).

15 See F. Gaspard (1990) *Une Petite Ville en France*, Paris: Gallimard, as cited by Castles and Miller (1993: 240).

16 In the regions mentioned, the support of the *Front National* was over-represented too. There seemed to be a clear connection between the level of racist incidents and the degree of support for the *Front National*.

17 *L'Est Républicain*, 10 December 1983.

18 On 7 May 1995, Chirac was elected President of the Republic of France (*de Volkskrant*, 8 May 1995).

19 *Le Monde*, 15 July 1983; as cited by Tahar Ben Jelloun (1984: 41).

20 MRAP pleaded for *a vivre ensemble avec nos différences* (Living together with our differences).

21 Klaus Barbie was one of the leading police figures during the Vichy regime and responsible – directly and indirectly – for the deportation and killing of thousands of Jews during the Second World War. He was tracked down in Bolivia in 1986 and brought to trial in France in 1987.

22 Ford (1990: notes chapter 3, no. 127).

23 *Le Monde*, 24 November 1989, as quoted by Ford (1990, no. 3.7.11).

24 *Le Monde*, 14 March 1990.

25 Normally, a 'round table meeting' is meant to have an 'open' discussion with all partners without pre-set agendas or preconditions and without positions taken and conclusions made before the meeting starts.

26 *Le Monde*, 14 March 1990.
27 *Le Monde*, 4 April 1990.
28 *Le Monde*, 4 April 1990.
29 *Le Monde*, 8 May 1990.
30 In two cases, the perpetrators were arrested and brought before court on account of murder – without the addition of the word 'racist'. In the third case, 34-year-old Saadi Saoudi was killed by a policeman after having been arrested for a fight. Investigation showed that he was shot in the neck and the back three times. There were bullet holes in his hands also. His family argued that it had been a true execution. The police however, argued that his death was the result of self-defence by the policeman (Guidice, 1992: 286–7).
31 *Le Monde*, 4 May 1990.
32 *Le Monde*, 4 May 1990.
33 *Libération* and *Le Figaro*, 11 May 1990; *Le Monde*, 12 May 1990; as cited by Ford (1990, no. 3.7.18).
34 *Le Monde*, 13–14 May 1990.
35 *de Volkskrant*, 15 May 1990.
36 *Le Monde*, 18 May 1990.
37 *Le Monde*, 23 May 1990.
38 *Le Monde*, 27–28 May 1990.
39 *Le Monde*, 29 May 1990.
40 *Journal Officiel de la République Française*, 14 July 1990, 8333, *Loi* no. 90-615, art. 2.
41 CNCDH 1991 report (1992); as cited by Lloyd (1993: 215).
42 *Le Monde*, 10 July 1991.
43 *Le Monde*, 10 July 1991.
44 Elbers and Fennema (1993: 62); *Le Monde*, 22 and 23–24 June 1991.
45 *Le Monde*, 21 June 1991.
46 *Le Monde*, 10 July 1991.
47 *Le Figaro Magazine*, 21 September 1991.
48 *Le Monde*, 19 November 1992.
49 *Le Monde*, 28 January 1992.
50 *Le Monde*, 18 February 1992.
51 *Le Monde*, 10 June 1992.
52 *Le Monde*, 15–16 November 1992.

CHAPTER 4

State responses to racist violence in the Netherlands

Introduction

And if he vents this by expressing himself negatively about his neighbours with abusive references to their skin colour, their Turkish, Moroccan, Surinamese or Antillean origin, then it would be wrong to call such a person a racist immediately. In most cases he is not. He is just stuck [living among different cultures in the inner city].[1]

Besides discrimination out of stupidity or wickedness, our society is also confronted with violent acts against members of minority groups, with even places of worship not spared. It is the state's task, more particularly that of the legislature and of the Justice Department, to mark the boundaries of the permissible.[2]

These comments were made by two political leaders of the Justice Department within a period of five months and marked the ambivalence in state responses to racism and racist expressions in the Netherlands in the 1990s. Until the early 1990s, racist violence was not perceived as a structural problem within Dutch society. The dominant local, as well as national, state response to a vast majority of incidents included denial of the racist nature of the incident and of any social character of the phenomenon. Although this type of state response dominated most of the post-war period. I want to distinguish five different periods. These are the 1950s and 1960s; the 1970s; from 1980 to the mid-1980s; the second half of the 1980s; and the early 1990s. Of course, as in the case of France and Britain, these periods are not mutually exclusive. Changes in relation to the key issues start in the previous period, and key features of a specific period are not completely omitted from discourses in later periods.

The 1950s and 1960s: racist violence as a non-Dutch phenomenon

In the 1950s and 1960s, racist violence never reached the public or formal agendas in the Netherlands. Responses to incidents were typified by a failure to acknowledge the racist nature and social (i.e. structural) character of the violence. Sometimes, however, the racist nature of an incident was so obvious, that denial would have been ridiculous. In these instances, a firm condemnation and expressions of disgust were included in state responses to the incident. Several instances showed the 'occasional recognition' of racist violence by state authorities. There was, however, no sign of perceiving of racist violence as a social problem, and incidents were regarded as isolated occasions. In sum, the perception of racist violence as a non-Dutch phenomenon, and an implicit denial of its existence in Dutch society with some exceptions of 'occasional recognition', constituted the key feature of this twenty-year period. This situation led to a lack of evidence resulting from under reporting or denial.

The reception of 'repatriates'

The reception of 'repatriates' from the former colonies in Indonesia, of whom a vast majority held Dutch nationality, has often been regarded both nationally and internationally as a model of 'smooth integration'. Since the mid-1970s, however, this image has started to show some small cracks. Subsequent studies have been more critical and have shown this 'integration' to be a forced assimilation rather than an automatic incorporation into the host society.[3]

Some facts have surfaced in these studies which show that racist behaviour towards Eurasians was no different. In August 1951, for instance, disturbances were reported in Middelburg;[4] in the late 1950s, in The Hague and Den Helder there were disturbances between groups of 'native' Dutch and Eurasians (van Amersfoort, 1974; Groenendijk, 1990). As far as could be ascertained, these were mainly blamed on rivalry between young men over girls, but still gave grounds for some official comments. For instance, Marga Klompé, Minister of Welfare and Social Affairs, argued in the British *Daily Telegraph* (1 October 1958) that 'a problem which we do not have in the Netherlands is racial tension like you [in Britain] have experienced. Once there was some jealousy between our teenagers and so-called Teddy Boys, when they saw young Dutch girls going out with coloured Indo-Dutch. But that was only natural, and nothing serious really happened.'[5]

Labour migrants

Labour migrants were recruited to ease the temporary labour shortage in the 1960s and 1970s. As elsewhere in Western Europe (see for instance Cohn-Bendit and Schmid, 1992), they were recruited as a labour force and perceived solely as such by the host societies and states. The labour immigrants were not expected to integrate into the host society. Given that their stay was supposed to be temporary, and that they took part in the production process at the employers' behest, the state at first rejected any responsibility for their living and other conditions.

However, despite this rejection by the state, the immigrants were not isolated by other sections of Dutch society. Religious charity organisations stepped in to take care of the new arrivals. These organisations were of predominantly Catholic origin and worked with the first groups of labour immigrants arriving from Spain and Italy.

People were treated according to their foreign background, and this was regarded as being the work of specialists (Rath, 1991: 152).

In publications, the work involved was referred to in terms of 'attitudes', 'nature', 'way of life', 'strangeness', 'customs', and 'adjustments'. Reports by different state and non-state authorities referred to possible problems arising from the reception of these labour immigrants.

In relation to the population density, life here is rather strongly regulated. We are not allowed much, but we do not notice that ourselves because we already have accustomed ourselves to it. But these Southern people, who grew up in less ordered societies, often cannot accept this so easily. Away from the closeness of their own regional culture, they are left on their own in a highly industrialised environment, in which speed, labour discipline and the large amount of free time are strange to them. besides, they do not speak the language.[6]

Labour immigrants were portrayed as people originating from a totally different society, with a 'more traditional' culture, which had its own 'nature'. Their 'attitudes' and 'customs' were regarded as being different from those of the Dutch. Due to their national origin, labour migrants were portrayed as constituting a separate group of people used to a different 'social-cultural way of life' in comparison to Dutch people – i.e. they were 'racialised'.[7]

The management of the larger companies in the Netherlands seemed to be more enthusiastic about the arrival of a new labour force than the Dutch population in general. This was shown by a survey in 1961 which reported almost half the people interviewed opposed to this type of labour recruitment. Over-population, preference for their 'own people' and the fear of downward pressure on wages were among their main arguments against it (Groenendijk, 1990).

The Twente 'riots' in 1961[8]

In the 1960s, several incidents occured involving Dutch and Italian or Spanish people.[9] Groenendijk (1990) made a historical case study of those disturbances – the Twente 'riots' in September 1961 – in order to study the response of local governments. In the Twente region, in the east of the Netherlands, tension had been rising for some days, especially after an Italian boy was attacked by four Dutch youngsters in Almelo. In this area, Italian and Spanish people were refused entrance into several dance halls. This was justified by referring to advances made on Dutch girls and claiming that Dutch customers were staying away due to the Italians' presence.

In early September 1961, the entire police force of the city of Oldenzaal were called to duty because of an increasing number of rumours about possible violent confrontations. A confrontation between Italians demanding their right to enter a dance hall, and a large threatening crowd of 'native' people gathered outside, led to fights. The local police could not handle the situation and asked for assistance from the military police and the police from the nearby city of Enschede.

In the days that followed, Italian and Spanish workers went on strike in the four big cities in the region – Almelo, Hengelo, Enschede and Oldenzaal. Their grievances were based on insufficient protection against the violence of Dutch youth, insults in the streets and being refused entrance to dance halls. The mayor of Enschede, Wim Thomassen, asked the public to understand the position of the labour immigrants and their feelings of insecurity and declared that they were highly appreciated as workers. Thomassen promised protection and banned the display of any signs at the entrance to dance halls saying 'No Italians allowed', declaring these to be aggravating and insulting and in fact a form of disorderly conduct. The mayor also promised that the police would take action against anyone behaving in this manner.

Three remarkable points can be distinguished in the first police report about the events (Groenendijk, 1990). First, there existed a minimum of communication between the police and the labour migrants. Secondly, every time violent or forceful measures by the police were reported, they had been directed against the labour migrants. Thirdly, the Dutch participants in the disturbances were called *burgers* (citizens). This was different from the reports in later days, when only 'youth' and 'rowdies' were mentioned.

This first police report was important partly because most of the media coverage of these early events was based upon it. Later news coverage was more independent. In the first media reports, labour migrants were portrayed as 'victims' of violence and unequal treatment. This perception, however, often coexisted with references to not entirely innocent victims. Editorial comments unanimously disapproved of the behaviour of the 'rowdies' and signs like 'No Italians allowed' were compared with similar signs during the Second World War ('No Jews allowed') and to signs in South Africa and the USA ('Blacks not permitted entrance'). Weekly magazines responded with more detachment, reporting 'strange events' and the 'youthful disease of modern times'.

The events came to an end after several days of violent attacks by 'youngsters'. The collective violence resulted in the departure of 122 out of some 800 Spaniards and of 46 out of some 300 Italians. The departure of labour migrants was regarded as shameful. The idea that one could speak of an outburst of racism, however, was rejected in editorials and it was presented as a 'vulgar riot by hooligans'. Scarcely an article of the weekly press did not analyse the events, portrayed as 'rowdy riots', as an unavoidable part of labour migration.

According to Groenendijk, an important lesson to be learnt from the local state responses to the disturbances was illustrated by the very different responses of the mayors of Enschede and Oldenzaal. The first responded immediately and unambiguously, condemning the 'no entrance permitted' signs and promising police protection. It took a whole week before the other mayor responded publicly, and then only to call for calm. The immediate response by the mayor of Enschede could be regarded as an obvious local example of 'including recognition' of racist violence, i.e. including the view of the Italian and Spanish communities as an inextricable part of the local society. The response by the mayor of Oldenzaal could be regarded as a total denial of racist violence, directing his main attention to restoring and maintaining law and order without any condemnation of the migrant population becoming the target of violence.

At the national-state level, little official response was reported. An inquiry into the causes of the events was suggested by one MP, while another MP questioned the conduct of the Oldenzaal police. The Home Secretary did answer parliamentary questions very briefly, but neither he nor the provincial authorities were convinced of the need for an inquiry. Another more general inquiry started, however, during this same period, investigating some of the questions raised by the presence of labour immigrants. At the end of 1962, a working group reported its findings resulting in nineteen recommendations (e.g. employers had to give more attention to educating immigrants; extra houses needed to be built; and immigrants must be encouraged to learn Dutch). The report was presented to Parliament without any further comment.

The only measures implemented in these years were to be found in the fields of welfare and social work. In the 'pillar system' of the Dutch nation-state (see Lijphart, 1979), these fields of welfare and social work are called the *maatschappelijk middenveld* (social midfield) and are important to note because this 'midfield' presents the typical way of dealing with conflicts and tensions in the Dutch society (this will be elaborated on in more detail later). The activities of these organisations, as well as the measures mentioned, were directed towards the labour immigrants and their way of life in the Netherlands, that is, towards the adjustment of their 'way of life' to the 'Dutch way of life'. Implicitly the 'other way of life' was perceived as one, if not the only, cause of social problems. Because these labour migrants were only expected to stay in the Netherlands temporarily, and to return to their countries of origin when the work (labour shortages) ended, small adjustments to their way of life in the Netherlands were perceived to be enough to prevent any serious trouble.

The welfare solution mentioned might be defined as a particular example of an 'exclusionist' perception of this group of immigrants. On the other hand, it could be perceived and defined as a paternalistic kind of (temporary) 'inclusion'. Racist violence, however, was denied to exist at all and did not constitute a topic on the public or formal agendas. It would give too much credit to the Twente 'riots' to portray them as unilaterally connected to these measures, but the 'shock' caused by them, probably did speed up departmental decision-making processes with respect to subsidies for organisations in the so-called social midfield (Groenendijk, 1990: 82).[10]

Anti-semitic violence

Partly due to the dominant discourses denying the existence of racist violence in the Netherlands, few incidents were reported during the 1950s and the 1960s. As mentioned before, racist violence was not regarded as constituting a real social problem during these two decades (phase A). The racist nature of several incidents, as well as the structural character of the violence, were denied and were perceived in general to be 'non-Dutch'. In reported instances of racist violence, the impact and importance of the violence was often played down by the assumption that it was the product of boyish pranks.

Let us consider the 1960s. On 5 January 1960, the Dutch newspaper *de Volkskrant* reported an 'outburst of anti-semitism' in Amsterdam. People were receiving letters stating that 'Jews were not wanted'. The newspaper asked whether this was the work of rascals, communists or reviving fascists. The Rabbi of the Dutch-Israelite denomination in Amsterdam, John Schuster, argued that Dutch Jews were not under any threat, 'because the character of the Dutch people vouched for this, so anti-semitic expressions would be thought damaging and they would be rejected'.[11]

Statements by the authorities about the incidents referred to the suspicion that a majority of incidents – most of which consisted of vandalising with swastikas and fascist or anti-semitic slogans – were boyish tricks. For example, after an old Jewish graveyard was seriously damaged, the police in Enschede argued that the incident had nothing to do with anti-semitism. The local Chief of Police, Bruining, thought the damage was caused by youths 'just for kicks'.[12] In many instances, perpetrators were regarded as drunken pranksters.[13] In keeping with this view, racist motives were denied or negated – implicitly or explicitly.

In some instances, the racist nature of an incident was so obvious that denial was impossible. In instances of the anti-semitic kind of racist violence especially, the 'occasional recognition' type of response by state authorities was experienced in the Netherlands. It should be stressed that in this study and in the definition used, racist violence includes anti-semitic violence (see also Chapter 1). Although aware of the complexity of underlying debates, this study is directed towards state responses to racist violence, and therefore it is an important factor when specific forms of racist violence are perceived and responded to more prominently than other forms. In the 1950s and 1960s, this was the situation in the Netherlands with respect to anti-semitic violence.

This might partly be explained by Dutch experiences during the Second World War, which will be elaborated on in more detail in Chapter 5.[14] However, it needs to be mentioned here that the post-war period in the Netherlands was characterised by a strong public, as well as political, opposition to anything connected with fascism or racism, and most certainly, anti-semitism. Any group with fascist or racist links and sentiments trying to organise itself was confronted with broad condemnation and criminalisation and media reports of such attempts immediately led to the end of such initiatives. Public, political and judicial attention and the consequent pressure to ban any such organisation were prominent elements within the post-war Netherlands (see van Donselaar, 1991).

In line with these dominant discourses, instances of violence, in which the racist (i.e. anti-semitic) nature of them could not be ignored, were firmly condemned in the public, media and political responses. These responses, however, always included a reference to the incidental character of the occurrence and statements that racist violence was not structurally present in the Netherlands.

In September 1963, a large swastika was discovered on the roof of a Jewish-owned factory in the city of Almelo. The swastika appeared to have been painted there some years before, and the police suspected it to be an anti-semitic action.[15] In 1964–66, a wave of desecrations of Jewish graves occurred, especially in the eastern Achterhoek region, where the synagogue of Aalten also was vandalised.[16] From September to November 1966, some 1,000 graves were desecrated and vandalised in the south and east of the Netherlands.[17] As mentioned, instances were reported in which the police, as well as the Jewish community, were quite certain that anti-semitism had been one of the underlying motives.[18]

In these instances, responses took the form of firm condemnation. As the above examples show, incidents rarely comprised violent attacks against individuals, but were mainly directed against places of worship and graves. There were many examples of responses by state authorities, as well as the authorities within the victimised communities, in which the impact and the racist nature of the violence was played down or denied. Most of the time, drunken pranks or youthful vandalism were blamed for the violence without any real knowledge or actual evidence concerning the motives or organisations behind it. Therefore, the 1950s and 1960s in the Netherlands were characterised by the denial of the existence of racist violence, with some exceptions, including instances of the 'occasional recognition'.

The 1970s: first signs of racist violence on local agendas

In the 1970s, state responses to racism and racist violence in the Netherlands presented a diffuse picture. In 1971, the ratification of the International (UN) Convention on Elimination of All Forms of Racial Discrimination led to the addition of statutory provisions outlawing discrimination in the Dutch Criminal Code. It should be noted that the first article of the Dutch Constitution prohibits distinctions made on grounds of irrelevant qualities or characteristics of persons, such as religion, belief, political opinion, race, or sex (Rodrigues, 1994: 383–4).

The denial of racist violence as a social problem continued and thus the issue remained in Phase A. This period, however, is distinguished from the previous one, because it shows some examples of the 'excluding recognition' of racist violence by local authorities. Several incidents of collective racist violence, especially the Rotterdam riots (1972) and the Schiedam riots (1976), were perceived to be caused by social problems closely related to the presence of minority groups, especially labour immigrants and their descendants, and people of Surinam origin. It is the denial of the existence of racist violence in mainstream public and political discourse and these local responses that constitutes the key features of this period.

A second reason to distinguish this period was the occurrence of terrorist actions by Moluccan youths. These actions themselves are not the subject here, but the assumed solutions to general social problems in relation to the presence of minority communities, as well as to the terrorist actions by the Moluccan youngsters, led to a change of state policies with the construction of general minorities policies. These policies consisted of an enormous extension of welfare and social work. The situation with respect to responses to racist violence will be elaborated upon first in this section. Thereafter, attention will be paid to the Moluccan actions in relation to the birth of a minorities policy.

Changing patterns of migration in the 1970s

After the mid-1960s, the main countries from which labour for Dutch industry was recruited were no longer Italy and Spain, but Turkey and Morocco. After a temporary decrease in the numbers recruited due to economic recession (1967), a substantial increase was noticeable between 1969 and 1972. The recruitment was almost entirely conducted by official recruitment offices (Penninx, 1979: 99). Dutch state authorities officially stated time and again that the Netherlands did not constitute an immigration country and that labour immigrants were here to stay only temporarily. This was reconfirmed in the *Nota Buitenlandse Werknemers* (White Paper on Foreign Workers, 1970) by the Ministry of Social Welfare and Public Health, in which it was stated that labour immigrants had to adjust to the Dutch way of life. At the same time, however, they were expected to preserve their own 'identity' in order to become re-adjusted in their mother country after their return. Labour migration diminished after the 1973 oil crisis (Muus, 1993: 72).

In relation to migration of people from Surinam, this decade showed two peaks. In 1974–75, over 50,000 Surinamese people immigrated to the Netherlands just prior to independence (1975). These people were all Dutch subjects. The next five years constituted a transition period in the decolonisation process at the end of which another peak in Surinamese immigration was noticeable with some 31,000 immigrants (Entzinger, 1984: 83; Muus, 1993: 54). During the 1970s, there also was a small but steady migration by Dutch subjects from the Dutch Antilles (Koekebakker, 1990: 76). A major difference in perception between the labour migration and that from the (former) Dutch colonies was that the latter was not one of temporary settlement, but the mainstream denial of the Netherlands as a persisted immigration country.

Racist violence and riots in the 1970s

Tension and hostile behaviour by Dutch people towards minority communities was reported throughout these years and sometimes surfaced quite openly. The victimised communities changed with the changing patterns of migration to the Netherlands. In the early 1970s, reported violence was mainly directed against Turkish and Moroccan individuals and communities. In 1969, The Hague was confronted with violent attacks against hostels in which Moroccans lived. In July 1971, Turkish people were attacked in the streets of Rotterdam after a previous violent attack on a Turkish hostel. In the same month, Turkish people were attacked in The Hague. In November 1971, a Portuguese seaman was almost lynched by a group of taxi-drivers in Rotterdam after an argument with one of them.[19] In the southern cities of Weert and Roermond, Moluccan and Dutch youths clashed violently, and in August 1972, Rotterdam was the scene of riots directed against Turkish people (Groenendijk, 1990). These riots were by far the most important with respect to media attention for their severity and scale.

On 9 August 1972, a Dutch woman and her three children were evicted from their house by their Turkish landlord in a rather heavy-handed manner. This turned out to be the trigger event for what became perceived in the Netherlands as the first 'race' riot in the country. A crowd of local residents who had gathered threatened some Turkish people and the landlord pulled a knife, injuring three locals. When the police finally arrived, they fired warning shots to keep the furious crowd under control. That night the windows of a Turkish restaurant were smashed, and the people living in three hostels owned by the restaurant owner had to flee. The next morning, youths attacked the hostels again and threw out all the household goods. The police were present but did not intervene. Several nights of unrest and attacks against hostels and houses of Turkish people followed. The rioting smouldered around Rotterdam for several weeks (see among others van Reenen, 1979: 238–52).

Responses to the Rotterdam riots

The mayor of Rotterdam returned immediately from holiday and visited the scene.[20] He was verbally abused upon arrival and his car was almost overturned. At first, the police acted neither consistently nor adequately. Only when the riots started to spread through the neighbourhood, and later into other parts of the city, did the police intervene and arrest some eighty people. The media covered the events broadly, talking about 'Turkish nights'. One newspaper even asked 'whether Rotterdam would turn into a Belfast', quoting local residents who said they were considering buying guns.[21] The main objection expressed by local residents was directed against the 'Turkish' hostels. One of the leaders of the first attack group argued that these were not 'race riots' against Turks. 'We did not do anything against those Turkish families, we were only after those hostels. First we took soundings in the neighbourhood as to whether we could get any support. After we had some fifteen people together, we gave those Turks a good dressing down. They did not have to leave, oh no, they just had to know their place.'[22] Later, the city of Rotterdam announced that the hostels would be closed down.

The riots led to a debate in the Netherlands – which has gone on ever since – as to whether there had to be a policy of dispersal or concentration with regard to newly arrived immigrants. The city of Rotterdam proposed the first kind of policy in the aftermath of the riots, with a limit of 5 per cent of immigrants for each neighbourhood population. Later, however, this city policy was reversed by the *Raad van State* (the Council of State).

The riots were perceived as an outburst of tension and irritation by the indigenous population, caused by the size of the present immigrant population (a Dutch version of the *seuil de tolérance*). The authorities, and most of all the police, did not yet know how to respond adequately. They failed to intervene immediately, which led to a situation in which severe rioting took place for several days and smouldered on for weeks. Intervention took place only after some days, when the situation threatened to become a matter of law and order for the rest of the city. Most measures implemented, or at least proposed, were directed against the assumed cause of the violence, the presence of victimised minority communities.

The city authorities responded in panic and directed their official measures towards the alleged main cause of the irritation: the Turkish hostels. They introduced the dispersal policy mentioned and closed down the Turkish hostels as demanded by the rioters. Further, the neighbourhood in which the riots occurred, was now 'covered by a huge blanket of social and cultural services'.[23]

This last item might be interpreted as a Dutch-style measure of law and order, aimed at covering up any tension and conflicts. State responses to the collective violence at a local level could be classified as 'excluding recognition' of racist violence. Implicitly, the violence was recognised as being directed against people (and their properties) as representatives of the Turkish minority community – not in their capacity as individuals.

At the national level, little state response was reported with regard to the collective violence. The only official response consisted of the judicial decision that the city of Rotterdam was considered to have crossed legal boundaries by proposing a forced dispersal programme. This (lack of) national state response could be classified as a total rejection of collective racist violence constituting a problem within

Dutch society. The violence was perceived as a local problem of law and order and nothing else.

The Schiedam riots in 1976

On 6 August 1976, two Dutch youngsters were stabbed, one of them fatally, after an argument between two Turkish and five Dutch boys in Schiedam. Nothing else happened that night, although several small groups of youngsters were reported to have planned attacks on Turkish people (Jansma and Veenman, 1977: 134–5). The next night, an aggressive group of youths, among them people from outside Schiedam, started smashing the windows of a Turkish bar.[24]

There was a police presence at the time, but no response until the rioters set fire to another Turkish bar some hours later. Then the police response was directed against the Turkish bar owner who threatened to defend himself with his rifle. When the police finally, at a later stage, started to take action against the rioters there was confusion and anger, and from that moment on the police were among the main targets of the violence. The riots lasted for another five to six days. Local residents were said to be among the leaders, providing molotov-cocktails and car tyres and giving shelter to rioters (Jansma and Veenman, 1977: 142).

Responses by national and local state authorities

Responses to the riots on the national level were mainly focused on the distribution of pamphlets by the *Nederlandse VolksUnie* (NVU, Dutch People's Union) which appealed to residents in Schiedam to support the party and its leader, Joop Glimmerveen, 'in their life and death struggle against the enemies of our people'. This led to questions in Parliament by MP Hans Molleman (PvdA) to the Minister of Justice, Dries Van Agt (CDA) over the possible role of the NVU in the riots and over the possibility of banning the party. The minister answered some weeks later that the role of the NVU in the riots could not be determined. But the minister also stated that the role of the NVU in distributing the pamphlets was under investigation. The criminal prosecution and possible disbandment of this party would depend on the results of this investigation (van Donselaar, 1991: 161).

Two weeks before the 1977 general elections, PvdA MPs Molleman and Aad Kosto again asked the Minister of Justice whether the NVU could be banned because the party used the rune logo in their propaganda material. The investigation mentioned earlier had little result, but the new questions by the two MPs were answered within a week by the minister who stated that the NVU would be taken care of by the Public Prosecutor in Amsterdam. Finally, on 8 March 1978, the Amsterdam Court the NVU was an illegal body (see for further details van Donselaar, 1995).

Responses to the Schiedam riots by local authorities did not differ much from those reported in the 1972 riots in Rotterdam. Explanations for the Rotterdam riots pointed to the poor social conditions of some neighbourhoods involved and at the number of immigrants living there. The Schiedam riots were more or less regarded as the work of hooligans and young thugs. Reference to racist motives for the violent attacks were not reported.

The only real policy changes implemented consisted of a huge build-up of social services, various organisations and – either overt or concealed – dispersal policies to prevent any concentration of immigrant populations. In the following years, a start was made on the renovation of some of the neighbourhoods involved in the Schiedam riots. One result was a much lower concentration of minority communities in these neighbourhoods. Questioned as to whether this had been the result of a dispersal policy, the mayor and the City Alderman for Housing rejected the term. 'It is just a side-effect of this renovation. Okay, they will be dispersed, but a policy, no.'[25]

As for the police, as mentioned earlier, they at first stood back, arms crossed, doing little but 'looking at how a rain of stones rearranged one small business into a ravage'.[26] Later the police responded harshly, and then became themselves a target of the rioters. The local authorities responded, via the mayor, with terms that referred to the rioters as 'just a bunch of trouble-makers' and 'riff-raff' – terms which obviously trivialised the impact of the riots and the motives for this violence.

Responses by local and national state authorities were not directed towards the occurrence of racist violence in the riots. The responses by national authorities were mainly directed against the position of the *Nederlandse VolksUnie* and the possible ban of this party, whereas responses by local authorities were mainly directed at community relations and law and order issues. During these years, the Netherlands seemed to be poised waiting for other violent clashes in its major cities. In 1976, the annual Social and Cultural Report, issued by an influential advisory institution concerned with future developments and state policies, forecast more riots such as those seen in Rotterdam and Schiedam. In 1977, a Turkish man was pushed into the water and left to drown and thus was regarded as the first fatal victim of racist violence in the Netherlands. Bovenkerk (1978: 15) argued that these years constituted a moment of 'fearful waiting for the next outburst of xenophobia. This all makes clear that terms like tolerance and obligingness belong to the past.'[27]

Actions by Moluccan youths

In the 1970s the Netherlands was confronted with four terrorist actions by small groups of Moluccan youths wishing to highlight political demands for a free and independent Moluccan Republic and the attention of the public and Dutch government to the situation of Moluccans in the Netherlands. In the years following the first action in 1970, it had become apparent that the Dutch authorities did not want to consider these problems as political, but preferred to regard them as social.[28] In 1975, Minister of Welfare Harry van Doorn stated that according to the government's opinion, the future of the Moluccans was in the Netherlands and they had to forget their political aspirations with respect to a Moluccan Republic (Schmid *et al.*, 1982: 39).

In that same year, Moluccan youths carried out two other terrorist attacks simultaneously, causing four casualties.[29] During these 1975 actions, the Moluccan population in several cities[30] had to be protected against acts of revenge by groups of white Dutchmen.[31] The police received some 6,000 phone-calls and letters in which people threatened to take violent revenge.[32]

Besides the political demands with regard to a Moluccan Republic, it was the growing discrimination and hostility among the Dutch population towards Moluccan youths, perceived to be terrorists and criminals, that definitely constituted one of the main causes of the 1975 actions (Schmid *et al.*, 1982: 40).[33]

A response: the birth of minorities policies

The Moluccan actions are important in this study because they serve as a marker in relation to the 'birth of Dutch minorities policy'. A significant feature of future minorities policy would be the belief that while minority groups had to integrate into Dutch society, they also had to preserve their own culture. This idea was partly based on the perception of migration as a temporary settlement.

Another important feature of future minorities policy would be the implementation of a special negotiation structure. National advisory institutions representing minority groups were to be set up and subsidised by the state to establish and maintain contact on a regular basis. The *Inspraakorgaan Welzijn Molukkers* (the Participation Council of Moluccans) was one of the first of these institutions. In parliamentary debates about this policy, especially directed towards the 'inclusion' of the Moluccan population in the Netherlands, it was questioned whether other 'categories' of immigrants could and should be included. For the time being, the Minister of Culture, Recreation and Social Work turned down this suggestion (Rath, 1991: 163). Therefore, at first the policy was directed towards the Moluccan population in particular, but later it was dircted increasingly towards other immigrant communities.

This feature of minorities policy was typically Dutch. The Dutch system as a whole was constructed along so-called pillars, strong 'group identities' along religious, liberal and socialist lines. The political and economic elites of these pillars held the key positions within the state authorities, with no single pillar holding an overall majority position. Tensions and conflicts within Dutch society were often handled through the previously mentioned 'social midfield' which was also a part of this pillar system. In a way, one could argue that the Dutch state organised and subsidised its own opposition. This led to a so-called negotiation structure in which the minorities now also started to be included by the state. It was the state that set up minority organisations, subsidised them and gave them a place within this negotiation structure.

Although a national minorities policy started to take shape, culminating in the 1979 report by the *Wetenschappelijke Raad voor het Regeringsbeleid* (Netherlands Scientific Council for Government Policy, see also Rath, 1991: 164–5), measures to combat racist violence were not introduced in the 1970s. Violence was not regarded as constituting a social problem in the Netherlands, other than individual (i.e. occasional) incidents stemming from inner-city neighbourhood problems or from problems common to young people (rivalry, high alcohol consumption).

Local responses to a 'changing climate'

At the local level, responses varied. There was not only the unambiguous condemnation by local authorities of such violence, but also many examples of the racist nature of the violence being played down in the same way as had been done in the 1950s and the 1960s. Together with increasing unemployment during the second half of the 1970s, youth unemployment and boredom were also portrayed as causes of violent racist incidents. For example, in 1978 fights broke out between young people from Schiedam and from neighbouring Vlaardingen. In an interview it was claimed that these fights were caused by Turkish youths in Vlaardingen taking over the local youth club.[34]

Sometimes local authorities took other approaches. On 20 October 1979, the *Nationaal Jeugd Front* (NJF, the National Youth Front) organised a meeting in Soest. Wearing military-like uniforms and carrying flags, slogans were shouted, such as 'Creoles [from Surinam] should stay in their stinking sewers' and 'Long live our Fatherland, in which Jews no longer are bragging and troubling an East Front Warrior'.[35] The police, who were present at the time, took no action. The local Chief of Police explained that this was due to the obscurity of what had been said. National political spokespersons later stated that they were shattered not only by the slogans, but also by this excuse from the local police. Two days after the incident, all political factions in Parliament signed a statement in which they claimed to be appalled by what had happened. In 1980, the speaker at the NJF meeting was prosecuted for discrimination on the basis of 'race' (van Donselaar, 1991: 169)

From 1980 to the mid-1980s: is racist violence a Dutch problem?

The fight against racism and discrimination increasingly attracted attention in the late 1970s and greatly influenced the minorities policy which was officially implemented in the early 1980s.[36] There was also an enormous increase in activity at the local level including state subsidies to anti-racsim groups. As support for the extreme right's political and racist agenda increased so did the number of anti-racist activities and so did the number of racist incidents reported in the media and by anti-racism groups.

The extreme right and racist violence

Sometimes the link between racist incidents and the politically organised extreme right was very obvious, such as when the NVU's pamphlets appeared at the Schiedam riots. This led to an investigation by the Justice Department, as mentioned earlier. But in 1980, an attack against a group of Moroccan people attracted even more publicity. This group of people was threatened with expulsion from the country and then given shelter by a solidarity committee in the Mozes and Aaron Church in Amsterdam. On 29 February 1980, some ten members of a meeting of the recently founded right-wing extremist party, the *Nationale Centrumpartij* (NCP, National Centre Party) went to the church 'to do what the police had failed to do'.[37] The attackers, however, were surprised by the number of people present – more than one hundred instead of the expected ten. Fights broke out and two of the three founders of the NCP were arrested and later found guilty of assault and battery (van Donselaar, 1993: 47).

This violent attack attracted much media attention and two days later the NCP was disbanded by its founders, who knew they stood no chance if their party was linked to violence. A few days later, a new party, the *Centrumpartij* (CP, Centre Party), was established (van Donselaar, 1991: 173–4). The media attention took two forms. On the one hand, one of the NCP leaders,[38] was portrayed as an intellectual trying to profit politically from increasing xenophobia in the Netherlands. On the other hand, the perpetrators were portrayed as Dutch people living under deplorable conditions including housing shortages and poor socioeconomic circumstances. Journalists reported that 'when we were trying to identify the political ideas of the NCP-members we could not find any ideology, only a predominant state of confusion'.[39] The racist nature of their discourse and behaviour was implicitly played down and trivialised. This would form the basis for the dominant perception of supporters of extreme right and racist ideas and political parties in the years to come.

Other incidents reported in 1980 – sometimes closely linked to a particular organisation – included the three following.

1 In June/July, several fights broke out in the city of Utrecht after migrant residents had been repeatedly intimidated by a group of white youths.[40]
2 At the end of November, a smoke-bomb was thrown into a restaurant in Hengelo, for which the *Nederlands Orthodox Reactionaire*

Front (Dutch Orthodox Reactionary Front) claimed responsibility. This organisation announced that more actions would take place 'to liberate the Netherlands of the coloured dirt'. Shortly afterwards, leaflets were distributed in the area by the *Nationale Jeugd Front* (NJF, National Youth Front).[41]

3 In December, two molotov-cocktails were thrown into a reception centre which provided shelter to more than one hundred Vietnamese boat-people. One week later, a building with other Vietnamese refugees was fired on.[42]

The Tilburg riots (1981) and responses

In this atmosphere of increasing attention to extreme right, racist violence, some violent events abroad also attracted attention in the Dutch media. The Brixton riots in London (April 1981) received enormous media coverage, and raised the question as to whether such riots could occur in the Netherlands. Just six weeks later, an affirmative answer seemed to be provided. In the southern city of Tilburg, several hundred local residents attacked a family of Surinamese origin, injuring three family members. The family was taken to safety at the police station but in the mean time a furious crowd raided their house, rampaging through it. A feature article by the newspaper *de Volkskrant* (9 May 1981) was headed: 'Fights result in race riot' and '*Vogeltjesbuurt* [the neighbourhood] has its own laws'.

In response to this violence, questions were put to the Home Secretary in Parliament. The main concern was the police conduct during the riots. The local Chief of Police blamed possible mistakes on the limited size of his force. The issue of a dispersal or concentration-type housing policy was raised once again in political debates – just as in the 1970s.

A spokesman for a Surinamese welfare organisation blamed state authorities for assuming that adaptation was assured by dispersing minorities throughout Dutch society. He noted that 'integration would only be possible through mutual understanding and respect of which there is no sign right now, as shown by this Tilburg incident'.[43] A spokesman for the local authorities' argued that the incident could not be regarded exclusively as one of law and order, but as a social problem for which no immediate solution had been found. He stated that through talks and meetings such incidents could be prevented from re-occurring. This spokesman also pointed out that the number of 'foreigners' in the neighbourhood was much too high.[44]

Finally, the family under attack was helped to find another house elsewhere. This led the Surinamese spokesman to warn against creating the impression – which might result from this policy – that 'if you do not want any Surinamese people around, you just have to throw them out and they will not return again'.[45]

Increasing resentment against minority communities

In August 1982, a similar incident occurred in the small city of Deurne in the predominantly Roman Catholic south of the Netherlands. Local residents protested against the possible settlement of a migrant family in their street. Some of them organised a petition against it, and one of the organisers argued that 'this street hates foreigners'.[46] The director of the local Housing Board stated that if protesters continued, they would be fought. The president of the Housing Association Board wondered why this protest had been raised at all, 'because this migrant family had already lived in the Netherlands for a long time and was well settled'.[47]

The city of Deurne was faced with a lot of incidents throughout the year. There were threatening letters and phone-calls (claimed by the *Viking Jeugd*),[48] swastikas were painted on a house, and a car owned by a member of the local anti-fascism group was set on fire. One 16-year-old boy was arrested, but the police stated that it was not possible he had acted on his own.[49] These and similar incidents did place racism and racist violence on some local and formal agendas – be it temporarily. Sometimes attention was paid to an incident at the national level – as happened with Tilburg. However, neither racism nor racist violence ever really entered on to the national public or formal agendas. This situation changed with the victory of the extreme-right *Centrumpartij* (CP): they gained one seat in Parliament and sent shock waves through the very core of Dutch politics and public opinion.

Extreme-right election victory

On 26 May 1981, neither the CP nor the NVU were successful in the elections, that is, neither won any seats. However, if the total vote of the two parties were combined, then support for the Dutch extreme right had increased by an average of 25 per cent overall, and up to 40 per cent in the cities (van Donselaar, 1991: 180). The struggle between the two seemed to be one of the main causes of their failure. But after the government coalition collapsed and new elections were held on 8 September 1982, CP leader Hans Janmaat entered into Parliament. The victory of the CP was celebrated in Amsterdam by party supporters, armed with iron and wooden bars, attacking a squatters' home and black people in the streets. Five people were reported injured.[50]

The political and public response to this extreme-right advance was one of shock. At the inauguration ceremony of the new Parliament, a demonstration against the CP was organised with several thousands of people attending. The other political parties agreed on isolating the extreme-right MP by ignoring him in parliamentary debates. In the media, a general unwritten agreement was made to keep any news coverage about the MP and his party low profile.

Increasing attention for racist violence

One of the major consequences of the election victory was the enormous increase in public and media attention to racism in the Netherlands. The media started to pay increasing attention to all kinds of instances of racism, including racist violence (phase B). During the early 1980s, much more information was collected and analysed with respect to racist violence in the Netherlands. Previously, most data were limited to 'major events' like the disturbances in Rotterdam (1972) and Schiedam (1976). In the 1980s, however, data about individual racist incidents were collected more frequently, and this contributed to an increasing awareness and concern about this phenomenon. However, it should be noted that this data collection was predominantly based on newspaper reports. No 'real' research was undertaken about the occurrence of racist violence in the Netherlands during those years.

The range of incidents reported by the media was quite broad, as was the response to specific incidents. This was shown by examples of very different instances of racist violence and also by the different types of responses they received during the period of 1982–83.

Examples of the first type consist of two incidents during football matches in 1982. The football club Ajax-Amsterdam increasingly became perceived and portrayed as a 'Jewish club' by supporters of opposing teams as well as by supporters of Ajax itself. Opposing supporters were often heard shouting slogans such as 'We go hunting Jews', and making references to the Holocaust. Ajax supporters often waved flags and banners with the Star of David. During a match between Ajax-Amsterdam and the FC Utrecht a photo was taken showing a 19-year-old Utrecht supporter holding a banner with anti-semitic signs. Newspapers published the photo and gave the story enormous coverage. Even national television talk shows discussed and condemned this behaviour. In 1983, the man was fined 250 guilders (about £100). Two weeks later, two other Utrecht supporters were convicted for shouting anti-semitic slogans. Each was sentenced to write an essay, one at the *Anne Frank Stichting* and the other at the former concentration camp in Westerbork – from whence many Jews had been transported to death camps during the Second World War. In response, the National Football Association sent guidelines to all associated clubs on how to deal with racism and anti-semitism (Holtrop and Den Tex, 1984: 8).

An example of the second type of response occurred in April 1983, when fights between Moluccan and Dutch youths were reported at a disco in Nijverdal in the east of the Netherlands. The fights resulted in three people being injured, of whom one later died. Some days later, shots were fired at the Moluccan Centre. The local Chief of Police claimed that the incident

was a mere bar brawl that got out of control. These things do happen often among youngsters. Coincidentally this also happens between Moluccans and Dutch. The Moluccans are not totally integrated; they attract attention sooner because they constitute a noticeable group, because of differences in nature and differences of skin colour. . . . Again, the Moluccans tend to group together and the whites tend to oppose that.

(Holtrop and Den Tex, 1984: 27)

Local responses to racist violence

The first examples, mentioned above, showed judicial responses to racist behaviour. The second example showed a response by a local authority to a violent incident in which the minority community was explicitly blamed for the occurrence of the incident. They were not 'integrated' and they grouped together, causing the 'opposition' and the violent reaction. The latter showed similarity to many of the recorded responses to racist incidents in the Netherlands in the 1980s.

Immediate state responses at the local level – nothing was heard at the national level – showed that a great deal depended on the awareness and consciousness of individual local authorities. The local responses, therefore, can be characterised as being very 'ad hoc'. This ad hoc response could either turn out to be an example of a 'total denial of a racist nature of violence' or a local example of the 'occasional, including or excluding recognition'.

Sometimes, a mixture of these responses did occur. The response in the Nijverdal incident, for instance, was an example of a mixture of 'total denial' and 'excluding recognition'. Ad hoc responses often occurred when local authorities were suddenly caught up in a racist incident without any clear prior assumptions or knowledge of racist violence.

There were exceptions, however. In February 1983, the city of Amsterdam published a report (*Tussen Witkalk en Zwarthemden*: Between Whitewash and Blackshirts) about the city's position concerning the increase of racist and discriminatory expressions.[51] In this report it was stated that the previous basic assumption had been that there should be no state interference in expressions of racism except when they broke the law. The report concluded that writers, politicians, artists and activist groups within the population had always played an important role in combating racism. The report explicitly recognised that the number of racist incidents was on the increase in recent years, but stated that racist violence still had an occasional character. This seems to be a clear example of 'occasional recognition' of racist violence by the (local) state authorities. The report continued by stating that broad awareness and 'being watchful' were necessary. Reference was made to the importance of a clear and public open stand against racism by state authorities 'even when it was just to show to the victims the attitude of the authorities in this case and that they would not leave the victims on their own. . . . It was the state's duty to protect threatened groups and to stand beside them' (1983: 3 4).

The report ended with recommendations including the creation of a central office to register complaints; that walls vandalised with racist graffiti should be cleaned immediately; a better prosecution policy; and plans to improve the information given to, and the education of, police officers.

At first the Amsterdam authorities' perception of racist violence seemed to be rather ambiguous. The report focused on the 'occasional' character of the violence on the one hand, but on the other, it placed the topic on the local formal agenda. Although major responsibility was still placed with the population itself, with regard to watchfulness and private initiatives, the Amsterdam report also formulated recommendations which characterised the 'including recognition' type of state response. The report, therefore, could be characterised at least as an example of the 'occasional recognition' with some indications towards the 'including recognition' by local state authorities.

The Amsterdam response to racist violence was illustrated not only by this report. Six months later, the city, and in fact the Netherlands as a whole, was shocked by a racist incident which showed local government responses in line with the report.

Kerwin Duinmeijer[52]

On 20 August 1983, in a cafeteria in Amsterdam, three white boys made racist remarks to Kerwin Duinmeijer, who was of Antillean origin. The abused boy and his friends left the scene but Kerwin was stopped on the street by the abusers and stabbed. A taxi-driver refused to take Kerwin to a hospital, because he did not want blood all over his car. After an ambulance was called, Kerwin was brought to a hospital where he later died. The 16-year-old murderer told the police that he stabbed Kerwin because 'he was black and dirty niggers should not look at me in an ugly way' (Holtrop and Den Tex, 1984: 27).

This murder, and also the conduct of the taxi-driver, caused enormous turmoil throughout the Netherlands. At the funeral service, the mayor of Amsterdam Ed. Van Thijn stated 'the writing is on the wall'. The mayor also headed an anti-racism demonstration. A spokesman for the *Anne Frank Stichting*, Bauco Van der Wal, said that he hoped and believed that this murder was merely an unfortunate incident.[53] In contrast, City Councillor Walter Etty argued that the murder of Kerwin was more than just that.

Racism and fascism do not fit in Amsterdam. You may disagree with one another on anything, but here we have to be clear. As city authorities you have to set the norm. It should be clear that we see the multi-cultural society, the different cultures, as an enrichment.[54]

Another kind of state response was shown by the judicial system. The murderer of Kerwin Duinmeijer appeared in juvenile court five months later and was not sentenced to imprisonment, but was put under psychiatric surveillance until the age of 21. The magistrate explicitly claimed that the murder was not racist and took into consideration the psychiatric report, which pronounced the murderer to be less than accountable for his conduct (Holtrop and Den Tex, 1984: 27), and to be coping with a 'disturbed aggression regularisation'.[55] In the magistrate's view, there was no proof of premeditation, and so it was not a question of murder, but rather a case of grevious bodily harm leading to the victim's death.[56]

Many organisations and individuals were astonished by this court decision, especially by the statement in the verdict about racist feelings not constituting the actual motive for the murder, which raised many questions.[57] Despite the legal decision, Kerwin's death was commonly perceived as a racist killing and has since been commemorated every year by an anti-racism demonstration in Amsterdam and by a statue placed in one of the best known parks in the city.

Responses by external actors: Anti Discriminatie Bureaus

Racism and racist violence in the Netherlands were not responded to solely by state authorities – on the contrary. Kerwin's murder brought racist violence as a topic to the public agenda. Many incidents were reported in the media, and anti-racism organisations and individuals turned up at numerous demonstrations. Of special significance in increasing awareness was the documentary *Kerwin, Een Teken van de Tijd* (Sign of the Times), which was shown several times on national television and had a major impact.[58]

Partly due to the increasing number of reported racist incidents, as well as to the new and unexpected success of the *Centrumpartij* (a gain of 9 per cent of the vote, and two seats in by-elections in the city of Almere on 21 September 1983) several local anti-racism activist groups set up so-called *Anti Discriminatie Bureaus* (ADBs, Anti-Discrimination Bureaux). Sometimes these bureaux were started partly by the local government, as recommended in the Amsterdam report (1983).

At an Anti-Discrimination Bureau, people could report complaints about discriminatory incidents and practices, and they received legal and other help in combating the discrimination – whether or not through judicial proceedings. The ADBs also organised several demonstrations and other activities against discrimination and racism and against political parties propagating racist ideas. During the 1980s, the number of ADBs and so-called Reporting Centres increased to about forty all over the Netherlands. Their activities included providing information to the public and authorities as well as putting pressure on local authorities to take discrimination, racism and racist violence seriously.

Extreme-right response to racist violence

In May 1984, the *Centrumpartij* indirectly responded to the increasing awareness of racist violence in the Netherlands. CP member W.J. Bruyn wrote a report in which he argued that the violent attacks against migrant minorities constituted a 'justifiable case of self-defence'. This was not the first instance in which he tried to make this point. During the 1961 'riots' in the Twente region, he had written a letter published in a Dutch newspaper in which he talked of 'justified self-defence of one's own interests and life style' (Groenendijk, 1990: 76). However, in 1961 Bruyn was a *ra'ra a'vis* (odd character); in 1984 he was a central figure in a movement.

In September 1984, judicial proceedings started against the author of the 1984 CP report. The Amsterdam court stated that in recent years there had been an increasing number of violent racist incidents in the Netherlands (Possel, 1987: 208), and the court declared it to be unlawful to label violence against 'foreigners' as an acceptable form of resistance. In the end, however, the author was not prosecuted because it was an internal report, not meant for publication. The attention paid to this report and to the judicial proceedings against it, however, seemed to cause considerable damage to the *Centrumpartij*, especially because the party leader Janmaat did not distance himself from it (van Donselaar, 1991: 187 and 191; van Donselaar, 1995).

National state response

In spring 1984, the *Anne Frank Stichting*, one of the main institutions in the anti-racism movement throughout the years, whose documentation centre had started collecting news coverage about racist incidents in the early 1980s, reported its concern about the rising level of racist violence in the Netherlands. The director of the *Stichting*, H. Westra, argued that the propaganda of the *Centrumpartij*, which still incited to racial hatred with impunity, was one of the main causes of this increase in racist violence.[59]

The fact that the *Centrumpartij* was still on a winning streak was proven by the results of the election for the European Parliament in June that same year. Although the CP did not gain a seat, its support was still increasing (2.5 per cent). With the same result in local elections, the CP would have gained seats on at least forty city councils.[60]

On 29 August, the *Vaste Kamercommissie voor Justitie* (Parliamentary Standing Commission on Justice) organised a hearing for the full spectrum of anti-racism organisations. This, along with growing awareness of racism in Dutch society, led to the establishment of the *Landelijk Bureau Racismebestrijding* (LBR, the National Office for Combating Racism). The office was set up the following year (1985) and reported on, and published information about, many cases of discrimination and racism and presented a number of procedures and strategies designed to combat direct and indirect discrimination. *Anti Discriminatie Codes* were developed to promote anti-discrimination practices in the labour market in particular. Besides these acitivities, the LBR trained people working for the local *Anti Discriminatie Bureaus* in, for instance, the judicial process of discrimination complaints.

In these years awareness and watchfulness with regard to racism and racist violence definitely increased in comparison to earlier days. It would be a mistake, however, to think this was a general recognition of the existence of racist violence in the Netherlands. Among the increasing number of reported incidents, many examples showed the local government still neglecting the racist nature of an incident.

Some examples of neglect on local level

On 22 February 1984, a synagogue in Eindhoven was vandalised with swastikas. Graves at a Jewish cemetery in the same southern city were desecrated. The local police stated that vandalism was the cause. 'No racism', according to the police, 'it could just as well have happened to a catholic or protestant cemetery' (Holtrop and Den Tex, 1984: 16). In May 1984, a leaflet of the racist and fascist NVU called for 'resistance with all means' to plans by the city of Leidschendam to set up a camp for caravan dwellers. The leaders of the local political parties reported this to the police. The local police argued that caravan dwellers were not a 'race' nor did they share a common religion. Only discrimination on the grounds of 'race' or religion could be prosecuted.[61]

These were two examples in which the local police denied the racist nature of the (threat of) violence. Sometimes, the police would not file a complaint. This was the case on 24 August 1984, when a partly disabled Surinamese girl was attacked and abused in Rotterdam by another woman who was waiting for her turn at a telephone box. With the telephone box already covered with blood, bystanders shouted to the attacker: 'Kick her to death'. The police refused to file the complaint.[62] Sometimes the police registered the complaint, but were not prepared to believe the victim's statements. In February 1984, the home of a Moroccan family in Culemborg was entered by three men. The intruders threatened the woman with a weapon and started to set fire to the house. The woman was told that 'she could leave the country now'.[63] The local police stated that 'the family had a good reputation, but language was a problem, of course, and we only had the statement of the woman' (Holtrop and Den Tex, 1984: 21).

Other examples showed different reasons (or excuses) for not responding to a racist incident. In June 1985, a Turkish family suffered verbal threats and also received a threatening letter. At their future home, four heads of pigs were hammered to the front door. The police claimed to know who had written the letters, but did not want to interfere because of possible escalation (Buis, 1988: 132).

Even in cases in which the police were convinced of racist motives, legal constraints caused the prosecutor to drop the case, and sometimes suspects were acquitted. On 29 September 1984, a 22-year-old black man was stabbed after having been verbally abused. The police stated that racist motives were involved. In January 1985, the perpetrator was convicted for attempted manslaughter. According to the public prosecutor, no conviction whatsoever with regard to racism was possible because the expressions used – 'dirty stinker' and 'rotten nigger'

– were insulting to an individual and not to any group.[64] In May 1985, a 12-year-old boy of Surinamese origin was shot at. The perpetrator had seen the boy tinkering with a moped and thought he wanted to steal it. To scare the boy off, he went for his gun and fired accidentally. Two Dutch friends of the boy, who were present, were not hit. The court magistrate decided that the shooting had no racist background.

These examples show that in a period of increasing awareness and debates about racist violence, including examples of 'including recognition' of racist violence by the same local authorities, not all authorities responded alike. This was a period in which racist violence constituted a topic on the public agenda, but not on the national formal agenda (phase C).

Second half of the 1980s: no longer an issue

From the mid-1980s on, the profile of racist violence declined in the Netherlands. The key feature of this period, is that racist violence disappeared from the public agenda and no longer constituted an issue. This disappearance coincided with the 'disappearance' of the politically organised extreme right from mainstream politics.

The extreme right falling apart

At the end of 1983, the director of the well-established polling *Interview*, Maurice De Hondt, predicted that the *Centrumpartij* could well form the fourth stream in the Dutch political spectrum. This controversial prediction, as well as the result in the Rotterdam by-elections, in which the CP gained eight seats in three boroughs, caused much debate and tension both in and outside the party. In late 1984, internal struggles led to their MP, Janmaat, being thrown out of the party. Janmaat himself claimed that the internal struggle had been caused by the intervention of the *Binnenlandse Veiligheidsdienst* (BVD, Dutch Secret Service).

Although the CP gained seats on the city councils of Amsterdam, Rotterdam, Almere, Lelystad and Utrecht in March 1986, the extreme-right movement in the Netherlands declined. In May 1986, Janmaat and his new party, the *Centrumdemocraten* (CD, Centre Democrats) lost their seat in Parliament. This seemed to underline the political theory concerning the extreme right, which holds that extreme-right political parties never outgrow the stage of minor party due to the nature of the extreme right itself. On the one hand, the extreme right strives to be regarded as a reasonable and acceptable alternative within the political spectrum. But becomes frustrated and threatened by internal appeals for more harsh and outspoken racist strategies (see among others van Donselaar, 1991). Developments within the Dutch extreme right since the mid-1980s have been commonly regarded as proof of this theory.

The second half of the 1980s could be characterised by declining attention to racist violence and a return to the level designated phase A: 'incidents involving individuals'. Van Donselaar claimed that there was a wave of racist violence during the first half of the 1980s which now 'appears to have diminished again' (van Donselaar, 1993: 51). He wondered whether there was a relationship between the level of violence and support for the extreme right. 'The correspondence was too striking to remain unnoticed, although one could approach it from another direction, i.e. the extent of which the media devoted attention to racist violence' (1993: 52).

The use of the term 'wave' referred to a series of events on a higher level, scale and intensity than before. Because data on racist incidents were gathered at the time, it is difficult to agree with the use of this term. As far as this study is concerned, however, it is not important whether there is actually evidence for such a wave or not. Important is that there had at least been a wave of media and public attention for the subject. And it could well be that the reported wave of racist violence was a result of this wave of attention. In this sense, and with the lack of actual knowledge about a decrease in the number of incidents in the late 1980s implicit in the use of the term wave, it is important to notice that this broad attention for racist violence decreased in the second half of the 1980s. This was illustrated by the troubling difficulty experienced by the *Advies Commissie Onderzoek Minderheden* (ACOM, Advisory Commission for Research on Minorities) to organise a study of racist violence in the Netherlands. Several attempts by this Commission failed to get such a research project started because racist violence was not considered an issue.

Racist violence in the second half of the 1980s

In the second half of the 1980s, the visible support for extreme right parties, as well as mainstream attention to racist violence in particular, did decrease as mentioned. This did not necessarily coincide with a decline in the number of reported racist incidents. A report by H. Buis (1988), financed by the state as part of a number of initiatives in the field of the study of racism and published by the *Anne Frank Stichting*, showed a whole series of incidents taking place during the period of January 1985 to January 1988. The initiative for this study had originally been the wave of attention for racist violence in the first half of the 1980s. Public and media attention, however, now decreased substantially. Racist violence seemed to be 'thrown back' to phase (A) – the individual problem – including, at best, some instances of 'occasional recognition' by local authorities.

The reported incidents since 1987, however, pointed out a new development in the Netherlands. The novelty lay in asylum-seekers and refugees increasingly being victimised. Where previously labour immigrants, immigrants from the former colonies and their descendants constituted the main targets of reported racist violence, after 1987, refugees became the main victims.

In the eastern city of Assen, a hostel housing Tamil refugees was severely damaged and one Tamil badly beaten. The local police, who arrested eighteen people, argued that it was a fight which got out of control. Racist motives were not involved. Seven suspects were sentenced later to work in an alternative disciplinary program (H. Buis, 1988: 141).[65] A week after the incident, leaflets were distributed directed against the presence of this particular group of refugees. The leaflets were signed by the *Actiefront Nationaal-Socialisten* (ANS, National-Socialist Action Front). It should be noted that during the second half of the 1980s, a widely publicised, negative image of Tamil refugees persisted in the Netherlands (see Dubbelman, 1987).

A number of incidents were reported throughout this decase. First, for example, in Tilburg the home of a Turkish family was set on fire. The next day, local residents stated that they did not want the family to return to their home. This gave the police grounds to suspect that 'a conflict between two cultures' was the cause of the fire (Buis, 1988: 142).[66]

On 21 December 1987, the 34-year-old Azam Choudry of Pakistani origin was stabbed to death in an Amsterdam bar. Before the fatal incident, he had been verbally abused with racist remarks and attacked. He left the bar, but returned later. A fight broke out and he was stabbed. The perpetrators claimed to have acted out of self-defence (H. Buis, 1988: 143).[67]

On 15 January 1988, Ahmed Hamouchi, of Moroccan origin, was stabbed to death in Haarlem. The police immediately responded by arguing that racism had nothing to do with this incident. Many people, however, thought differently, and an anti-racism demonstration was held on 5 February.[68]

In April 1988, two Moroccan men were beaten up in the streets of Utrecht. One victim died of his injuries. A representative of the victim spoke of 'undeniable racist motives'.[69]

Responses to racist violence

In the late 1980s, racist violence had once again returned to the status of an individual problem. Buis' (1988) study concluded that people who complained about a racist incident often had no support when they filed a complaint. Often, the first response by the police was to ignore it or wait a long time before any action was undertaken. Institutions and/or authorities often did not know their responsibilities with regard to providing a response, if indeed they wanted to respond at all.

Buis presented three possible explanations for this passive attitude: (1) the racist nature of the incident was often a matter for discussion; (2) there was no tradition of behaviour and attitudes with regard to neighbourhood conflicts; and (3) there was no clear idea of the different steps and measures which could be taken (H. Buis, 1988: 96–7). These conclusions, the examples of incidents, and the responses to the incidents mentioned show the ad-hoc nature of state responses to racist violence in the Netherlands during this period. A vast majority of responses turned out to depend on whether racist violence was an issue on the public and/or formal agenda at that specific time; the authorities involved and their position towards racism; coincidental relations between different authorities at that moment; and often on a stroke of (bad) luck (one major exception was the Amsterdam report of 1983).

These very uncertain and unpredictable elements offered authorities a chance to respond in any way possible. Some responses constituted a firm, unambiguous and public condemnation of the experience of racism, discrimination and racist violence. More often, the responses showed a total lack of understanding concerning these phenomena. Often the only concern noticeable was directed at the maintenance of law and order or preventing the case from being 'blown out of proportion'. In many instances, this led to a total negation of the incident.

The early 1990s: two-faced responses

In the early 1990s, racism and racist violence returned to the core of the public and even to the formal agendas (phases C and D). State responses developed in two different ways. On the one hand, racist incidents were firmly condemned as such. This response, however, remained a mixture of firm condemnation together with playing down the importance and impact of racist violence in Dutch society. Most of the public statements pointed to the 'occasional' character of racist violence in the Netherlands, often mentioning the situation abroad. These references (mainly to Germany) presented racist violence to be on a high level there, compared to the Netherlands where the level was said to be very low, if one could speak of a level at all. Examples of the 'occasional recognition' of racist violence by the state were manifold.

On the other hand, there were signals that inside state institutions racist violence was beginning to be regarded as a serious matter which had to be given special attention and priority. Police forces and local authorities were instructed by national state authorities to be alert, watchful, and to report incidents. I shall elaborate on this later in the chapter. Examples of this increasing attention to racist violence by several state institutions were noticeable. In many of these instances, state responses were clearly directed against suspects as well as against the circumstances in which racist violence was perceived to flourish – for instance football matches, nazi skinhead concerts, and demonstrations. We may characterise these state responses as examples of the 'including recognition' of racist violence.

Besides these two types of state responses, the early 1990s also showed statements made and measures implemented by state authorities which could be grouped within the 'excluding recognition' type of response. Proposals concerning restrictions on migration, and especially on asylum policies, were formulated and implemented in these years. Often it was argued that these measures were necessary to improve the position of migrants and their descendants, as well as to counterattack the racist discourse and increasing support for racist parties. Statements and debates along these lines led to a criminalisation and marginalisation of minority populations in the Netherlands.

Increasing support for the extreme right again

One plausible reason for the increasing attention to racist violence in the early 1990s consisted of the re-emergence of the extreme-right racist movement. In the parliamentary elections in 1989, Janmaat, now party leader of the *Centrumdemocraten* (CD), regained his seat in Parliament. The return of Janmaat did not cause much of a shock in the public, media or political arenas. There was shock, however, a year later, when the CD and the *Centrumpartij '86* (CP'86: a continuation of the *former Centrumpartij*) had huge and unexpected success in the local elections on 21 March 1990 – ironically the International Day against Racism. In nine out of ten cities in which they participated, these racist parties won seats, amounting to fifteen in total.[70]

Not only were these two extreme-right, racist parties represented on nine city councils, but some of their seats were occupied by people with outspoken racist, violent ideas, such as M. VanderPlas – former member of the *Actiefront Nationaal-Socialisten* (ANS), Mordaunt – member of the *Nationaal Jeugd Front* (NJF), and the earlier mentioned Bruyn – author of the report on 'the right of self-defence'. These election results caused much confusion – once more – in the Netherlands.

Speculation about possible explanations for this success was rife. Most explanations referred to social and socioeconomic phenomena, such as the increasing presence of migrants, unemployment, bad housing conditions and other inner-city problems. The considerable losses of the *Partij van de Arbeid* (PvdA, the Dutch Labour Party) were among the alleged causes for the success of the extreme right. These explanations were prominent within the public, political and media discourses, although my research into the matter showed that simple correlations between these social, socioeconomic and political phenomena, on the one hand, and the success of the racist parties, on the other, did not hold for the nine cities involved (see Witte, 1991). Most explanations, therefore, were proven to be too simplistic and one-sided.

The National Debate on Minorities

The first three years of the 1990s could partly be characterised by the so-called National Debate on Minorities. On the one hand, this debate

residents came out to 'teach that Turkish bunch a lesson'. Three months previously, the local police had first received warnings that the neighbourhood would take action themselves against 'Turkish drug dealers'. The police officer in charge stated that 'anti-Turkish sentiments were the work of some hot-headed people from not the best of social environments. . . . And, yes, the weather had been perfect for a fight too.'[77]

However, it took events abroad to bring racist violence back to the public and even to the formal agendas (phases C and D) in the Netherlands. The enormous increase of reported racist incidents in Germany attracted the attention of the Dutch media and public. This was very apparent in August 1991, the period of the racist riots in Hoyerswerda. The mass media attention in the Netherlands helped to create an atmosphere in which questions were raised as to whether such racist events could happen in this country too. In that same month, a group of Surinamese youngsters were attacked by a group of some one hundred local youth near a disco in Landsmeer, just outside Amsterdam.[78] This incident attracted quite a lot of attention, as if it could be regarded as the Dutch version of 'race riots'. The actual motives and causes for the Landsmeer incident were never clarified. Explanations differed relative to the main perceptions one had concerning racism, racist violence and the idea that 'Hoyerswerda' could or could not happen in the Netherlands.

The incident showed the influence of the circumstances and events in Germany on the Dutch discourses and perceptions. Not only was this influence reflected by the expectations and explanations by the media and general public, but also the events in Germany, especially Hoyerswerda, seemed to have inspired new groups of perpetrators. In the following months, October and November 1991, several bomb alerts were received at asylum reception centres throughout the Netherlands, such as Alkmaar and Goes.[79] Although no bombs exploded, the threatening phone-calls to these centres seemed to be a kind of 'copy-cat' action.

Waves of racist violence in the Netherlands

In the first half of 1992, a wave of racist violence, reported to be far larger than ever before (van Donselaar, 1993: 51; F. J. Buis and van Donselaar, 1994: 65–6), spread over the Netherlands. People were attacked, buildings of minority organisations and mosques were set on fire and vandalised, bomb alerts directed at asylum reception centres were numerous, leaflets containing aggressive abuse were distributed and so on. Some of these incidents attracted massive media attention, while many others got, at best, a three-line article in a regional newspaper.

Two separate waves were distinguished during this period (van Donselaar, 1993). The first was marked by the choice of place – The Hague – where the attacks were executed. It all started with an arson attack on a 'minorities office' on 4 January 1992. This incident was succeeded by several of the same kind in the city within the next three months: four bombings, three cases of arson, three (false) bomb alerts, four cases of destruction of property, and several cases of assault (van Donselaar, 1993: 54). Some of these latter incidents were solved upon the arrest of five skinheads in connection with two of the cases and the arrest of a man with regard to some of the arson attacks.

The second wave involved attacks distinguished by their target: mosques. None of these cases have been solved by the police. On 26 January 1992, a mosque in Amersfoort was set on fire. The family of the Imam, who lived above the mosque, was brought to safety. A South African version of the swastika was painted on the wall of the mosque. This specific incident caused some considerable commotion in the Netherlands. The daily newspaper, *de Volkskrant*, argued that the anxiety was caused by the question of whether this incident marked the beginning of 'German circumstances' (Hoyerswerda) and by the increasing xenophobia in Europe.[80]

Immediate state responses to (waves of) racist violence

In relation to the attack in Amersfoort, state authorities expressed their aversion and condemnation. The Minister of Justice, Hirsch Balin, was appalled by the incident and stated 'that it was fundamental that religious people could profess their religion in freedom here'.[81] A meeting, including the Minister of Justice and seven minority organisations, was organised by Home Secretary Ien Dales, who declared herself to be appalled and annoyed. She also stated that luckily there was no evidence of a connection between the Amersfoort incident and earlier incidents in The Hague. She called upon all mayors in the country to improve relations with minority populations.

After the meeting with minority organisations, the Home Secretary asked the *Commissarissen van de Koningin* (Provincial Representatives of The Queen, who also chair the Provincial Councils) to inform the cities in their Provinces of the results of their deliberations. In the statement, the minister stressed the unorganised nature of the racist incidents, which appeared to be individual acts of vandalism, and claimed that structural protection measures were considered necessary. Although there seemed to be no clear indication for it, the minister stated that if a case of organised violence arose, one certainly had to provide adequate protection. Secondly, local authorities were asked to meet with local minority organisations to avoid the re-appearance of this kind of violence and to convey a positive attitude on feelings of security. Thirdly, the minister asked local authorities to report both violent and non-violent incidents to the ministry in case these incidents could be related to those which had just occurred.[82]

Another example of the state taking the possible occurrence of racist violence seriously was reflected in the judicial prosecution of suspects once apprehended – although this did not happen often. On

1 February 1992, four 'skinheads' attacked a man of Haitian origin in The Hague and he was badly beaten. The next day, two 'skins' attacked people 'who seemed to be foreign' standing at a bus stop in the same city.[83] Once caught the legal authorities decided to bring the attackers to court immediately; within a month all six 'skinheads' were convicted and sentenced to several months' imprisonment. At their trials, some of them explicitly expressed their political extreme-right, racist sympathies.[84]

The day after the attack upon the Amersfoort mosque, Mayor Van Thijn of Amsterdam, attending an Auschwitz memorial, spoke of the increasing violence against asylum-seekers in Germany, the march of Le Pen's *Front National* in France and of the *Vlaams Blok* in Belgium, and the attacks in the Netherlands. He questioned whether 'our political leaders are conscious of the fact that they are the most responsible in preventing the existence of any breeding for xenophobia'.[85]

Responses by minority organisations

The Jewish community in the Netherlands immediately paid a visit to the mosque in Amersfoort to show their solidarity with the Muslim community. Rabbi Hermans stated on this occasion that 'it felt as an attack against a synagogue'.[86] Other minority organisations also responded to the incident. The *Turks Inspraak Orgaan* (Turkish Advisory Commission) expressed its concern about the increasing aggression towards 'foreigners' and argued, with reference to three racist attacks in the Netherlands, that one could no longer speak of 'occasional incidents'. They demanded measures to protect immigrants and their property.[87]

An arson attack against a Turkish shop in May 1992 constituted the trigger event for the *Nederlands Centrum Buitenlanders* (NCB, the Dutch Centre for Foreigners) to write a letter of warning to the Home Secretary.[88] They demanded recognition that these kinds of attacks caused feelings of insecurity among minority communities in the Netherlands. The NCB forcefully demanded acknowledgement that the latest incidents showed that violence against minorities did not constitute an occasional phenomenon. They argued that the violence was planned and systematic and insisted, therefore, that all police forces and mayors should be constantly on the alert, and they also proposed the establishment of a 'preventative alarm system' involving the police and minority organisations.[89] Organised and subsidised by the state, these minority organisations are characterised by the aforementioned, specifically Dutch negotiation structures and the importance and influence of the social midfield. Here we see an example of 'how the Dutch state organised its own opposition'.

Discussion about the assumed level of organised racist violence

The first response by state authorities and other sections of Dutch society was one of plain condemnation and shock. After the initial commotion over the Amersfoort-incident passed, responses were increasingly directed towards the alleged impact and seriousness of this incident. The newspaper *Het Parool* headed an article with 'Who will wash away that stupidity?' and 'The losers on the warpath'.[90] In the article, the incident was played down and was represented as the badly executed work of riff-raff, emphasising the backwardness of the vandals.

After several days, the Minister of Justice stated that the attack had not been carried out 'professionally'.[91] Some weeks later, the Home Secretary claimed that these attacks against minorities in no way represented the work of extreme-right organisations. 'The perpetrators have to be looked for within groups of deprived youth.' Therefore she perceived these incidents to be occasional incidents. The attacks and arson were 'a masterpiece of awkwardness'.[92]

The non-organised character of the incidents seemed to be proven by the arrest of an individual in The Hague in connection with several of the incidents mentioned. The Home Secretary again expressed her position that one could not speak of organised racist violence. 'Nothing, or at any rate nothing in police investigations indicates a country-wide campaign.'[93] At the end of 1992, she repeated this opinion in an interview: 'When the matter is investigated, it appears to be a case of one man acting on his own. There have been incidents, but there is no reason for talking about the growth of right-wing organisations planning this kind of thing'.[94]

These remarks by the minister typified the Dutch political discourse at that time. The arrest of one man, who was obviously responsible for some incidents, was perceived and presented as proof of the non-organised character of all the incidents in the first half of 1992. This man, however, was suspected of just some of the incidents in The Hague. His arrest did not make it possible to conclude anything about the vast majority of the reported, but yet unsolved, racist incidents.

Public and back stage responses

State authorities often publicly compared the Dutch situation with regard to racist violence with that in other European countries. The results always presented the Dutch situation in a good light. This was part of the public response of the authorities. Included were remarks presenting the incidents as acts of individuals without organisation or any intelligence.

Back stage, however, some state authorities, such as the Ministries of Justice and Home Affairs, did adopt a line of response of extra vigilance and they did set up a system of close communication in case anything did happen. The letter to the mayors of all cities by the Provincial Representatives of the Queen, issued by the Home Secretary, was an example of this. Another example was given by the *Binnenlandse Veiligheidsdienst* (BVD, the Domestic Secret Service) which asked all police forces to inventory all 'possible vulnerable targets' like asylum reception centres.[95]

The Christian Democrat Minister of Justice stated at a conference entitled 'Combating Discrimination: A Different Problem' that 'besides discrimination out of stupidity or wickedness, our society is also confronted with violent acts against members of minority groups, with even places of worship not spared. It is the state's task, more particularly that of the legislature and of the Justice Department, to mark the boundaries of the permissible.'[96] The minister claimed to have given immediate high priority (April 1992) to legislation and action by the police and the Public Prosecutor against discrimination. The minister ended his speech by 'calling on everyone to help foreigners against whom such discriminatory behaviour is directed.'[97]

These two types of response by state authorities were shown also to have negative side-effects. The letter by the NCB (18 May 1992) mentioned earlier showed that publicly playing down the violence led to feelings of insecurity and isolation among the victimised communities. The serious concern and awareness expressed 'behind the scenes' did not reach the potential victims. Similar concerns arose over whether the police would be informed about the intentions and measures expressed in this way. In 1992, there was evidence that police action was not always adequate nor in line with the Minister's position. In February, a report (Holthuizen, 1992) was published showing the police still refusing to file a considerable number of complaints with regard to discrimination. In a letter in 1985, the Minister of Justice had already ordered that *all* complaints had to be passed on to the Public Prosecutor. The police were ordered not to make any selection themselves. The report also claimed that the Public Prosecutor dismissed 50 per cent of those complaints he finally received. One year later, similar findings resulted from a report by the research institute of the Ministry of Justice (Bol and Docter-Schamhardt, 1993).

In a publication about vandalising doors and shops with swastikas and racist slogans in the south of Amsterdam it was claimed that in the first four months of 1992 a considerable increase in the number of anti-semitic expressions was registered.[98] The police, however, had filed these incidents under the category 'other incidents' for the sake of convenience. An article in the newspaper *de Volkskrant* (12 May 1992) showed that although complaints about police behaviour in general had decreased in 1991, complaints about discriminatory behaviour by the police themselves had been increasing.

In the summer of 1992, two racist incidents showed police responses to racist violence, including the 'traditional' playing down of an incident and a response not at all in line with the aforementioned back stage approach.

On 16 July 1992, a 17-year-old black man was badly beaten in Purmerend by five skinheads. The 'skins' jumped out of a passing car and started to beat him up, shouting racist remarks. The man needed hospital treatment. Acting Chief of Police, Yntema, stated that while one should speak of an incident, it should not be given more attention than other cases (of abuse). 'We should not discriminate against skinheads. We are investigating this incident, but we are not willing to give any extra attention to this maltreatment.'[99]

On 22 August 1992, two asylum-seekers from Nigeria were attacked and severely beaten in Hoorn. The police claimed that the victims were almost lynched. The perpetrators had heard a friend having an argument with 'somebody with a dark skin'. They ran out of the pub and started beating up the two asylum-seekers, who had had nothing to do with the argument. When the police turned up, they had a hard job to rescue the two victims. The police spokesman Weeda claimed that this fight had nothing to do with racism, 'Anybody could have been hit. This group of suspects have absolutely no idea of ideologies or any deeper thoughts. They just hit immediately.'[100]

The responses by authorities in these instances seemed to contrast with the decree by the Ministers of Justice and Interior to be extra alert to any incident in which racism could have played a motivating role. However, there were also some examples of police conduct attempting to prevent racist violence and other racist expressions from occurring.

On 26 September 1992 the Rotterdam police, in cooperation with the local *Anti Discriminatie Bureau* (RADAR), did everything possible to prevent the occurrence of a Nazi skinhead concert in the area of Rotterdam. The concert by a German skinhead band was announced in a skinhead magazine. Skinheads arriving from Germany, Poland and Britain were arrested and sent back home.[101]

On 10 October 1992, eight extreme-right radicals were arrested by the police when they left Arnhem railway station, supposedly on their way to a demonstration about asylum policies. They were armed with iron bars, knives, knuckle-dusters and the like.[102]

The public and 'behind the scenes' responses were especially directed towards the occurrence of racist violence in the Netherlands. Besides these state responses to racist incidents, the Home Office initiated a so-called General Declaration against Discrimination and Racism. In cooperation with the anti-racism umbrella organisation *Nederland Bekent Kleur* (literally: The Netherlands acknowledge colour; meaning: The Netherlands taking a stance against racism) the Home Office produced a Declaration stating that discrimination is prohibited; that respect for anyone living in the Netherlands, a democracy, is fundamental; and that everyone signing this Declaration agrees to set a good example, to promote anti-discrimination codes and to take action against anyone or any organisation involved in intentional or unintentional discriminatory behaviour. This Declaration was officially and first signed by the Home Secretary, Dales, followed by many MPs.

Since summer 1992: a continuation of the processes described

After this wave of racist violence attention in the media, the public
and the political arenas to this violence waned. However, the decrease
in attention did not reflect a decrease in racist violence. This was also
shown by behind the scenes activities. In May 1993, the Dutch Home
Office, in this case the *Binnenlandse Veiligheidsdienst* (BVD), assigned
a research project to the *Leids Instituut voor Sociaal Wetenschappelijk
Onderzoek* (LISWO, Institute for Social Research) of the University
of Leiden to present an overview of existing academic knowledge on
right-wing extremism in the Netherlands, with special attention to the
connection between electoral support and violence. The resulting study
by F.J. Buis and van Donselaar (1994) is the first academic study
focusing on racist violence in the Netherlands. Their report shows an
increase in racist and right-wing extremist violence from 1992 – 270
recorded incidents – to 352 incidents in 1993.

For 1993, the authors record a change of right-wing extremist
involvement in this violence – including an increase in threats, destruction and arson and a decrease in their involvement in cases of abuse.
The study also shows an increase in the overall number of incidents in
which (properties of) visible minorities were targeted – 58 incidents in
1993 in comparison to 17 in 1992. In 47 of the 58 incidents right-
wing extremist involvement was recorded (F.J. Buis and van Donselaar,
1994: 72–3).

The increase of racist violence in 1993 was also reported by the
Centrale Recherche Informatiedienst (CRI, the Information Service of
the Central Department of Criminal Investigation). The CRI reported
612 incidents, which was three times the number of incidents in 1992.
Of these incidents, 40 per cent were maltreatment, arson, false bomb
alert and physical and verbal abuse. Half of the other incidents involved
threatening letters or phone calls, while the remaining 30 per cent
consisted of insulting behaviour and the distribution of pamphlets.[103]
In its 1993–94 report, the independent *Fascisme Onderzoek Kollektief*
(FOK, Fascism Research Collective) also recorded that 'the wave of
racist or right-wing extremist violence, which occurred in the Netherlands
in late 1991, has not decreased in the past two years' (FOK, 1995:
89). What did decrease, according to the report, was the attention
given to this violence by the media and in a number of cases by the
state and the police.

Local responses to racist incidents

The level of attention does not always coincide with the level of
severity and intensity of the violence. An example of this was a series
of arson attacks against 'foreign' restaurants in the area of Nijkerk,
which did not attract any publicity. A more severe example was the
murder of a 32-year-old resident of The Hague on 13 September 1994.

He was killed by two persons after their random search for a victim with a dark skin (FOK, 1995: 89).

In the autumn of 1993, on the other hand, a whole wave of threatening letters sent to individuals within minority communities all around the Netherlands did attract much attention by the media. In the city of IJmuiden, people of migrant origin received letters stating 'Foreigner, we are living in a recession and that is caused by you shrewd foreigners with your dirty, ugly hypocritical muslim culture. Move out of the Netherlands before it is too late. Otherwise, irregularities like in Germany are not out of the question.' The local mayor argued that she 'would prefer to keep silent about these letters – but we have passed that point. Publicity will play into the hands of the authors, but, on the other hand, the local community is so shocked that one must respond. Our whole community is touched by it, and will have to fight against it.'[104]

Besides IJmuiden, threatening letters were recieved by minority individuals in the cities of Waalwijk,[105] Dordrecht, Sliedrecht, Papendrecht, Alblasserdam,[106] and Reuver[107] – several were signed by White Power. Several instances of racist graffiti also attracted media attention in the autumn of 1993. In some of these, the police did suspect the involvement of the CP'86, for instance in actions in Rotterdam-Tarwewijk.[108] In other instances in which Nazi symbols were painted, the police argued that it was probably the work of hooligans (in Leiden),[109] or that they had no reason to believe that it was directed against 'foreigners' (in Amsterdam).[110]

Racist violence attracted much attention by the media and politicians in 1992, but though the following year this attention decreased, the violence did not. Responses to specific incidents had to be looked for at the local level and showed a great diversity, from examples of the 'including recognition' of racist violence (IJmuiden) up to examples of ignoring the incident or playing down its impact on victimised communities.

Responses at the national level

Racist violence did not constitute a main topic on the formal agenda after 1992. Still, the issue never completely disappeared from the public agenda (phase C) partly due to the enormous attention paid to the predicted increase in support for the extreme right. Every now and then, discussions were held about these parties and their supporters, and debates comparable to the earlier Debate on Minorities took place. The response to political right-wing extremism was threefold. First, many examples were shown in which 'ordinary' supporters were portrayed as people living under difficult conditions. The increase in support was explained in a way that played down or even ignored its impact on society in general, and (implicitly) on specific sections of that society, that is, minority communities in particular. Secondly, especially during the 1994 election campaigns, statements by prominent members of established political parties were notably in line with (former) extreme right-wing arguments and images. Thirdly, the politically organised right-wing extremists increasingly had to face firm action by state authorities, especially when there was a case to prosecute in connection with incitement to racist hatred or racist violence.

In relation to the supporters of extreme-right political parties, the dominant discourse in the Netherlands was that these were not racists, but people with socioeconomic problems who needed attention and help. Often these socio-economic problems were perceived and portrayed in close relation to the presence of certain minority communities. The Dutch version of the *seuil de tolérance* increasingly occupied a dominant position within mainstream discourses from right to left wing parties and people. An early example of the broadly taken position on this matter was the formulation by the Social Democratic State Secretary Kosto in September 1992:

If an original resident of an old big city neighbourhood, in Amsterdam, Rotterdam, The Hague or Arnhem, if he [*sic*] sees his neighbourhood radically changing *because* of the entrance of many strangers with a completely different culture, then he is stuck. And if he vents this by expressing himself negatively about his neighbours with abusive references to their skin colour, their Turkish, Moroccan, Surinamese or Antillean origin, then it would be wrong to call such a person a racist immediately. In most cases he is not. He is *just* stuck.[111]

Another example of such arguments was presented by a professor emeritus in constitutional and administrative law, S.W. Couwenberg. He argued that

what often is considered to be racism, like restricting the flow of migration to prevent the people from being harmed, is not racism, but ethnic protectionism. And this is an aspect of the new protectionism which originates in the development of the welfare state and is directed to the protection of one's own welfare against the competition by foreign products and by foreigners in one's own country in the labour and housing markets.[112]

These are only two examples of statements in which racism and racist abuse (and implicitly racist violence) were portrayed as 'understandable'. Implicitly, racist attitudes were de-racialised and presented as normal, natural behaviour towards specific minorities within a problematic situation. Within the early months of 1994, that is, in the leadup to local and national elections (March and May 1994), several statements were recorded in which this dominant discourse was underlined. These often reflected opinions which before were thought to be monopolised by political right-wing extremist parties. In February 1994, for instance, the leader of Christian Democrats (CDA), Elco Brinkman, argued that the 'illegality among foreigners should be exterminated'.[113] And two weeks later, the Christian Democratic Prime Minister Ruud Lubbers argued that 'members of minority groups themselves have to work enormously hard to find a job. Not just learn how to get social benefits, but also learn how to find work.'[114]Another top member of the CDA, Jan Van Houwelingen, stated that 'the problem of allochtonous people is that often they are not willing to look for work'.[115]

Asylum-seekers and asylum policies as well as the illegal residence of people were central issues during the election campaigns.[116] In a television programme, the VVD party leader, Bolkestein, attracted special attention when he presented a six-point programme having argued that the problems caused by the arrival of asylum-seekers were no longer manageable. The six points were (1) asylum-seekers had to be taken care of in 'their own region'; (2) a list should be constructed of so-called safe countries (from which people could no longer ask for asylum); (3) within the region asylum-seekers should be distributed proportionally; (4) relief should in principle be temporary; (5) asylum policies and measures within Europe should be harmonised, and (6) illegal residents should be actively located.[117] The first point was interpreted by many as Europe should be reserved for the Europeans. Government members responded to these proposals by stating that five of them (points 2–6) were already elements of existing policy, and that the first one mentioned was in defiance of international law.

Besides these responses to an increase in support for right-wing extremist thought and parties, the racist organisations and parties themselves were increasingly confronted with firm repression by state and other authorities. A triggering event was a statement by the party leader of the *Centrum Democraten* (CD), Janmaat, after the sudden death of Home Secretary Dales. Janmaat said that he did not feel sorry for her death. 'We will not shed a tear about her death. Perhaps she has shown the way for the whole PvdA [Dutch Labour Party].'[118] This statement attracted much media attention and strong condemnation. An interview with Janmaat by the weekly magazine *Elsevier* aroused even more turmoil when he stated that the Minister of Justice should resign, because before the Second World War his Jewish father had taken refuge from Germany in the Netherlands.[119] 'I do not want to blame Jews for travelling around like nomads, but they should not hold a public position.' Janmaat made reference to the political programme of the *Centrum Democraten* in which people are not allowed to hold public positions if they are not 'third generation Dutch'.

The Public Prosecutor investigated whether any of these statements were liable for prosecution. Responses were moted in several sections of society. For instance, the *Federatie Nederlands Vakverbond* (FNV, Federation of Dutch Trade Unions), the *Christelijk Nederlands Vakverbond* (CNV, Christian Dutch Trade Union) and the *Christelijke Boeren en Tuindersbond* (the Christian Union of Farmers and Market Gardeners) said they would expel union members who were actively involved in the right-wing extremist parties (CD and CP'86). In December 1993, the FNV had already expelled two of its members for this reason.[120] The Chairman of the FNV, J. Stekelenburg, sent an open letter to all members in which he emphatically asked them not to vote for a racist party.[121]

The Dutch Reformed Protestant Synod and the Roman Catholic Episcopal Commission Justitia et Pax both declared that membership in their churches was incompatible with membership in a racist party (FOK, 1995: 94). And the hotel and restaurant industry started an action against Janmaat by sending him 160,000 postcards which said 'And this time no one can say that he did not know'.[122] A football club, Limburgia, declared a referee to be *persona non grata* from now on, because of his CD membership.[123] In April 1994, the police in the south-east of the province of Brabant started a campaign against racism.[124] Public servants in several Dutch cities set up a *Landelijk Netwerk Ambtenaren tegen Racisme* (a nationwide network of public servants against racism).[125]

Within the *Centrum Democraten*, Janmaat's statements also led people to resign. In the polls, support for the CD dropped from 5 per cent of the vote (eight parliamentary seats) to 3 per cent (five seats). *De Volkskrant* headlined its article about this 'Support for CD decreases, but ideas gain ground'.[126] This was even more the case when several party members (among them Janmaat himself) were prosecuted for discrimination, for incitement to racist hatred and for racist violence. In Purmerend, the local councillor for the CD, Michel vanderPlas, was arrested for beating up the author Adriaan Vennema, who had written several books about people collaborating during the Second World War

The *Centrumpartij'86* also faced prosecutions. In February 1994, two local leaders of the CP'86 in Arnhem were sentenced to six and three months respectively because of the possession of weapons and maltreatment. In Zwolle, six members were fined 1,000 guilders each for incitement to racist hatred. The local leader of the CP'86 in Amsterdam, W. Beaux, was fined 1,000 guilders for using the slogan 'Our People First', which was also used by the successful *Vlaams Blok* in Belgium.[127]

A major incident in this respect was the arrest of the local leader of the CD in Amsterdam, Yte Graman. A free-lance journalist infiltrated the Amsterdam CD and filmed Graman stating that he had been responsible for two arson attacks in 1972 and 1979 that led to five people being injured. In the video-taped conversation, Graman also referred to a so-called death list, including the Minister of Welfare, Public Health and Culture, Hedy d'Ancona, and the new Home Secretary, Ed. van Thijn.[128] In July 1994, Graman was prosecuted for attempted murder and the sentence demanded by the Public Prosecutor was eight years' imprisonment. In September 1994 Graman was sentenced to six years.[129]

The Graman case led to a split within the Amsterdam division of the *Centrum Democraten*, and both Graman and vanderPlas, were expelled from the party. These cases together with Janmaat's statements obviously damaged the party's chances of electoral success. The polls had shown an increase in possible parliamentary seats for the CD from one (in the 1989 elections) to seven in December 1993 and had it been parliamentary instead of local elections in March 1994 the CD would have gained five seats. These local elections in March however still were an enormous success for the right-wing extremist parties. The CD gained seventy-seven seats in city councils (compared to eleven in 1990), and eighteen seats in five boroughs in Rotterdam. The CP'86 gained nine seats (compared to four in 1990), and in Utrecht the former CD member Wim Vreeswijk regained his seat as party leader of the *Nederlands Blok*.[130] One of the seventy-seven seats for the CD, in Purmerend, turned out to be won by another journalist who had infiltrated the party. In the spring of 1994, it turned out that three journalists had infiltrated the CD (see e.g. Rensen, 1994). As shown in the Graman case, this infiltration not only gave better insight into the party and more publicity for the situation ('behind the scenes') within the CD, but also provided information which was helpful and useful in judicial prosecutions.

On 2 May 1994, the *Centrum Democraten* gained three seats in parliamentary elections and the other right-wing extremist parties did not enter Parliament. The main response to the CD, winning two seats compared to the last election, was one of relief that the CD had not won the seven seats predicted only six months before. On 4 May 1994, the National Commemoration Day and two days after the elections, the CD was fined 10,000 guilders, Janmaat 6,000 guilders and a second MP for the CD (and Janmaat's partner), Wil Schuurman, 1,500 guilders because of incitement to racist hatred and discrimination. The Public Prosecutor was said to be investigating whether the CD could be banned. In July this turned out not to be possible due to insufficient evidence.[131] Then Janmaat and the CD again were summoned to appear in court because of alleged discriminatory statements and incitement to racist hatred.[132] In the second half of 1994, media and judicial attention focused more on the *Centrumpartij'86*, especially when the local leader in Rotterdam, Freling, argued during a meeting of the city council that 'all foreigners should have to leave the Netherlands including the [black] football players, Blinker and Taument, of Feyenoord'.[133] In November 1994, CP'86 were often in the news because they started to organise demonstrations which increasingly were prohibited for reasons of public order. And when CP'86 demonstrators did show up, they were arrested.[134]

Partly due to the increasing criminalisation of the right-wing extremist parties, the parties experienced internal dissent and people resigned or were expelled. Since their success in the 1994 local elections had brought them a large number of council seats, they began to have difficulty either holding the seat when a particular member was expelled or had resigned, or finding anyone else to take it over. In several city councils, seats of the CD and/or CP'86 remain unfilled. This not only led to vacant seats, but also meant that the parties did not receive the fees connected with these seats. In some cities, for instance Breda, Almelo and Alkmaar, the councils decided to transfer these fees to the local anti-racism organisations.[135]

Some success in clarifying racist incidents

F.J. Buis and van Donselaar (1994) conclude in their study that the rate of clarification in racist and right-wing extremist incidents has increased in 1993 compared to 1992 – from 19 per cent up to 34 per cent. This increase holds true for incidents involving destruction (from 33 per cent up to 66 per cent) and arson (from 20 per cent up to 53 per cent). The clarification of incidents involving confrontations of groups, however, decreased from 88 per cent in 1992 to 57 per cent in 1993. The clarification of maltreatment remained similar in both years (52–53 per cent). In 1994, some incidents that attracted media attention were solved.

In January 1994, five men between the ages of 17 and 19 were arrested for having written and sent threatening letters signed *White Power* in Waalwijk.[136] In February 1994, a 16-year-old leader and his 'gang' of four, who presented themselves as the *Nazi Front Zeeland*, were sentenced to several months in a disciplinary community institution.[137]

In that same month, five men between the ages of 24 and 38 were arrested and held responsible for at least ninety criminal acts. They presented themselves as a group of friends, united by their heavy drinking bouts. The Public Prosecutor, however, proclaimed them to be a criminal organisation and that they committed their crimes from a racist point of view. They used the name of the *Nijmeegse Bevrijdingsfront* (Nijmegen's Liberation Front) and, according to anti-fascist organisations, three men were members of the CP'86. The five men were each sentenced to one or two years' imprisonment.[138]

Conclusion

Racist violence in the Netherlands did not constitute an issue on the formal agenda until the early 1990s. In the first post-war period, i.e. 1950s to 1960s, racist violence was not perceived as a social problem (phase A), and therefore it was regarded as a 'non-Dutch problem'. Specific incidents were considered to include racist, especially anti-semitic, elements and were openly condemned by the public, the media and state authorities. However, this condemnation always coincided with a strong emphasis on the alleged occasional character ('occasional recognition') of the incident.

Parallel to the increasing attention and support for the extreme-right racist political parties, racism and racist violence increasingly received public and political attention in the early 1980s (phase B). This, however, was often restricted to discrimination practices and less attention was paid to racist violence itself. The racist murder of Kerwin Duinmeijer changed this discourse, but only for a short while. In the early 1990s, racist violence reached the public and formal agendas. This was partly due, once again, to the increasing support for extreme-right racist parties, as well as to international developments and events, especially those in Germany.

The state responses to racist violence were somewhat ambiguous and can be described as two-faced responses by state authorities. Within the context of public debates on the arrival and presence of minority communities, several policy measures were implemented which can be classified as the 'excluding recognition' of racist violence by the state. These policy measures mainly consisted of restrictions on asylum and migration policies. Moral panics frequently were part in the public debates.

But examples were also shown of the 'including recognition' of racist violence by state authorities. Here, however, the state followed two lines of response. On the public stage, state authorities presented all kinds of statements which explicitly or implicitly played down the occurrence and impact of racist violence in the Netherlands, even though an initial firm condemnation of the specific incidents often was made. Behind the scenes, however, several state authorities took the violence very seriously and ordered lines of response to police and local authorities.

State and police action was taken against suspected perpetrators of racist violence, as well as against circumstances in which this kind of violence might flourish. Especially in 1994, firm action was directed against politically organised right-wing extremists. On the other hand, minority communities reported an increasing feeling of insecurity, partly due to a lack of noticeable state action. Another effect was the fact that not all state authorities (especially police) were aware of the behind the scenes measures or acted in accordance with them.

Notes

1 Part of a speech given by State Secretary on Justice, Kosto, 30 September 1992, as published by the *AO-weekly*, no. 244, 4 December 1992, pp. 11–12.

2 Opening speech of the Christian-Democratic Minister of Justice, Hirsch Balin, at the conference 'Combating Discrimination: A Different Problem', 9 April 1992, The Hague, conference file p. 11.

3 See for example Lucassen and Penninx (1985), Cottaar and Willems (1984; 1987), Rath (1991), Schuster (1996).

4 *Keesings Historisch Archief*, no. 1051, p. 9530.

5 As cited by Cottaar and Willems, 1987: 127.

6 De Graan of the Sub-Department for Co-ordinating Institutions and Migration of the Ministry for Social Work, as quoted by Rath (1991: 152).

7 Rath (1991: 154) argued that we should define this process as an example of 'minorisation'. The debate on whether one may speak of 'minorisation' or 'racialisation' is discussed on pp. 194–195.

8 The word 'riots' is placed in inverted commas, because these disturbances should not be perceived as anything similar to riots in the USA (in the 1960s and 1992) or in Britain (1958 and the 1980s). Riots similar in scale, severity and level of violence did not occur in the Netherlands.

9 The first 'major' group of labour immigrants originated from Italy. In 1960–61, the number of migrants from Italy and from Spain also increased substantially with support of the Dutch government. Most of the Italian immigrants were aged under 35 and unmarried. This was one of the terms for recruited unskilled labourers ordered by the state. The Spanish migrants in general were skilled workers and therefore many of them were aged over 35 and married. Thus, differences in composition of groups of labour immigrants were due to regulations and procedures of recruitment.

10 At first, contributions of the Ministry of Welfare and Social Work to welfare organisations covered 40 per cent of their budgets. In 1969, this contribution was raised to 70 per cent and in 1972 to 95 per cent. In 1975, the ministry finally covered 100 per cent of these budgets (Rath, 1991: 157).

11 *de Volkskrant*, 6 January 1960.

12 *Deventer Courant*, 5 October 1962.

13 For instance, *Nieuw Israëlisch Weekblad*, 3 July 1964.

14 During the Second World War, the Jewish population in the Netherlands diminished. Only some 15,000 of 140,000 Jews living in the Netherlands before 1940 were still living in this country after the war (see also Chapter 5).

15 *Algemeen Handelsblad*, 10 September 1963.

16 In the Achterhoek region, the support for the pre-war Dutch National-Socialist party (NSB) had been relatively substantial.

17 *Het Vrije Volk*, 27 December 1966.

18 See for example *Trouw*, 12 January 1965.

19 *NRC Handelsblad*, 4 November 1971.

20 The mayor of Rotterdam happened to be the same man who had been the mayor of Enschede during the 1961 disturbances in the Twente region (see p. 117).

21 *Het Vrije Volk*, as cited by *Haagse Post, De Afrikaanderbuurt*, 24 October 1984, pp. 34–43.

22 *Haagse Post*, 24 October 1984, pp. 37–8.

23 *Haagse Post*, 24 October 1984, p. 39.

24 *Haagse Post, Schiedam-West. Assimilatie of Terugkeren*, 31 October 1981, p. 35.

25 *Haagse Post*, 31 October 1981, p. 41.

26 *Haagse Post*, 31 October 1981, p. 35.

27 Bovenkerk's *Omdat Zij Anders Zijn* (1978) received much publicity because it provided proof that discrimination occurred in the Netherlands, especially in the labour market.

28 On 31 August 1970, some days before the Indonesian President, Soeharto, would visit the Netherlands, Moluccans took the Indonesian residency in Wassenaar. One policeman was killed during the action which ended after twelve hours. This action raised much publicity and turmoil. A majority of the Moluccan population in the Netherlands supported the action.

29 On 2 December 1975, a train was hijacked in the east of the Netherlands and four days later the Indonesian Consulate-General in Amsterdam was taken.

30 At their arrival in the Netherlands (1950s), the Moluccan population was placed in camps – left over concentration camps from the war. After distrubances in these camps in 1957 and comments by a special advisory

commission – the Verwey-Jonker Commission – special Moluccan neighbourhoods were built in some fifty to sixty cities all over the country (Penninx, 1979: 17–19; Entzinger, 1984: 76–7).

31 *Het Vrije Volk*, 9 December 1975; as cited by Schmid *et al.*, 1982: 62.

32 *Rotterdams Dagblad*, 8 December 1975; as cited by Schmid *et al.*, 1982: 62.

33 There would follow another two terrorist actions. In May 1977, a school and train in the east of the country were taken over by Moluccan youths. The actions were ended by military force resulting in the death of nine train hijackers and two hostages. In March 1978, a fourth terrorist attack on the Provincial Hall in the city of Assen resulted in two casualties.

34 *Haagse Post*, 31 October 1981, p. 35.

35 *de Volkskrant*, 23 October 1979.

36 In 1983, the governmental *Minderhedennota* (White Paper on Minorities) was the final answer by the Dutch government resulting from the 1979 WRR report. There were no substantial changes between the two publications.

37 *Vrij Nederland*, 15 March 1980.

38 The leader was the political science researcher, Frits Henry Brookman, at the University of Amsterdam.

39 *Vrij Nederland*, 15 March 1980.

40 *Het Parool*, 8 July 1980.

41 *de Volkskrant*, 27 November 1980.

42 *de Volkskrant*, 24 March 1981.

43 *de Volkskrant*, 9 May 1981.

44 It should be noted that most of the Surinamese people in the Netherlands were Dutch subjects.

45 *de Volkskrant*, 9 May 1981.

46 *Eindhovens Dagblad*, 31 August 1982.

47 *Eindhovens Dagblad*, 31 August 1982.

48 Viking Jeugd was a youth organisation led by former SS-men (van Donselaar, 1991: 206).

49 *Het Parool*, 15 September 1982; *Afdruk Kroniek*, 1982–83.

50 *Nieuwe Amsterdamse Courant*, 9 September 1982.

51 *Tussen Witkalk en Zwarthemden*, B & W Amsterdam, 22 February 1983.

52 Officially, Kerwin's last name was Lukas. He became known as Duinmeijer, named after his foster parents at the time of his murder.

53 *Utrechts Nieuwsblad*, 17 September 1983.

54 *Utrechts Nieuwsblad*, 17 September 1983.

55 *Haagse Post*, 9 December 1989.

56 *de Volkskrant*, 24 January 1984.

57 *Brabants Dagblad*, 24 January 1984.

58 *Kerwin: Een Teken van de Tijd*, Froukje Bos, Video Nederlands Filminstituut, 1984.

59 *de Volkskrant*, 1 March 1984.

60 *NRC Handelsblad*, 19 June 1984; as cited by van Donselaar, 1991: 193.

61 Art. 137, of the Dutch Penal Code.

62 *Het Vrije Volk*, 21 August 1984.

63 *Utrechts Nieuwsblad*, 28 February 1984.

64 *Binnenhof*, 9 January 1985.

65 And *de Volkskrant*, 3 January 1987.

66 And *Afdruk*, no. 41, February 1988.

67 And *NRC Handelsblad*, 12 January 1988.

68 *Afdruk*, April 1988.
69 *NRC Handelsblad*, 10 August 1988.
70 Previously they had had only four seats in city councils. The nine cities were Amsterdam (6.8 per cent), Rotterdam (7.2 per cent), The Hague (6.4 per cent), Utrecht, Purmerend, Almere, Haarlem, Schiedam and Dordrecht. Tilburg had been the only city in which they could not gain a seat.
71 See *de Volkskrant*, 12 September 1991.
72 Statement by Kosto on 30 September 1992 as published by the *AO-weekly*, no. 2444, 4 December 1992, pp. 22–3.
73 The Chief of Police presented this estimated figure according to findings of an anti-drugs investigation in the area. The figure had been discussed and criticised numerous times and hard evidence had never been given. Still, it was a very important event during the previously mentioned criminalising debates about minorities in the Netherlands in 1991 and 1992.
74 Many newspaper articles during the whole of March 1992, among which *de Volkskrant*, 21 March 1992.
75 *Handboek Minderheden*, no. 25, December 1992.
76 *de Volkskrant*, 8–11 August 1990.
77 *de Volkskrant*, 10–11 May 1990.
78 *de Volkskrant*, 26–28 August 1991; *Alkmaarsche Courant*, 27 August 1991.
79 *Alkmaarsche Courant*, 18 October 1991; *de Volkskrant*, 25 November 1991.
80 *de Volkskrant*, 28 January 1992. The newspaper also stated that the data of the *Anne Frank Stichting* had shown that the year 1986 had seen a peak of racist incidents. The years before 1986, however, seemed to have shown even more reported incidents. But maybe because of the fact that racist violence was never before a really important issue, this had been a case of short memory.
81 *Alkmaarsche Courant*, 27 January 1992.
82 A letter of the Provincial Representative of the Queen of the Province *Noord-Holland* to the mayors of the cities in this Province, 29 January 1992.
83 *de Volkskrant*, 4–5 February 1992; *NRC Handelsblad*, 3 February 1992.
84 *NRC Handelsblad*, 19 February 1992; *de Volkskrant*, 20 February 1992.
85 *Trouw*, 27 January 1992.
86 *Trouw*, 27 January 1992.
87 *de Volkskrant*, 27 January 1992.
88 This centre is a nationwide organisation supporting immigrants from the Mediterranean area. Its objective is to improve the social position of immigrants and is especially aimed at influencing policies in favour of, and the emancipation of, the immigrants.
89 Letter from NCB to the Minister of Home Affairs, 18 May 1992, reference DB92–121, subject 'Violence against Ethnic Minorities'.
90 *Het Parool*, 27 January 1992.
91 *de Volkskrant*, 29 January 1992.
92 *de Volkskrant*, 25 March 1992.
93 *de Volkskrant*, 29 January 1992; as cited by van Donselaar, 1993: 55.
94 Monthly *Opzij*, vol. 20, December 1992, p. 151; as cited by van Donselaar, 1993: 55.
95 *NRC Handelsblad*, 28 March 1992.

96 Hirsch Balin's opening speech at the conference 'Combating Discrimination: A Different Problem', 9 April 1992, The Hague, p. 3.

97 ibid., p. 11.

98 *Het Parool*, 9 May 1992.

99 *Alkmaarsche Courant*, 22 July 1992.

100 *de Volkskrant*, 26 August 1992; *Alkmaarsche Courant*, 29 August 1992. On 1 December 1992, the Public Prosecutor demanded imprisonment of seven years for the main suspect of this fight. He said racist motives had not been proven to exist, although many racist remarks were made. The demand was based on the fact that the suspect was already in prison for several (long) periods because of violent behaviour (*Alkmaarsche Courant*, 2 December 1992).

101 *de Volkskrant, Het Parool* and *Alkmaarsche Courant*, 25, 26 and 28 September 1992.

102 *de Volkskrant, Het Parool* and *Alkmaarsche Courant*, 12 October 1992.

103 *Trouw*, 9 March 1994.

104 *Het Parool*, 25 November 1993.

105 *Brabants Dagblad*, 3 November 1993. Five men, between 17 and 19 years of age, were arrested in January 1994 for writing and sending these threatening letters. They explained their behaviour by stating that they 'only wanted to play a joke on people' (*de Volkskrant*, 8 January 1994).

106 *Algemeen Dagblad*, 12 November 1993.

107 *Limburger*, 30 November and 1 December 1993.

108 *NRC*, 14 October 1993, and *Trouw*, 25 October 1993.

109 *Leidsch Dagblad*, 3 November 1993.

110 *Het Parool*, 1 November 1993.

111 Statements by Kosto on 30 September 1992, as published by *AO-weekly*, no. 244, 4 December 1992, pp. 11–12 (my italics).

112 *NRC*, 9 February 1994.

113 *NRC*, 8 February 1994.

114 *NRC*, 24 February 1994.

115 *de Volkskrant*, 25 February 1994.

116 *Nieuwsblad Migranten*, vol. 7, no. 15, 6 May 1994.

117 *de Volkskrant*, 14 March 1994.

118 *Het Parool*, 11 January 1994.

119 *Elsevier*, 22 and 29 January 1994.

120 *de Volkskrant*, 3 January 1994; FOK (1995: 93).

121 *de Volkskrant*, 12 February 1994.

122 *Nieuwsblad van het Noorden*, 16 February 1994.

123 *Trouw*, 21 January 1994.

124 *Brabants Dagblad*, 6 April 1994.

125 *Utrechts Nieuwsblad*, 7 April 1994.

126 *de Volkskrant*, 19 February 1994.

127 *NRC*, 18 March 1994; *Algemeen Dagblad*, 12 April 1994; *Leidsch Dagblad*, 25 April 1994.

128 *NRC* and *de Volkskrant*, 29 April 1994.

129 *NRC*, 20 July 1994; *NRC*, 13 September 1994; *de Volkskrant*, 28 September 1994. In appeal, Graman was sentenced to two years' imprisonment (*de Volkskrant*, 9 May 1995) because the Higher Court decided that the attempted murder was not proven.

130 *Algemeen Dagblad* and others, 3 March 1994.

131 *NRC*, 4 May 1994; 5 May 1994; 14 July 1994.

132 *Algemeen Dagblad*, 23 July 1994.

133 *Haagse Courant*, 9 November 1994.
134 In Zoetermeer, for example, *Het Parool*, 19 November 1994.
135 *NRC*, 19 May 1994; *Tubantia*, 12 July 1994.
136 *de Volkskrant*, 8 January 1994.
137 *Algemeen Dagblad*, 17 February 1994.
138 *de Volkskrant*, 3 February 1994; *Trouw*, 17 February 1994.

CHAPTER 5

Comparing state responses to racist violence

Introduction

In Chapters 2, 3 and 4, state responses to racist violence since 1945 were described in three different nation-states. In this chapter, these responses will be compared and analysed. In Chapter 1, three main sets of questions were raised:

1 What are the similarities in state responses to racist violence and is there a general perception of the problem?
2 What are the differences and are there specific national responses? How can these be accounted for?
3 Is there a trend in the state responses to racist violence in Britain, France and the Netherlands?

The state is not a monolithic unity, and activities by state authorities comprise a complex series of actions by persons within one or more state agencies. These activities result from internal struggles and compromises and are constantly subjected to very different influences from both outside and inside the state apparatus. State responses to a specific phenomenon are conceived of as relatively autonomous, and the scale and nature of the phenomenon is not the sole determining factor. Rather, state responses are determined by a number of historical, political, socio-economic and ideological processes. In turn, state responses to racist violence form a major influence on future expressions, levels and perceptions of the violence.

To discuss and analyse similarities, differences and trends in state responses, reference will be made to both general and specific historical, political, socio-economic and ideological contexts and processes. It should be noted that several academic debates are centred around the relation between racism (and racist violence) and the contexts and processes mentioned. This is not the place and it is not the intention of this study to discuss and take a stand in all of these debates. References will be made to these debates and relevant literature when the specific contexts and processes are discussed in relation to state responses to racist violence. Simple, one-sided causal relations are not to be found. This section does not present an exhaustive, detailed explanation of the similarities and differences in state responses. Rather indicators are given as to the direction in which explanations might be found. Each of these background explanations should be examined and studied more closely in future studies to analyse their specific influence on particular state response(s).

In Chapter 1, five reasons were mentioned for choosing the three nation-states involved. To summarise, they had the following in common: (1) the historical emergence of capitalism (including colonialism); (2) they were among the most advanced capitalist countries; (3) similar political and welfare states; (4) a similar history of migration; and (5) the presence of migrant settlers and their descendants. The overall conclusions of this chapter take into account these elements, as well as experiences during the Second World War. The latter proving important with respect to the understanding of racism, racist violence and self-image (self-perception) as major elements in mainstream discourses within these three nation-states.

This comparative chapter is divided into three sections related to the questions mentioned concerning similarities, differences and trends in state responses to racist violence, and ends with a conclusion.

Similarities in state responses

Since 1945, incidents have been reported in all three nation-states in which people were victimised because of their real or alleged membership of an imagined minority community based on phenotypical characteristics and/or religious, national or cultural origin. All three nation-states, however, have had long periods in which this kind of violence was not perceived as a specific social problem. Four phases in a theoretised process of racist violence en route to the political agenda have been distinguished. These were (A) racist violence as a problem experienced by the *individual*; (B) racist violence perceived as constituting *a social problem* by different groups in society; (C) racist violence on the *public agenda*, and (D) racist violence on the *formal agenda* (see Chapter 1).

In all three countries, long periods have been identified in which the phenomenon of racist violence has been stuck at phase A. In this phase, racist violence is not commonly perceived as constituting a social problem, and the perceptions and experiences of it are mainly restricted to those groups of people who are actual or potential victims.

Neglect and denial of racist violence in phase A

One of the consequences of this situation is that state responses to instances of violence are mainly registered at the local level and by local authorities. A common characteristic of the responses in this phase in all three states is their ad hoc nature. The actual responses in every single incident depend largely on the knowledge, insight and perceptions of the individual local authority with regard to racism and racist violence. This has led to the broad range of responses by local authorities shown in Chapters 2, 3 and 4.

Given the lack of perception of racist violence as a social problem in this phase, it is not surprising that local authorities have often denied or neglected references to racist elements in any of the incidents. All three countries have shown many examples in which the racist background of the violence was implicitly or explicitly denied. In response to the violence, local authorities immediately directed their responses towards the individual incident in which discussions centred around the real or alleged motives of the perpetrators. In the course of these discussions, the incidents were often trivialised or their significance played down. This frequently occurred by explaining that the suspect's motives had little to do with racism.

Perpetrators of racist violence were often perceived as young men acting out of boredom and/or frustration. For instance in Britain, the Teddy Boys in the 1950s and perpetrators of 'Paki-bashing' in the early 1970s were portrayed as 'thugs' or 'hooligans' trying to attract media and public attention or to shock public and political spectators. Frequently, the violent behaviour was explained (away) in all three countries with references to alcohol consumption and rivalry over girls. Racist motives were denied also when the perpetrators were described as not being intelligent enough to act with a preconceived notion, or were not capable of having an ideological understanding of racism or fascism. In addition, there are examples from each of the countries where the involvement of racism was simply denied. But by focusing all the attention and discussions at an individual level, we can now say, with the benefit of hindsight, that the general social problem – the racist character of these societies – was kept out of sight.

In this type of response the individual victim or victimised communities were often referred to as hypersensitive. Frequently, their individual victimisation was explained as a matter of bad luck – it could have happened to anyone. It was often said that victimised communities defined anything negative which happened to them as racist. In statements like these, the racist nature of a specific instance was implicitly denied.

Other instances have shown examples of perceived victim precipitation, i.e. local responses in which the victims themselves were blamed for the violence. This blame was often explained by their individual or group behaviour. Examples include: 'they should not react so aggressively to verbal abuse, people with red hair also get abused'; 'they should not have been there at that specific place and time, they provoked the violence by being there'; 'they should not group together, people feel threatened and become violent'. Some similarities are noticed here with responses to domestic violence, rape and homophobic violence. The element of 'blaming the victim' was particularly present in instances in which victims tried to defend themselves. Several times this even led to the arrest of the victims instead of the attackers (for instance Liverpool, 1948; Rotterdam, 1972; Scheidam, 1976).

These responses and the fixation on the individual nature of each incident, similar in all three countries over time, were also reflected in the hesitancy of the judicial authorities to include racist elements in judicial procedures – even when legislation provided the opportunity to do so. Many instances were indicated in which perpetrators were arrested and prosecuted, but any racist element was left out. In the courts, consideration was given only to the violent aspects of the crime. Sometimes, the lack of judicial attention to the racist nature of the crime was blamed on the problematic construction of hard evidence for this, and the work and time it would demand. The possible failure to find evidence of a racist nature was perceived as threatening, or even damaging to the whole case.

Self-perception

The implicit or explicit denial of the racist nature of the violence involved has been shown to be the overall starting point in state responses in all three countries. This meant also denying the possibility that racism is an inextricable part of the society. Such a perception was mainly based on the self-image, the self-perception of the states involved. Without going into detail, it could be argued that these self-images revolved around those countries being world leaders of democracy and civilisation. These notions have a long tradition and were among the main justifications given for colonising other parts of the world. This perception was clearly reflected in the statement by British Prime Minister Margaret Thatcher in 1978 that the 'British character has done so much for democracy, for law, done so much throughout the world'.

Reports about genocide, torture, extended violence and racist behaviour during the processes of colonisation and decolonisation were difficult to cope with and reconcile with these self-images. More than once, actual events, instances of misconduct, oppression and killings were covered up and ignored. Despite the large number of examples of undemocratic, uncivilised and racist behaviour, the dominant self-perception in each of the three nation-states remained one of a democratic, 'civilised', open and non-racist society. This was further strengthened in mainstream self-perceptions about fighting and beating fascist Germany, Italy and Japan during the Second World War. The dominance of this self-image at least partly explains the striking similarities in state responses to racist violence in which the existence of the racist and/or structural nature of this violence was often denied. Such recognition would conflict sharply with the self-image.

Racist motives were implicitly denied except in some (not all) instances in which the perpetrators explicitly portrayed themselves and their motives as racist. In turn, in societies with the dominant self-images mentioned, it was not likely that the majority of perpetrators of this violence would portray themselves as racist – the only exception perhaps being obscure neo Nazi groups. This completed the circle: 'We are not racist. Therefore, violence perpetrated for racist reasons cannot be a structural problem in our society and often has other grounds. And because there is no structural racist violence, we are not racist'.

The other side of the coin: anti-racism in phase B

There has been another side to the coin in all three countries. Certain sections of the three societies have been sensitive to appeals about racist violence, partly because the anti-racist self-image was in such sharp contrast with what was happening. Instances have been shown in all three countries in which racist violence came to be perceived as constituting a social problem by several sections in society (phase B). Activities by minority and anti-racism organisations have been shown to be of eminent importance here. Although state responses to these organisations and their activities and demands did not constitute the major subject of this study, a few points first need making about the organisations themselves.

In all three countries, minority and anti-racist pressure groups brought the phenomenon of racist violence to the surface and began to organise activities to attract public and political attention and to formulate demands and measures. These initiatives often included an appeal to the above mentioned non-racist self-image. Influence and pressure were directed towards state authorities directly through political parties and to media representatives, as well as to the public in general. Activities took different forms, such as demonstrations (CARF/Britain, 1970s; *SOS Racisme*/France, 1980s; *Nederland Bekent Kleur*/Netherlands, 1990s) and petitions (West Indian Standing Conference/Britain, 1970s; MRAP/France, early 1970s; NCB/Netherlands, 1992).

Besides direct actions, anti-racism and minority organisations in all three countries began to collect data on racist incidents, in order to convince the government and the public that racist violence constituted a problem (Institute of Race Relations/Britain, 1979; *Anne Frank Stichting*/Netherlands, 1987; *SOS Racisme* and MRAP/France, 1980s). Of course the impact of each demonstration and report did differ. In general, however, the impact of these organisations and their activities in relation to the future entrance of the topic on to either the public or formal agendas was very important.

Several minority and anti-racist organisations directed their work at the local level. Many were locally organised, as well as responsive to local racist incidents. The Local Anti Racial Harassment and Attacks Networks and the local Monitoring Groups in Britain, the local *SOS Racisme* committees in France and the local *Anti Discriminatie Bureaus* in the Netherlands were all private organisations concerned with putting pressure on local authorities, even when racist violence was not considered a topic on the national public or formal agendas. Their activities have been shown to be important in the process of establishing racist violence as a social problem and in following-up proposals and the implementation of local anti-discrimination policies. They were also important in attracting broader public attention to the impact of this violence on everyday life and in establishing procedures and networks to protect people from being victimised, sometimes even by setting up self-defence groups and networks.

State responses to these organisations and pressure groups and their activities differed and this is elaborated upon later. However, it should be noted that in all three countries instances have been shown in which minority and anti-racist organisations influenced individual internal actors and contributed to changes in the perception of racist violence within mainstream discourses.

Increasingly caught between two sides in phase B

In the second phase (B) of the model, racist violence was commonly denied as constituting a social problem, and state authorities responded ambiguously in all the countries to the demands of minority and anti-racist organisations and to individual racist incidents. This ambiguity was caused by the fact that authorities found themselves caught between anti-racism movements and their demands on the one hand, and the political extreme right threat and their increasing public support on the other.

A similarity among the three countries was the emergence of large-scale anti-racist movements, coinciding with a reported increase in support for extreme right political parties. This has been shown in Britain during the second half of the 1970s with an increasing support for the National Front, in France (*Front National*) in the 1980s, and in the Netherlands during the early 1980s (*Centrumpartij*) and in the early 1990s (the *Centrumdemocraten*). In these circumstances, state authorities have shown themselves to be more open to supporting certain anti-racism organisations, more willing to listen to them and to implement some of their demands in political programmes. This was seen also in the cooperation between major mainstream political parties and anti-racism movements. This strengthened the 'civilised' self-image of these nation-states as being tough against fascists. Of course, this response by state authorities was also influenced by the growing impression among established political parties that such support would lead to the political defeat of extreme right parties, which were increasingly regarded as being real and feared competitors for votes.

In relation to the emergence of the extreme right and racist ideologies, another related factor was that established political parties themselves had originally been the pioneers, initiators and/or copiers of similar sentiments, slogans and policies.

Since the early 1970s, world economic restructuring and increasing international cultural interchange have been experienced by many sections of the populations of developed countries as a direct threat to their livelihood, social conditions, life style and national identity – an interpretation eagerly encouraged by the extreme right, but also by many mainstream politicians.

(Castles and Miller, 1993:30)

Within this political climate specific issues were increasingly dominating the public and formal agendas, such as crime, violence, migration, 'integration' of immigrants, and the like. State authorities had a decisive influence on the creation of these agendas and introduced and directed dominant elements and perceptions into mainstream discourses. This led in all three states to the creation of links between these individual issues and to the presentation of them as causal correlations. Concrete influence by state authorities in all three countries has been reported in processes of politicisation of law and order and migration and processes of racialisation, marginalisation, problematisation and criminalisation of specific minorities.

All three countries have also provided examples of responses by state authorities (especially established political parties) which have included both definitions of the situation, as well as points included in the programmes of these extreme right parties. In all three nation-states racist violence was perceived and presented by state authorities as a consequence of the (increasing) presence of victimised communities (for instance Britain, late 1970s and 1980s; France, 1980s and 1990s; and the Netherlands, locally: early 1970s; nationally: early 1990s). Under these circumstances, increasing support for right-wing extremism as well as an increase in racist violence has been reported. On the other hand, this also contributed to a situation of increasing public awareness of racist violence and of an increasing number of racist incidents being reported; this was closely related to the emergence of anti-racist and minority movements and their increasing influence as mentioned (pp. 167–168).

These similarities in state responses to the emergence and demands of anti-racism and minority movements, on the one hand, and the emergence of extreme-right parties on the other, can be partly explained by the political systems of the three countries involved. These systems are similar in their 'open', competitive, democratic nature and their sensibility to pressures from outside the state apparatus (see Richardson, 1993a). Both the growing pressure of, and increasing support for, anti-racism movements, as well as the increasing support for extreme-right political thoughts and parties, established reasons of concern for state authorities in all three nation-states.

The media in the three countries also played an important role in relation to the increasing attention paid to the phenomenon of racist violence. Influential reports were divided into two main categories: reports on specific racist incidents (for instance in Britain, early 1970s on 'Paki-bashing'; Marseille/France, 1973; Carpentras/France, 1990; Netherlands, early 1990s) and on the living conditions of (victimised) minority communities (Britain, 1950s and late 1960s; France, late 1950s and early 1960s). Of course, recognising that these reports were influential does not mean that they did not differ greatly in content. Some were even regarded as inciting yet more violence (for instance Marseille, 1973). In fact, the overall media treatment of the issue reflected an ambiguity similar to that of state authorities and also reflected the (politically and ideologically) broad coverage in the three nation-states. At least, however, media reports brought racist violence to the attention of a broader public and they were partly responsible for the appearance of this issue on the public agenda (phase C).

Trigger events or accelerators at the entrance of phase C

At times of increasing support for racist thoughts and extreme-right parties, as well as of increasing pressure by anti-racist and minority movements, specific incidents acted as trigger events which brought the issue of racist violence on to the public agenda (phase C). We could, in other words, call these trigger events the 'accelerators' in the process of the formation of a social problem (see Chapter 1). In the British case, after some years of increasing support for the National Front, these accelerators took the form of the disorders which broke out in 1979 (Southall) in the course of an anti-racism demonstration against the National Front, by the New Cross fire and the ensuing anti-racist demonstration in 1980, as well as by the 1980–81 disorders. The inquiry by Lord Scarman into the Brixton disorders (1981) highlighted the impact of discrimination and racist attitudes on the day-to-day life of minority populations. These accelerators contributed to the entrance of the issue of racist violence on to the British public agenda (and finally on to the formal agenda, culminating in the 1981 Home Office report on 'racial' attacks).

In the Netherlands, two periods have been distinguished. During the first half of the 1980s, the emergence and increasing support for the *Centrumpartij* coincided with an increase in reported racist incidents, as well as the setting up of local *Anti Discriminatie Bureaus*. The racist murder of Kerwin Duinmeijer triggered off several national and local demands and initiatives designed to combat this kind of violence. In the early 1990s, this pattern repeated itself intensively within an increasing amount of support for the *Centrumdemocraten*, and a reported wave of racist incidents in 1992. In France, similar accelerators have been shown in 1982–83 (the emergence of and increasing support for the *Front National* and a reported wave of racist violence), as well as in 1990, when the Carpentras incident most definitely brought racist violence – albeit temporarily – on to the public (and even onto the formal) agenda.

Responses to the entrance on to the public agenda (phase C)

A striking similarity in state responses to the entrance of racist violence on to the public agenda was the portrayal of racist violence as indicating the need for migration control and restrictions in all three countries. In Britain (late 1950s and 1970s), France (1970s and 1980s) and the Netherlands (1990s), responses by state authorities were recorded explaining the occurrence of racist violence as just more proof of the already dominant notion that 'too many migrants would lead to social conflicts and violence' or translations of the notion of *seuil de tolérance*. Often the majority of reported racist incidents were directed specifically against those groups of people who were already at the centre of the debate on migration – for instance, people of North African origin in France (1954–1962 and early 1970s); Afro-Caribbean people (late 1950s) and those of Asian origin (late 1960s and early 1970s) in Britain; Muslims during the Gulf War in Britain and France, and asylum-seekers in France and the Netherlands in the early 1990s.

Another striking similarity in state responses in phase (C) was the attention given to discrimination, which is a much broader category and was conceived of in more general terms than violence itself. These state responses underlined the self-image of the state as working with a standard of fairness. In Britain (second half of the 1970s), France and the Netherlands (both early 1980s and early 1990s), anti-discrimination legislation was implemented and extended at those times in which racist violence entered the public agenda. Other forms of responses by state authorities in this respect consisted of the establishment of specific national organisations for combating discrimination in general (CRE/Britain, 1976; LBR/Netherlands, 1984) or for registering racist incidents in particular (CNCDH/France, 1988). It should be noted that these responses also included several differences which will be discussed later (pp. 179–184).

These two similar lines of state response in periods when racist violence constituted a topic on the public agenda may be explained by the above mentioned position state authorities found themselves in, that of being 'caught between two sides'. The responses were not directed towards the phenomenon of racist violence, but towards political 'issues' which were perceived to be related to this phenomenon. This perception will be elaborated upon at a later stage in this chapter (pp. 187–195). It should be noted, however, that the ambiguous response by state authorities not only reflected the position the authorities were in, but also reflects the fact that state authorities do not constitute a monolithic unity, and therefore could and did respond in different directions.

One last similarity involved the influence of actions by specific internal actors – either directly or indirectly. There were hardly any examples found in the three states in which internal actors took the initiative themselves in order to attract attention for the specific issue of racist violence. The British MP Paul Rose, who kept records of extreme-right violent incidents in the mid-1970s, and the meeting organised by the Dutch Parliamentary Committee on Justice in 1984, were among the very few examples of initiatives taken by internal actors in bringing attention to racist violence in this phase. More numerous are examples in which internal actors initiated action to attract attention to issues problematising and criminalising victimised communities. Ironically, this may have at times indirectly contributed to increased public attention to racist violence. Examples of this were speeches by Powell (late 1960s and 1970s) and Thatcher (1979) in

Britain, Chirac (1970s and 1980s) and Pasqua (early 1990s) in France and Bolkestein (1991) in the Netherlands.

Some will argue that these speeches mainly contributed to the problematisation and criminalisation of vitimised groups of people, and even to a reported increase in racist violence. However true this may be, it is important to note that internal actors of established political parties were actively involved in the creation of a political climate in which racist violence would (eventually) enter the public agenda in all three countries. Whether this was through incitement to racist violence leading to more violence (leading to more attention), or whether this was by creating a climate in which more of the public paid more attention to racist violence as a kind of counter-response, remains a subject for future research. The limited action undertaken by internal actors reflected the weak position of the victimised minorities within the power/political structures in these respective societies.

Explanations of violence in response to entrance on to the public agenda (phase C)

From the moment that denial of the racist nature of violent incidents was perceived to be virtually impossible and the issue of racist violence entered the public agenda (phase C), state authorities were increasingly forced by public pressure to respond and to give some explanation of the violence. Many explanations included references to specific geographic areas – inner cities – and to specific groups of people, i.e. unemployed, young and badly educated people. Explanations were manifold in the three nation-states, and some are elaborated upon here in more detail. They are categorised under several headings referring to the alleged main causes of the violence:

- demographic (increase of migration and concentration of minority communities in specific places: capability of host society to 'absorb')
- international (migration flows and events abroad)
- geographic (inner cities)
- economic (crisis, unemployment and deprivation)
- political (extreme-right parties and ideologies)
- media (copy-catting)
- psychological (low intelligence of perpetrators)
- age (youth) and gender (male)
- cultural (incapacity to 'integrate').

Demographic
In Britain (1950s), France (1970s and 1980s) and the Netherlands (locally: 1970s; nationally: 1990s) state responses to racist violence utilised explanations of demography. The most outspoken example of this was the French notion of *seuil de tolérance*, although this was not restricted to the French discourse alone. Examples were shown in all three states which implicitly or explicitly represented the notion of a

threshold of tolerance. This notion has often been used in relation to specific groups of people entering the country, for example people of Algerian and other North African (Maghreb) origin in France, people of Afro-Caribbean and Asian origin in Britain, and people of North African origin and African and Asian asylum-seekers in the Netherlands.

According to this notion, whenever the alleged natural threshold was crossed, social conflict and disorder (including racist violence) would be inevitable. This perception was found in the report by the Royal Commission on Population in Britain (late 1940s), in the report of the Social and Economic Council in France (1969), cited in Freeman (1979: 88), and in local policies by Rotterdam (1972) and Schiedam (1976) and indirectly in the NSCGP report on Immigrant Policy (1990) in the Netherlands. These explanations have been heard since in statements by representatives of state authorities of very different backgrounds (Hattersley (1965), Powell (1968), Thatcher (1979), Chirac (1983 and 1990), Mitterrand (1989), Kosto (1992) and Bolkestein (1994), to name but a few).

International
The presentation by state authorities of international migration as a threatening development was another similarity in the three countries. There were numerous examples in which, for instance, politicians of established political parties presented an image in which the country was threatened by a 'flood': Thatcher (1979), Chirac (1983) and Bolkestein (1994). Examples of state authorities presenting different aspects of migration as threatening elements which needed priority attention were also numerous (for example Stoleru on family reunion, 1976; Cresson and Lang on 'illegals' (Le Monde, 10 July 1991); several leaders within the Dutch Labour party on 'illegals' in 1992; Bolkestein on Muslims in 1991 and on asylum-seekers in 1994). The migration issue always appeared on the agenda as a potential source of social and economic problems. The presence of specific groups of people, especially the increase in their numbers, as well as the presence of a second generation, were portrayed in political, media and popular discourses as main sources of social problems such as crime, (increased) unemployment, disorders and deprivation. Such a situation often coincided with times of economic depression, social unrest, moral panic about the presence or arrival of specific groups of people and with the increasing support for extreme right-wing, racist political ideologies and/or parties. Explanations about the emergence and existence of these notions in relation to migration and *seuil de tolérance* will be elaborated upon in the next section.

Geographic
The predicted social unrest and problems arising from it (including racist violence) were presented as being concentrated to the inner cities, an area in which many of 'these people' lived. The reference to geographic areas is explained by the fact that the entrance on to the

public agendas of the issue of racist violence always coincided with a period of time in which migration already constituted a topic (for example in Britain: 1958, late 1970s and early 1980s; in France: 1973, 1980s and 1990; and in the Netherlands: early 1990s). The reference to specific groups of people in the inner cities assumed to perpetrate violence was not a new phenomenon in the history of Britain, France and the Netherlands. In the dominant discourses within these capitalist nation-states, working-class citizens in the inner cities were often portrayed as the 'dangerous classes', consuming too much alcohol and 'not really civilised' – that is, liable to vent their emotions, frustrations, problems in an elemental, violent way instead of talking, discussing, negotiating. This was especially the case with respect to young people, who were perceived as being more 'spontaneous', primitive, violent and 'wanton.' Explanations referred mainly to the density of minority communities in the inner cities, as the main source of problems. Thus racist violence was seen as a problem involving those on the outer edge of society which did not threaten the core of present mainstream society, culture, or the state. This perception and presentation also gave grounds to the notion that combating racist violence was mainly a matter of law and order and of effective (community) policing.

Economic

Another explanation focused on the supposed influence of socioeconomic conditions. Economic crisis, mass unemployment and deprivation of specific geographical areas (inner cities) were presented as constituting the core of social problems, which led people to vent their frustrations and emotions in a violent manner. This explanation of the violence parallels the arguments mentioned in connection with the geographic explanation.

Political

Often a link was perceived as existing between the occurrence of racist violence and the political far or extreme right. Actually, this line of thought worked in two directions. On the one hand, the success of extreme right-wing racist parties was regarded as establishing a situation in which racist violence would flourish. On the other hand, repression of the political extreme right was often argued against as such repression would lead supporters to take violent action.

Media

Several reported racist incidents were perceived to be copy-cat actions after the mass media had paid extensive attention to a specific incident. One of the consequences of this explanation has been a great deal of concern among mass media representatives over reporting such incidents. In addition, statements have been noted in which the media are advised not to pay any attention to this violence, as this only increases the problem. A similar view was expressed by President Pompidou in the early 1970s, when he argued that France should not become entangled in the snare of racism. 'Sometimes the simple fact of saying the word summons up the idea, and reality, unfortunately, often follows the idea' (see Chapter 3).

Psychological
The intelligence of the perpetrators involved in racist violence has often been questioned. This is in line with the explanation concerning the geographical area in which racist violence is mainly believed to occur, i.e. not really civilised people who vent their emotions and frustrations in a violent manner instead of dealing with them by talking, discussing and negotiating.

Age and gender
Boyish pranks are often regarded as leading to racist violence, and this violence is not portrayed as racist, but merely an outcome of the male maturation process. Some remarks about this explanation have already been made in the context of the denial and neglect of racist violence (see p. 165).

Cultural
At times when racist violence was an issue on the public agenda, the above mentioned mechanism of 'blaming the victim' was also reported. This has been especially reflected in public and political debates about both the lack of, and need for, integration by minority communities, presented in relation to the occurrence of the violence. This implicitly puts the blame for the violence on the victimised communities. Consequences of this perception have been proposals and initiatives by state authorities for firmer policies on (forced) integration as an answer to increasing tension and violence.

Responses to entrance on the formal agenda (phase D)

Once racist violence was perceived to be a social problem which had to be dealt with by the state and to which priority was given, the issue entered the formal agenda. Two main state responses were distinguished in this phase (D): the 'excluding' versus 'including recognition' of racist violence by state authorities implicitly or explicitly referring to the perceived position of the victimised groups in society. All three countries have shown that the 'excluding recognition' of racist violence was dominant in the state responses when racist violence entered the formal agenda for the first time.

In short, in Britain, France and the Netherlands there have been instances when the racist nature of the violence involved was regarded as being impossible to ignore any longer and was finally recognised. These situations often occurred after a series of specific racist events (accelerators) which led to an increase in pressure by migrant and anti-racism movements in order to get the issue of racist violence on to the formal agenda. The issue of migration control had already been placed there. Therefore, racist violence was often perceived as a more or less natural consequence of migration, perpetrated by the 'less civilised', unemployed working class (especially youth) in the deprived inner cities, as well as a sign of increasing support for extreme-right political ideologies and parties. The main state responses in these instances consisted of the implementation of migration restrictions. Sometimes state responses also included some form of condemnation of the violence, but nearly always alongside explanations or references to the deprived and problematic conditions under which the suspected perpetrators were living. In turn, these conditions were portrayed as closely related to the presence of specific minority communities.

The dominance of this perception in itself was not remarkable, since the entrance of racist violence on to the formal agenda coincided with the migration issue. The popular and political discourse within this context of debates on migration restrictions portrayed the victimised minority groups as the main source of the alleged problems. Racist violence was mainly seen as just more proof of the already dominant perception (Britain: 1958 and mid-1980s; France: 1973 and early 1980s; Netherlands: early 1990s). In a situation in which the victimised groups were excluded from specific social, economic and political rights and resources, the dominant ideological discourse made it difficult – if not impossible – to perceive these groups as an integral part of society and to implement measures accordingly.

The aforementioned does not mean that there have been no examples of the 'including recognition' type of state response in Britain, France and the Netherlands. State authorities often found themselves caught between increasing support for extreme-right political thought and/or parties on the one hand, and an increasing anti-racism movement on the other. Partly because of this, anti-discrimination legislation has been proposed and implemented, as well as improvements in existing legislation, adjustments and improvements in the instructions for police conduct in matters of racist violence, condemnations of the racist violence, inquiries by the state, and even the implementation or at least proposals of policies aimed at combating racist violence specifically (Britain: mid-1980s; France: 1990, Netherlands: 1990s). However, one striking conclusion has to be that these measures and proposals always coincided with measures expressing the 'excluding recognition' type of state responses, such as migration restrictions, tightening of measures and policies against 'illegals', restrictions on asylum policies, public and political debates on criminal behaviour by second generation immigrants, on Muslim fundamentalism, and so on. State responses in which both types of response have been registered were referred to as 'two-faced' state responses.

Differences in state responses

'Occasional recognition' in phase A

The major difference in state responses in the phase in which racist violence was not commonly perceived as constituting a social problem (phase A) consisted of the relatively frequent 'occasional recognition' of racist violence by the Dutch state authorities. This 'occasional recognition' referred to instances in which the racist nature of a particular incident had been recognised (implicitly), but the structural character of racist violence had at the same time been denied. In these instances, racist violence was perceived as constituting an exceptional, rare occasion. Chapter 4 on the Netherlands has shown several examples in which local as well as national authorities recognised and condemned the racist nature of an incident openly and unambiguously. These statements were immediately followed by arguments that neither racism nor racist violence constituted a regular (and therefore problematic) part of 'Dutch everyday life'. Examples of this 'occasional recognition' have rarely been shown in the histories of British and French state responses to racist violence.

In explaining this major difference, we have to direct our focus to the experiences of the three nation-states during the Second World War and the way in which these countries coped with these experiences. The three states experienced the war in very different ways. Britain was among one of the major 'liberators' and 'defenders of the free world' and, together with the United States and Canada, constituted the core of the victorious winners of the war in Western Europe. Although German bombings had damaged major areas of British cities and many British soldiers died, the United Kingdom had not experienced the kinds of psychological and economic hardships brought about by several years of occupation. More to the point, Britain had not experienced the direct consequences of the Holocaust.

The experiences of the Dutch and French populations were different. The Netherlands were invaded by Hitler's army and within a few days the country was fully occupied, leading to five years of occupation and fascist terror. One of the main consequences was the mass murder of the vast majority of the Dutch Jewish population. With the assistance of the Dutch civil registration system (developed before the war), Dutch Jews were easily traced and consequently transported to death camps. After 1945, just 10 per cent of the Dutch Jewish population had survived Nazism.

The German invasion into France seemed to meet little resistance as well. After the occupation of the northern parts of the country, a deal was made with Hitler. Consequently, southern parts of France were governed by the Petain regime during the war. This regime was directly responsible for the death of many thousands of French Jews and of French resistance fighters.

In France as well as in the Netherlands, many memories evoke the heroic role of the resistance. The role of collaborators, however, received some attention in the Netherlands, but hardly any attention at all in France. The difference in this respect between France and the Netherlands – both of whom experienced occupation resulting in great losses, particularly within the Jewish communities – are explained by the different ways in which these two countries 'came to grips' with these experiences. 'Cover up' and 'amnesia' seemed to have formed the main elements in the French method of coping in the first post-war decades (see e.g. Hansson, 1991:43–4; *de Volkskrant*, 25 February 1995). Only since the mid-1980s has extensive attention and literature been dedicated to this part of French history. It is significant that it was two North American historians, R. Paxton and M. Marrus, who 'pioneered the detailed investigation into Vichy and the Jews in a book published as late as 1981' (Kushner, 1994: 6).

Since the 1960s, the Dutch have shown a broadly felt and well-documented knowledge, shame and, to some degree, feeling of guilt with respect to these experiences. They contributed to a dominant discourse which has been sensitive to preventing and repressing any utterance or instance of racist and/or fascist thought and behaviour in the post-war years. From 1945 until the 1980s, organisations perceived to be based on racist or fascist sentiments, ideologies or programmes have been under enormous pressure due to media, popular and political concern and actions to ban them (see van Donselaar, 1991, 1993). Within this context it is not remarkable in itself that incidents with an 'undoubtedly' racist character were condemned by the broad public, political and state authorities. The relatively frequent occurrence of the 'occasional recognition' of racist violence in the Netherlands, in comparison to Britain, could be explained by these different war experiences and, in relation to France, by different ways of coping with these experiences.

The role of anti-semitic racist violence

Another distinction in relation to the Second World War is the specific impact and attention paid to anti-semitism and anti-semitic violence in France and the Netherlands. France has had a very strong tradition and experience of domestic anti-semitism (Kushner, 1994: 32). However, in the post-war period, partly because of the experiences of the French and Dutch Jewish populations during the war and especially since the Second World War experiences started to be discussed publicly (in the Netherlands since the 1960s, and in France since the 1980s), the French and Dutch public, media and state authorities have been specifically alert for instances of anti-semitic violence. This has been shown in series of incidents during the 1960s and, for example, the desecration of a cemetery in Vlissingen (1993) in the Netherlands. Several incidents, most prominently the Carpentras incident (1990), have shown a similar singular alertness in France, especially since the mid-1980s, when increasing attention was paid to French history during the Second World War.

In state responses to anti-semitic racist violence in both countries, relatively more notice was given to the perception of, and the impact on, the victimised population. In Britain, anti-semitic violence was given relatively little special attention in either popular or political discourse until the early 1990s (see also Kushner, 1994). In Chapter 1, the problematic and much debated relationship between racism (racist violence) and anti-semitism (anti-semitic violence) has been mentioned, and the latter has been included in the concept of racist violence. This is not the place to go into detail on this relationship and debate, but it should be noted that anti-semitic violence has been given special attention in France and the Netherlands and has directly (as accelerators) or indirectly (by growing awareness and concern) contributed to the overall attention to racist violence.

Anti-racism and minority organisations

Anti-racism movements in general have had a major influence on the changing position of the issue of racist violence with respect to the public and formal agendas (see pp. 167–168). Their role, however, has not been the subject of this study and deserves to be studied in greater detail (see for instance an analysis of debates within the anti-racist movements in Britain and France: Lloyd, 1994). None the less, their influence and place in society and in the political structures of each individual country have been important in relation to differences in state responses to racist violence. For these reasons, the next remarks will be short and somewhat unsubstantiated and are mainly based on experiences during the execution of this study on state responses.

A first striking difference among the three countries is that these organisations in France mainly consisted of people from minority communities. The only exception of importance was the 'intellectual Left' in the early 1970s, developed in response to some specific racist incidents. The vast majority of participants and staff in the Dutch anti-racism movement have been members of the white majority population. In Britain, there has seemed to be a mixture in this respect, including strongly monitored minority organisations and political left-wing organisations, mainly staffed by people from the majority population.

In the Netherlands, many people within the white native population not only warned about, but also have been active against, signs of racism and discrimination. In France, on the other hand, victimised minority groups were thrown back on their own resources to fight racism and violence. In the Netherlands, racism and racist violence were perceived – at least by certain groups of people outside state authorities – as a 'Dutch problem' when they surfaced, whereas the French situation has shown racist violence to be 'their' problem (i.e. the victimised communities). In Britain, perceptions were divided along dominant political lines. In the 1970s, anti-racism was mainly politically organised. This situation was caused not only by those who did the organising, but also by those who took a position of not wanting to participate in such an organisation. British anti-racism movements have shown a higher degree of mixture with respect to different communities involved.

Another difference consisted of the way in which the issue of anti-racism was politicised. Although known for its very closed bureaucracy (Richardson, 1993a: 3), the British case indicated a rather strong relationship between parts of the anti-racism movement and mainstream (Labour Party) politics. In France, this was so to a much lesser degree. And it hardly existed at all in the Netherlands. The anti-racist movements in the latter two were much more affiliated with youth culture and were organised by the youth when they were first set up in the countries early 1980s. This has been especially true with respect to the anti-racist organisations active at local levels (*SOS Racisme* in France and the *Anti Discriminatie Bureaus* in the Netherlands).

A third difference concerned the nature of the organisations themselves. The Commission for Racial Equality (CRE) in Britain and the *Landelijk Bureau Racismebestrijding* (LBR) in the Netherlands were two organisations which were mainly set up and supported financially by their respective governments and they were more or less affiliated with the state. In France, such a national anti-racism organisation has never existed. Of course, there were *SOS Racisme, France Plus* and the *Mouvement Contre le Racisme et Pour l'Amitié Entre les Peuples* (MRAP) in France. But these more or less matched their counterparts in Britain and the Netherlands, such as Campaign Against Racism and Fascism (CARF), the Newham Monitoring Project (NMP), the Institute of Race Relations (IRR) and the Runnymede Trust as well as the *Anti-Racisme Informatie Centrum* (ARIC), the *Anne Frank Stichting* and the local *Anti Discriminatie Bureaus* (ADBs).

These distinctions are shown to be important with respect to the main issue of this study. They led to a situation in which anti-racism organisations and activities in Britain and France were much more isolated from large parts of mainstream politics and state authorities compared to the Netherlands. In Britain and France, this situation depended greatly on the specific government at a specific time. In Britain especially, main parts of the anti-racism movement and the main (Conservative dominated) state authorities since 1980 have not been 'on speaking terms' with each other for all kinds of reasons. This has partly been due to Thatcher's attempt to challenge the influence of pressure groups in general (Richardson, 1993b: 88).

In France, the anti-racism organisations and state authorities were barely speaking, although this was restricted mainly to the Socialist Party. The isolation of the French anti-racism movement in relation to the present centre-right government is more or less similar to the British situation. Contrary to France and Britain, the anti-racism movement in the Netherlands has established and maintained a lot of contacts with state authorities, including all the major political parties – right wing and left wing – irrespective of political changes in government. Several Dutch state authorities – to differing extents – maintained and continued relations with anti-racism movements and supported these, or at least specific activities, financially. In addition, more than once state authorities joined in activities organised by these organisations (for instance in Amsterdam, 1983) or even took over the initiative (for instance the introduction of the Declaration against Discrimination and Racism by the Dutch Home Secretary, Dales, in 1991).

The role and impact of anti-racism organisations

It is self-evident that these differences have been important in relation to the influence and impact of anti-racism organisations and activities on state actions in general, and on state responses to racist violence in particular. The two extremes consisted, on the one hand, of private British and French anti-racist organisations 'not being on speaking terms at all' with their respective state authorities and, on the other, private Dutch anti-racism organisations working together and discussing plans for how to handle issues with state authorities.

Explaining these differences in itself should be a subject for another study, and therefore exhaustive explanations cannot be given here. However, more general remarks in this respect can be made with reference to the decisive influences the different political systems concerned have.

One of the striking differences between Britain, France and the Netherlands lies in their political structures. There are various debates centred around the differences and similarities of political systems in Europe (for an overview of political systems see G. Smith, 1980; Rieu and Duprat, 1993; for debates on party systems in Europe see Mair, 1990; and for debates about the role and influence of pressure groups in Western Europe see Richardson, 1993a). As mentioned above, references are made here to plausible explanations of differences concerning the influence of anti-racism and minority organisations in relation to state responses to racist violence. Therefore, we can say that France is characterised by its very centralised state structure, whereas state structures of Britain and the Netherlands are better characterised by a mixture of centralised and decentralised elements. Aside from this, it is difficult to compare Britain and France with the Dutch state. The Netherlands, being much smaller in geographic size, may hardly be compared without falling into sterotypical references such as 'the Dutch village'.

These differences are important here, because the centrality of the state structure could be influential to the chances of external actors (for instance anti-racist organisations) attracting state attention and contributing to having their demands and issues placed on the political agenda. Because of the centralised state structure, this will be much more difficult to achieve for French external actors, than for

British, and even more so, Dutch external actors. It should also be noted that in France, contrary to Britain and the Netherlands, pressure from organised interest groups 'is still viewed by many in France as a source of bias, injustice and inefficiency' (Hall, P.A., 1993: 160). And pressure groups in France are often much more factionalised internally and they more often turn to the streets for massive demonstrations threatening public order which the state cannot ignore instead of influencing the decision-making process within the institutions (Hall, P.A., 1993: 163–4).

Regarding the political systems, the three nation-states differ remarkably. Britain and France have known either right-wing or left-wing governments. The two countries more or less mirror each other with respect to the frequency of government change. The British government frequently changed from Conservative to Labour and vice versa until 1979 when the Conservative Party took office and is still in at time of writing (1995). The French government was dominated by the centre-right political parties until Mitterrand's victory in 1981. Since then, the French government has changed back and forth between the left and centre-right parties. The Netherlands has always found it necessary to form coalition governments. Due to a proportional representation system and the large number of participating parties in Parliament. Dutch governments have always consisted of more than one party. Since the Second World War, the Dutch Christian Democrats have consistently been one of the governing parties (until 1994). Dutch coalition governments have changed every now and then from a centre-right to a centre-left coalition.

These differences in change and content of governments have been important. In Britain, fifteen years (to date) of Conservative government did not contribute much to a constructive relationship between private anti-racist organisations and national state authorities, but rather led to a situation in which they are not 'on speaking terms'. Despite Britain's long tradition of pressure groups, many anti-racism and minority groups started their work in a period (1970s and 1980s) in which increasingly the influence of pressure groups in general was attacked. Therefore, the not yet realised power position of these newer groups was even harder to accomplish (Richardson, 1993b: 86–99). Increasingly pressure groups turned to the local level at which authorities are increasingly less powerful in comparison to other European countries (Richardson, 1993b: 89).

In France, the years of opposition by the Socialist Party have contributed to the implementation of demands by anti-racist organisations in their election programmes and in government plans in 1981. But, it also has contributed to the gap between anti-racist organisations and state authorities when this party was not in office. The more multi-political Dutch climate has contributed to more contact and relations between anti-racist organisations and state authorities. The state of relations in all three countries does of course either contribute to or worsen the chances of external actors (anti-racist organisations) achieving success with their demands and positions.

The political systems of the three nation-states also mirror the more general structures of the societies in question (see e.g. Finer, 1970; Smith, G., 1980). In Britain with a polarisation around social class (Smith, G., 1980: 30), a very strong class discourse exists between the labour and bourgeois classes. Although French society is also highly divided, this is less so, with the dominant discourse emphasising French culture as one unity. In comparison with the Netherlands, Britain and France each represent a much more competitive political state structure and society. Of course these distinctions are made between dominant elements of social structures. It does not mean, for instance, that no class discourse exists in the Netherlands. In comparison to Britain, however, it is much less prominent in mainstream discourses. The Netherlands can be portrayed as having a structure of negotiation with low class consciousness.

The Dutch system (see Lijphart, 1979) has been constructed along so-called 'pillars' based on strong group identity, along religious, liberal and socialist lines. The political and economic elites of these 'pillars' formed and staffed the state authorities with no single pillar holding a majority position. Major social fields like education, unions, political parties, and even recreation activities have been organised along these divided lines. Although this 'pillar system' has become increasingly less prominent, the Dutch political system remained an example of a negotiating political state structure and society. The key feature of this structure has been that social problems, conflicts, and so on were not so frequently debated in open politicised and polarised discussions, after which the majority 'ruled' what to do. Rather, such issues were left to be handled by the so-called 'social midfield' in which a consensus was looked for, and then functioned as a starting point for action. This social midfield consisted of all kinds of welfare and education organisations representing the aforementioned 'pillars'. Conflicts in the Dutch situation were taken care of by social arrangements, negotiations, consensus and through welfare services and subsidies. This is in contrast, for instance, to the British judicial tradition in which a prominent place is given to legislation, presumably due to the competitive and bipartisan structure of the British nation state.

In the Netherlands, the so-called negotiating coalition system, as well as the general condemnation of everything that 'smells like racism or fascism', contributed to the establishment of contacts and exchange of ideas between the state authorities and anti-racism organisations. An example of this consists of the frequent communication between local politicians and the police with the local *Anti Discriminatie Bureaus*, and the frequent contacts between national anti-racist organisations and national state authorities. The Dutch state has also been very active (one may even say 'paternalistic') including minority organisations within a specific negotiating system which formed an important element in the minority policies in the 1980s (see Rath, 1991). This negotiating system was also used in situations of increasing concern with respect to racist violence such as in 1992.

These general differences in the political structures and societies involved have been shown to be of importance in the different ways in which racist violence reached the public and formal agendas in the three countries. In this respect, it is important to note that major disturbances, an increase in the number of 'threatening' examples of self-defence groups and increasing attention for racist violence perpetrated by state authorities (i.e. the police) contributed to the progression of racist violence to the next phases (C and D) in Britain. These were all factors which were regarded as destabilising society in one way or another. In France, racist violence entered into the next phases after severe incidents occurred which attracted massive media attention and which therefore could no longer be neglected (series of racist murders in 1973 and 1982–83 and Carpentras in 1990). Another influential factor was the emergence of the *Front National* when it began to be perceived as a serious threat to French political stability (Castles and Miller, 1993: 133).

In the Netherlands trigger events have also been influential (the murder of Kerwin Duinmeijer in 1983; Amersfoort in 1991), although the scale and intensity of the reported violence was relatively low compared to France or Britain. The increasing support for the extreme right seemed to constitute another (more influential) triggering factor for increasing attention to issues of discrimination and racism, and indirectly, for racist violence. This influence was not so much caused by the fear of political instability. In fact, to deny this influence has always been a motive for authorities and others who did not want to pay too much attention to the extreme right. Rather, the emergence of the Dutch extreme right functioned as a trigger in the same way, and for the same reasons, as did the occurrence of the 'occasional recognition' type of state response to racist violence.

In other words, the general differences in political structures and in closely connected relations between state authorities and anti-racist organisations were reflected in the chances these organisations had of achieving their goals. This has also been reflected in the (threatening) severity and intensity of specific events and processes which accelerated the construction of racist violence as a social problem and brought this issue on to the public and formal agendas.

Not (only) a state task in phase C

In the first half of the 1980s, the French, but more so the Dutch, showed examples of state responses in which racism in general, and racist violence in particular, were recognised not only as constituting social problems, but also as something which should be mainly tackled by external (non-state) actors. In France, the main state responses consisted of the adjustment of existing anti-discrimination legislation, making it easier for organisations such as MRAP to continue their anti-racism work with the use of judicial procedures. In the Netherlands, state responses included the 'top-down' initiative by state authorities in establishing the National Office for Combating Racism (LBR) and initiatives in supporting the local *Anti Discrminatie Bureaus* financially. Because these initiatives were directed at improving the work of external actors and because of the lack of other concrete state action, the perception remained that combating racism/racist violence was primarily a task for these non-state organisations rather than for state agencies. This was also explicitly referred to in the report by the city of Amsterdam in 1983, which stressed the major responsibility of actors, writers and other well-known people in this respect.

The difference here between the French and Dutch situation is the fact that the support by the Dutch state for anti-racism (and other) organisations reflected the importance given to the so-called social midfield. Therefore, this emphasis on the role of external actors as a 'natural' consequence of mainstream state and society discourse. It has been noted that in France the implementation of changes in legislation in favour of the work of these private organisations was predominantly the result of the particular Socialist government at the time. It did not constitute an example of 'normal practice' in French society as it did in the Netherlands.

The British situation in this respect has been quite different. The Race Relations Acts 1965 and 1967 were not implemented at times when racist violence constituted an issue on the public (or on the formal) agenda, and the British state itself set up organisations to implement these Acts (for instance the Commission for Racial Equality). Besides that, other private anti-racism organisations in Britain did not receive financial support at all from the state and were often labelled as 'radicals', 'leftists', 'extremists' by state authorities and media. The British situation in this respect showed the dominant perception that conflicts had to be regulated (partly at least) by legislation, and that the introduction, as well as the implementation, of this legislation were predominantly state (controlled) tasks.

Riots as accelerators

Riots, disorders, or disturbances have played an important role in increasing public awareness of the living conditions of minority communities including their policing because many major riots were said to have been instigated by racist incidents and racist policing. An important difference in this respect was that in Britain (early 1980s) and France (1980s and 1990s) riots have mainly been portrayed as clashes *between* minority (youth) communities and the state authorities themselves (mainly the police). While in the Netherlands (in the 1970s) they were mainly perceived as being between different communities with the police as by-standers. In the Netherlands, the police became targets only when they began to attempt to intervene. Their initial passiveness was perceived by certain rioting groups as tacit support for their actions. It should be noted that this occurred when the rioting groups were Dutch, not when they came from within minority communities. Similar developments have been reported in the British situation during the late 1940s and 1950s, but have not been repeated since. The distinction between community-community clashes and community-state clashes is important because it either led to, or emphasised notions in, mainstream discourses about minority communities.

These discourses will be elaborated upon later, but it should be noted that major clashes between perceived representatives of these communities and the state (police) have been presented in political and media statements as examples of the alleged violent and criminal character of these communities. In the major clashes in the Netherlands, emphasis has also been put on the alleged causes within these communities (non-conformity, grouping together, and so on), but less emphasis has been placed on the connection with aggressive, violent or even criminal characteristics. On the contrary, in the Dutch perceptions of these riots, minority communities have at least partly been presented as victims. These respective perceptions of minority communities either as perpetrators of violence and crime themselves or as victims have played an important role as accelerators at those times when racist violence entered the public agenda. It has meant that mainstream perceptions of minority communities as perpetrators of violence and crime have been difficult to reconcile with the perception of 'them' as victims (of racist violence). This has been the case in France and more so in Britain, but less in the Netherlands.

No panic in phase C and D

The Dutch negotiation structure and the way in which social problems, conflicts and tensions were 'handled' and left to the social midfield has helped to develop a high level of sensitivity within the political elite and general Dutch mainstream discourse and the view that panics, for whatever reason, had to be prevented. This was especially true for subjects connected to racism, resulting from a historical sensitivity towards this topic, explained earlier.

Examples are numerous in which public opinion leaders and state authorities urged the public not to 'exaggerate' the level, intensity and significance of the violence in the country. This was a dominant element in state responses in all phases through which racist violence passed on its way to the formal agenda, but especially when the topic reached a level of broader concern (public agenda). The relative frequency of the 'occasional recognition' of racist violence might partly have been a consequence of this sentiment too. Thus, the notion of preventing any panic and exaggeration was often accompanied by a general perception of condemnation and disapproval of the possible racist nature of an incident.

Although nothing points at 'a lust for panics' in Britain and France, the prevention of such panic was relatively unimportant in these latter two countries. Here state responses to the entrance of racist violence on the public agenda were no different from responses in earlier phases. Responses did depend largely on the specific trigger events which brought the issue onto the agendas, as well as the specific state authority responding. From a Dutch perspective one could argue that French and British authorities often waited a long time before they started to respond, and sometimes until the perceived situation 'really got out of hand'. The Dutch perception of the situations in France and Britain in this respect functioned as an argument for 'nipping it in the bud'.

Defining racist violence in phase D

When the topic of racist violence entered the formal agenda, state action was considered and often implemented. Before turning to the actual content of the action, however, an important difference between the three states has to be discussed in relation to the specific notion of the violence itself, because the specified notion at least partly determined the resulting action. The figures in the Appendix show the enormous differences in the numbers of recorded racist incidents. One reason for the large discrepancy is that different notions and definitions are used in the three countries. In Britain, many debates and discussion have been directed at the definitions and terminology. The official state reports referred to 'racial violence' emphasising the difference of 'race' between the perpetrator and victim of the violent incident and the 'racial motivation' of the perpetrator.

The 1981 Home Office report on *Racial Attacks* introduced this official notion and the perception and definition linked with it. Gordon argued that this meant a redefinition of the problem:

It was not about racist attacks as such – that is, attacks motivated in some way and to some extent by racism. Rather it was about *interracial* incidents or attacks and was thus equally concerned with attacks on white people either by Afro-Caribbeans or Asians as it was with racist attacks properly speaking. It [the 1981 Report] chose instead to follow popular 'common sense' racist ideas which equate attacks on black people with ordinary criminal attacks on white people where the attacker was thought to be black.

(Gordon, 1993: 170)

This was shown by the perception of the British police of 'racial violence' also, in the late 1970s and early 1980s, in which the notion 'race' was connected with the presence of 'black' people rather than with the presence of racist ideologies and practices. At first, 'racial violence', according to this perception, even included concerted action directed against the police (Bowling, 1993b: 10–11).

In the Netherlands, as well as in France, the notion of 'racial violence' has never been used to describe this violence. If recognised as motivated by racist ideas, a violent incident has been perceived to be a matter of 'racist violence'. In both states, however, racist violence has often been perceived exclusively as being perpetrated by marginal groups or organisations, both inside and outside the country. As Lloyd noted in the case of France, the 'problem with this official view is that it removes a general responsibility from French society, regarding racial violence either originating in marginal groups (the extreme right or pathologist social groups such as skinheads) or in external events (again, a pathologist category of international or foreign affairs)' (Lloyd, 1993: 215). The same could be said about the Netherlands.

These French and Dutch perceptions and implicit definitions have had several implications. First, the motives of perpetrators of racist violence were required to be clearly racist (politically and ideologically) before an incident was recognised by state authorities as racist. Secondly, the perceptions and definitions were oriented only to the real or alleged perpetrators and no notice was given to the experiences and perception of the victim(s). Also no attention was paid to racist violence, contrary to some other kinds of violence, as directed towards specific minority communities which feel themselves threatened and victimised whether or not they actually are attacked individually. Thirdly, the relatively small number of 'clearly racist' incidents were officially condemned by the state, but the resultant small extent of the 'problem' was immediately emphasised. Fourthly, the official state recognition of racist violence as a social problem has been much harder to achieve, because racist violence was perceived, by definition, as a characteristic of the (marginal) periphery of society. The accelerating function of anti-semitic violence in this context has been explained above.

In explaining these different notions, as well as the different outcomes in state actions, we have to turn to three major historical processes which all have had an influential and even determining impact. These are the processes of *(de)colonisation* and *migration*, as well as *the Second World War*.

One of the consequences of the experience of the Second World War was the total exclusion of the notion of 'race' from public and political discourse in the Netherlands and France. The notion of 'race' was perceived as a synonym for, and an inextricable symbol of, the racist Nazi discourse of German occupation and was therefore totally banned from popular discourse after the war.

The negative connotations of the notion of 'race' [in France and the Netherlands] have helped to ensure that it has largely disappeared from official political and much everyday discourse. Explicit references to human differentiation in terms of a fixed biological ranking and sustained by assertions of congenital inferiority are equally rare (although belief in the existence of 'races' remains widespread).

(Miles, 1993: 82–3)

The situation in Britain has been very different. The notion of 'race' remained in use, referring to categories of people who differed from one another with respect to phenotypical and ethnic characteristics.

These differences among the three countries of course had a determining impact on the perception and definition of 'racist violence'. Before explaining the different impact, however, we have to include other major influences on the mainstream notions of this violence which differed among the three countries.

In the context of this study, it is important to stress the differences among the three countries in relation to the processes of colonisation and decolonisation. There is a continuous debate about the relation between colonialism and today's racism and whether or not one may speak of 'new' racism in the 1990s (see e.g. Hall, S., 1978; Barker, 1981; Miles, 1989; 1994a; 1994b; Rattansi, 1994; Solomos and Back, 1994). In short, the debate concentrates on whether colonial racism and today's racism are similar. Increasingly, but still highly contested, the idea that one should talk about various historical racisms, always in a process of transformation has gained ground. The expression and content of these racisms are closely related to different socioeconomic, political, historical contexts. However, this also means that racism in the three countries today cannot be seen without taking into account their history as colonial empires, although nowadays differences in expression and content are obvious.

Generally speaking, British and Dutch colonialism was referred to as 'exploitation colonialism', targeted mainly at the economic exploitation of the colonies and their populations and characterised by indirect rule. French colonialism, however, was characterised by direct rule and consisted of a form of 'settlers' colonialism' in which economic exploitation coincided with the intended implementation of the French 'way of life and culture' (see for more details on these processes, e.g. Fanon, 1952; 1961; Phizacklea and Miles, 1980; Miles, 1982; Rex, 1983; 1986; Nederveen Pieterse, 1989; Fryer, 1991; Hiro, 1992). 'In actual practice the British [and the Dutch] were detached and pragmatic, while the French set about the task of propagating their culture with true missionary zeal' (Freeman, 1979: 32).

This constituted an important element in the dominant French 'One People, One Culture' discourse in the post-colonial era which did not allow room for rapid recognition of racist violence as a structural problem in French society. In France and Britain, people from (former) colonies once settled in the mother country were confronted by racist expressions closely related to elements of the colonial discourse. In the Netherlands this is also the case, yet to a much lesser degree (see Schuster, 1996). This is important in relation to broader contexts in which migration, and later racist violence, entered the formal agendas. This issue is elaborated upon in more detail in connection with the processes of migration in the three countries.

After the Second World War, all three nation-states, in their roles as colonial empires, were confronted with the process of decolonisation. The road to independence for the French colony of Algeria consisted of a long and bloody war from 1954 until 1962. This was was not restricted to Algerian territories, but had violent and murderous consequences within France too, as shown. Although the decolonisation of the Dutch Indies involved military action (so-called police action), it was not comparable in scale to the French experience. The decolonisation of the Dutch Caribbean colony of Surinam and that of the British colonies (except in the case of Malaya and Kenya) were not accompanied by military engagement with armies of the colonised states. The latter decolonisation processes were more or less 'arranged' and 'negotiated' instead of forced by military means.

Migration

Since 1945, the three nation-states have witnessed four distinct migration movements: (1) of owners of wealth and managerial and technical staff of international companies; (2) of (industrial) workers; (3) of subjects originating from (former) colonies, often nationals of the host society; and (4) of refugees and asylum-seekers. The total percentage of these migrants is more or less similar in all three countries – some 5–7 per cent of the total population. All three states have been actively involved in attracting labour migrants. However, the British recruitment scheme was fairly small and operated only until 1951 (Castles and Miller, 1993: 68). And it should be noted that the overall net flow of migration to Britain has been an outward one during the whole post-war period (Layton-Henry, 1992: 2). In contrast, the French and Dutch state administrations were actively involved in attracting labour migrants to work in their expanding industries in the 1950s and 1960s (Miles, 1993: 151). Particularly in France, this was due to the enormous loss of people in the war(s). Both state administrations were actively involved in recruiting, although many labour migrants arrived in both countries due to economic recruitment outside state procedures. The main migration movement of labour in these two countries decreased considerably due to economic developments in the aftermath of the first oil crisis, as well as to the fundamental restructuring of the labour process (see Castles, 1993: 22–3; Castles and Miller, 1993: 77).

One of the consequences of these different levels of state involvement in labour migration was the feeling that immigration was connected to the perceived utility of foreign labour. In the 1970s, the French generally perceived immigration as economically useful, while the British did not (Freeman, 1979: 266–7). The Dutch situation more or less reflected that of the French, although it was felt less strongly in the Netherlands (Groenendijk, 1990).

To varying degrees and starting at different times, all three states have attempted to exclude migrants from former colonies from entering the 'Mother Country'. At first, these specific groups of immigrants were entitled to the nationality of the 'Mother Country' due to colonial occupation rules. The perceptions of these different types of immigration and the reception of the various immigrant communities were different in each case and between the three nation-states. However, all three have shown instances in which immigration in general, and specific 'categories' of immigrants in particular, have been problematised. Immigration and specific immigrant populations have increasingly been perceived and handled as potentially problematic and as having to be 'managed' by the state.

In Britain, this process of problematisation began to be prominent in mainstream public and political discourses in the 1950s. In France, this started in the late 1960s; in the Netherlands, first indications of this process were evident in the early 1970s. This coincided with the emergence of 'common' public and political awareness of the permanent settlement of immigrants from former colonies and with moments of perceived or real threats of socioeconomic setback or even depression. These processes became more acute in Britain in the 1970s, and in all three countries from the 1980s onwards. Reference has been made here to mainstream public and political discourses. Cabinet and other political state discussions and debates 'behind closed doors' on alleged social problems in relation to immigration already existed before the periods mentioned. Processes are shown in which state authorities responded to alleged problems of which they themselves (at least partly) have been the initiators (the problematisation process).

The character of the immigration changed due to global and national economic and political changes and decisions.

The ensuing recession [1973–4] gave impetus to a restructuring of the world economy, involving capital investment in new industrial areas, altered patterns of world trade, and introduction of new technologies. The result was a second phase in international migration, starting in the mid-1970s and gaining momentum in the late 1980s and early 1990s.

(Castles and Miller, 1993: 65)

Predominant images that were held about these groups of immigrants were based on the idea that their presence caused negative social developments, especially isolation, deprivation, crime and disorder. These were mainly grounded in assumptions that these immigrants were of different culture, 'race' and/or religion – factors which were perceived to be incompatible with the way of life, 'race', culture or religion of the host society. In other words, these groups of immigrants and their descendants were regarded as unable to adjust to the imagined community of the nation-state. The issue of (certain movements of) immigration reached the formal agenda repeatedly in all three countries – increasingly so in recent times. Later, immigration consisted predominantly of EC citizens, refugees and asylum-seekers from Eastern Europe and the Asian and African continents or were due to family reunion of earlier migrant settlers. Immigration control and restrictions have been implemented by all three states. Immigration debates and implemented restrictions not only influenced the chances of those trying to enter the three nations, but also directly influenced everyday life of groups of the people, or their descendants, who were already living in these countries.

The perception of immigrants in general, and from former colonies in particular, however, did differ in each nation-state. In France, over 2 million people 'returned' from the colonies. Among them were not only French settlers (*colons*), but also Algerians who had never been in France before (*pied noirs*). One effect of the Algerian War was the extremely negative context within which the position of Algerian workers in France was questioned and discussed publicly (Freeman, 1979: 81–2). In the Netherlands, Dutch settlers, as well as Eurasian people from Indonesia who had never been in the Netherlands before, 'returned'. Their immigration, however, was not so much perceived as the consequence of Indonesia going independent after a lost war, but more as the result of international political pressure (especially by the United Nations and the United States) on the Netherlands to withdraw from the Dutch Indies. Therefore these immigrants were perceived as repatriates (most of them with Dutch nationality) and as refugees who had to be welcomed and taken care of. The reception of Eurasians, therefore, was a task executed by the Ministry of Welfare. Several public statements by government ministers and officials have been made in which the Dutch population was called upon to feel responsible for receiving these people in a positive manner (see Schuster, 1996).

The situation in Britain was very different again from that in the Netherlands and France. Here, people from former colonies migrated to the 'Mother Country' as British citizens and were perceived as labour migrants. In fact, the recruitment scheme for labour immigration was stopped in 1951, because 'it was easier to make use of colonial workers' (Castles and Miller, 1993: 68). The immigrants were perceived and protrayed as arriving of their own volition in search of economic security. This presented them in terms of extra competition in labour and housing markets but their arrival was seen neither as a consequence of losing colonies nor as an inevitability for which the people involved could not be blamed and therefore they had to be looked after.

In all three nation-states, certain 'categories' of immigrants and their descendants have been perceived as 'sources of social and economic problems'. With the increasing awareness of the permanent character of immigrant settlement, all three nation-states have emphasised the obligation of these problematised migrant communities to integrate or to assimilate. The symbolic use of the concept of integration has a corresponding result in the representation of certain perceived social problems, such as unemployment and crime, as consequences of immigration and as characteristic of migrant populations (Miles, 1993: 180). Therefore, chances of successful integration always have been connected to (further) immigration restrictions.

These political responses and immigration policies, and the manner in which measures were taken, created and validated prejudices and racism among the general public in all the three countries. However, the similar emphasis on integration raised differences too. While the word might be the same in translation, and might have the same general object, the idea of integration had discrete nuances and refers to distinct practices in each nation state. In other words, while the French, Dutch and British states all claim to be implementing a policy of integration, what is meant differs because the structure of the nation, and the nature of its imagining, varies.

(Miles, 1993: 176)

In Britain, specific groups of people of immigrant origin were perceived as belonging to 'a different race'. Relations between the specific immigrant communities and the mainstream white British communities were perceived as 'race relations' – in other words, as relations between different 'races'. Implicit in this discourse is the notion, that 'They' and 'We' might have good or bad relations, but remain 'different by nature'. In this discourse, 'racial discrimination' could be combated by legislative measures, but 'natural differences' could not. In France, the dominant discourse perceives all French citizens as belonging to 'one people' with 'one culture'. For years, the exclusionist and discriminating practices directed against certain groups of immigrant origin have been neglected or explicitly denied as existing. 'In other words, the best way to combat racism was to keep it buried from view' (Freeman, 1979: 109). Accordingly, state responses could only include immigration control and measures to prevent concentrations of 'foreigners' in particular settings (Freeman, 1979: 161). Central in French discourse was the notion that immigrants had to integrate, and actually assimilate. For that reason, specific rights or policies directed towards minorities would directly lead to racism (Castles and Miller, 1993: 225).

The situation in France and Britain was different from that in the Netherlands. In the late 1970s, it was obvious that groups of immigrant origin were 'here to stay' and especially after terrorist actions by Moluccan youths, so-called minority policies were developed to 'help' these groups integrate into Dutch society. The experiences with the Moluccan community showed the direction in which this integration was expected to develop. 'Integration with the preservation of one's own culture' was the key element in the minority policies of the late 1970s and early 1980s. The preservation of one's culture still referred to the assumption that many immigrants would at some point return to their country of origin. Anti-discrimination regulations and subsidies for cultural activities of these communities were major elements of these policies. In the late 1980s, however, this discourse changed when the emphasis shifted increasingly to problems of the labour market position of a majority of these communities and especially to their own 'responsibility' for their bad socioeconomic position. 'Integration' became one central aspect of policy, immigration control the other. The emergence of the integration issue pointed implicitly to an increasing awareness that the immigrant communities were here to stay.

Discourses and racialisation

In all three nation-states processes of racialisation are shown, although these processes have been portrayed and discussed in different ways in each country. These differences are partly due to different experiences during the Second World War, the way in which (de)colonisation took place, the colonial and racist discourses and the dominant discourse in relation to perceived 'political correctness'.

To describe the Dutch situation, Rath (1991; 1993) distinguishes the process of 'racialisation' (see Miles, 1989; 1993) from what he calls 'the process of minorisation'. Minority groups in relation to racialisation are perceived as 'unadjustable by nature' to the 'indigenous way of life'. Minorisation points to the perception of groups as 'capable of adjustment', especially after involvement by the state and welfare organisations. The key element of minorisation in the Netherlands is the image of minorities as not conforming to the Dutch 'middle-class way of life'. According to the dominant discourses, this sociocultural non-conformity can and ought to be changed. According to Rath, this is in contrast to a situation of racialisation (especially in Britain) in which people cannot change their 'race'.

Rath refers to the so-called anti-socials in the Netherlands – a category of indigenous people who constitute the lowest sections of society and who exhibited undesirable behaviour, according to (and categorised by) the state and private institutions, during the 1930s and 1950s to 1960s. They were perceived as capable of 'adjusting' themselves, albeit through so-called adjustment training programmes. Minorities are also perceived, and approached, in this way in the Netherlands, according to Rath (1993: 222–3).

Rath, however, leaves out one important and decisive distinction between these so-called 'anti-socials' in the 1930s to 1950s and minorities in the 1970s to 1990s. This concerns the alleged phenotypical and cultural differences between the two constructed categories of people. The former category of 'anti-socials' was not constructed by reference to visibly different characteristics – minorities are. In other words, even if minorities are constructed in the dominant Dutch discourse as 'capable of adjusting to the dominant Dutch way of life', they remain perceived (in the street, in the minds of a majority of employers, politicians and elsewhere) as groups of 'unadjusted' people.

They are categorised by non-conformity which is indirectly constructed around alleged phenotypical and cultural characteristics. Their actual categorisation is based on their national, religious, and cultural origin which is negatively evaluated as 'not being adjusted or integrated'. This dominant Dutch discourse – and practice – does not allow for a distinction between individuals within these minority groups who 'are adjusted' and those who 'are not' (yet). It is precisely for this reason that individuals from within these groups – even those who are highly educated and have a perfect knowledge of the 'Dutch tongue' (the main reason according to the dominant discourse for exclusion in the labour market) – are often still excluded, for instance when they apply for a job (Bovenkerk, 1992). We can therefore speak of racialisation in the Netherlands too.

More or less the same can be said with respect to France. 'Culture' and not 'race' constitutes the dominant characteristic used to describe and perceive specific minorities in France. The French mainstream discourse presents

the 'cultural' characteristics and, in the same process of perception, assumes them to be physical or physiological. This mode of entry merges with the former way of perceiving 'race'. The syncretic core of racist ideology remains intact. The cult of 'difference' means that we can perceive 'race' through cultural characteristics instead of physical ones. This is still on the same ideological level since both posit a different and irreducible 'nature' of human groups.

(Guillaumin, 1991: 13)

In summary, the categorisation of specific minorities in the dominant discourse constructed on 'culture' is similar to that based on specific 'unchangeable' – i.e. phenotypical – characteristics, which are evaluated negatively (i.e. 'non-assimilative'). Thus, what we see in the three countries involved is a similar process of racialisation, which is based on the notion of 'race' in Britain, and on the notion of culture and ethnicity in France and the Netherlands. Of course, the different notions at the core of these racialisation processes are important to understand the process of each individual country. But it is important to understand that such a process occurred in all three countries. What we see here is that racialisation processes manifest themselves in plural and complex forms. In the words of Solomos and Back (1994: 156): 'This means that racisms may be expressed through a variety of coded signifiers.' One such expression is the coding of race as culture in France and the Netherlands.

These differences in discourses are due also to different levels of politicisation of issues like immigration. In France – and for that matter in the Netherlands too – these issues were less politicised than in Britain, due to differences in the structure of the policy machineries (see e.g. Freeman, 1979: 118–19). 'A major difference between the immigration policy processes of France [as well as the Netherlands] and Britain is the greater extent to which British policy has been formulated in the public arena and embodied in major legislative acts' (Freeman, 1992: 30). These differences have an uneven effect in the three nation-states and on the different ways in which the three states have been responding to the phenomenon of racist violence.

Seuil de tolérance *in phase D*

A difference in state responses to racist violence among the three nation-states consisted of reference to the so-called *seuil de tolérance* – 'employed mainly as part of a strategy of spatial or territorial exclusion' (MacMaster, 1991: 14). In state responses to racist violence, this reference has been especially used in the Netherlands and France, but hardly heard of in the British situation. This may be explained by the different perception and position with respect to integration and assimilation in the three countries. Since the late 1980s, French and Dutch state authorities have been emphasising the necessity of integration (and assimilation) of specific minority communities. In this context and in instances of violent clashes and incidents, state authorities have often argued that the size of the minority population needed to be restricted to a certain percentage of the total local/neighbourhood population. In the Netherlands as well as in France, discussions were raised every now and then about policies to prevent the concentration of immigrant communities within individual neighbourhoods.

These discussions have been remarkable because the critical limits mentioned have differed over a period of time in accordance with the actual average percentages of people present. After the Rotterdam riots in 1971, for instance, statements were heard in which the percentage of the minority population in individual neighbourhoods should be limited to some 5 per cent. In the late 1980s and early 1990s, the argued limitation figures went up to some 15 per cent, which coincided with the actual average percentage of the minority population in the larger cities at that moment. Despite the presentation of *seuil de tolérance* as a 'natural' threshold, the state responses cited a need to halt further immigration, whatever the present resident percentage, rather than use arguments about the neighbourhood's capacity for absorption.

The situation in Britain has been quite different because of the dominance of the 'race' and 'race relations' discourse. Although discussions on territorial quota existed in Britain too, the discourse of 'race and race relations' implies that integration, or even assimilation, were much more difficult to achieve, if possible at all. Within the dominant discourse, including the existence of distinctive 'races' based on unchangeable characteristics, the only 'reasonable' policies were directed at a peaceful coexistence between the different so-called races. Therefore, the improvement of 'race relations' has been perceived as one of the few concrete goals of the state with respect to racist violence.

The influence of the political, ideological and popular discourses on the 'excluding recognition' of racist violence by state authorities has been reported with respect to the notion of *seuil de tolérance* in order to preserve law and order. In France and the Netherlands, measures have been proposed, and sometimes even implemented, to limit or reduce the size of minority communities present in certain areas, in order to give a 'better chance' to the 'assimilation/integration' perceived to be necessary. In Britain, measures have been implemented to improve relations between different communities.

'Including recognition' in phase D

The way in which the 'including recognition' type of state response has been enacted has been different in the three nation-states after racist violence entered on to the formal agenda. In the 1981 Home Office report, British state authorities officially recognised racist violence as constituting a social problem which had to be combated by the state. In the continuation of this report, the so-called multi-agency approach has been developed as an instrument to combat racist violence. The 1981 report, as well as the multi-agency approach, are examples of the 'including recognition' of racist violence, because the main goal was to prevent and to suppress circumstances favourable to perpetrators of racist violence and to do so with the cooperation of the victimised minority groups. The last point, however, remains a point for criticism, because there have been examples of representatives of victimised groups being excluded from participation on political grounds. None the less, the multi-agency approach could be characterised as an example of 'including recognition' by state authorities. Experiments have been executed and plans and procedures have been refined and extended. In 1995, this approach is still presented by state authorities as the single best answer to the issue. The multi-agency approach could be perceived as the local answer to improving local community relations. The British 'race (relations)' discourse is an eminent achievement in the 'including recognition' of racist violence.

In France, some attempts have been made to introduce programmes to combat racist violence in the 'including recognition' manner. The Rocard proposals in early 1990 were examples of such an 'including recognition' of racist violence by state authorities. However, most of these proposals were not implemented. This failure has been due mainly to a failure to attract the support of all established political parties and the perceived need to do so. Very quickly discussions concentrated on the assumed link between anti-racism measures and immigration restrictions and on the debate as to whether anti-racism measures could be discussed and implemented at all without debating and restricting migration. So far, real examples of 'including recognition' measures by the French state have rarely got any further than the proposal stage or at best to a better recording of racist violence. No real measures have been implemented to combat racist violence in an 'including recognition' way. Some symbolic statements and actions by state authorities have been noted mainly against political racism and the *Front National* (for instance in 1990 in the direct aftermath of the Carpentras incident), but these symbolic actions were never translated into state policies against racist violence in France. This situation typifies the dominant French discourse which has made it impossible – up until time of writing (1995) – to distinguish between groups of people within their 'One French People' ideal, even when specific groups are perceived to be victimised by specific crimes, i.e. racist violence.

In the Netherlands, the 'including recognition' of racist violence by the state constituted one of two lines of response. In 1992, with the recognised occurrence of a wave of racist violence, state authorities responded on two levels: the public and the behind-the-scenes. In public, the violence and racist nature of incidents were condemned immediately. A declaration against discrimination and racism was even drawn up and signed by state authorities. However, soon statements were made by state authorities playing down the same incidents, arguing that the violence was not organised, that the assumed perpetrator(s) were stupid and that the Dutch situation was not serious compared to the situation abroad – especially in Germany (after Hoyerswerda, 1991). This public response has more or less been a case of denial of the racist nature of the violence, with some examples of the 'occasional recognition' of racist violence.

Behind the scenes however, instructions were sent out to police forces and local and provincial authorities to be very alert and to report any incident which might include an element of racism. Several examples of this alertness were demonstrated by the police, arresting police who tried to disturb anti-racist or multicultural happenings, or who tried to organise a Nazi skinhead concert or arresting people shouting racist slogans during football matches. This behind the scenes approach was a clear example of an 'including recognition' type of state response to racist violence. Predominantly, the intention of the public response appears to have been to prevent panic about racist violence and to prevent the perception of racist violence as a serious social problem in the Netherlands.

The intention of the behind the scenes response was to take every sign of racist violence very seriously and to try to prevent any incident from occurring. The specific characteristics of this Dutch double way of responding was to make it seem to the outside world as if nothing serious had happened. To prevent feelings of insecurity or mistrust within minority communities, minority organisations were invited to a meeting by the Home Secretary, who informed them that the state was taking the situation seriously. This reflects the dominant position of the role of the social midfield in Dutch society, given and organised by the state itself, but it did not prevent some minority organisations from questioning state action, or lack of it, after some months of police investigations did not produce any results.

Timing of all the phases

One of the main differences in the history of state responses to racist violence in Britain, France and the Netherlands were differences in timing. These differences have been shown in all phases of the construction process of racist violence on its way to the formal agenda. In the late 1960s and 1970s, racist violence began to be recognised as a social problem by several sections within British society (phase B). This was not the case in France until the first half of the 1980s, and in the Netherlands only temporarily in the early 1980s, but mainly since the early 1990s.

The entrance of racist violence on to the British, French and Dutch public (phase C) and formal (phase D) agendas also took place at different periods of time. In Britain, racist violence was perceived to enter the public agenda in 1979–81 with debates on assumed causes of the riots, including racism in general, and racist violence in particular. In France, racist violence entered the public agenda due to major demonstrations by anti-racism movements after a series of incidents was reported in the early 1980s, and at a later stage, by specific racist incidents in the late 1980s and early 1990s. In the Netherlands, the murder of Kerwin Duinmeijer brought the issue of racist violence to the public agenda temporarily in 1984, and so did events in Germany and in the Netherlands in the early 1990s.

As for the formal agenda racist violence in Britain officially entered this stage temporarily in 1958, and more permanently in 1981. In France, racist violence found a place on this agenda in a totally different context during the Algerian War (1954–62), and later in 1990. In the Netherlands, racist violence was never really an issue on the formal agenda until the early 1990s.

These differences in timing might be explained by differences in several processes mentioned above. The arrival of racist violence as 'political terrorism' on the French formal agenda is explained by the historical context of the Algerian War of Independence. But in the construction of racist violence (as such) as a topic on the formal agenda, differences in timing have to be explained by differences in the socioeconomic processes as well as differences in (mainstream) discourses, especially those concerning specific periods of immigration and minority populations.

The entrance of the topic on the British formal agenda in the late 1950s was caused by an increasing awareness of, and concern for, the permanent settlement of (colonial) labour immigrants in relation to the early onset of economic stagnation in Britain (Castles and Miller, 1993: 71). An accelerator in this construction process were the 1958 disorders, with the Commonwealth Immigrants Act 1962 the eventual concrete outcome of this process. The arrival of immigrants from the (former) colonies was perceived differently in France and the Netherlands compared to Britain (as explained on pp. 190–193). The main perspective on labour immigration in France and the Netherlands was the alleged temporary presence of the immigrants. The awareness and concern about permanent settlement of (labour) immigrants did not reach the surface until the mid-1970s. The ensuing recession in the early 1970s (after the oil crisis in 1973–74) marked a turning point in the French and Dutch mainstream perception on immigration and immigrant communities. At that same time in Britain, a process of problematisation and criminalisation of specific minority communities had already been set in motion. These processes did not become dominant in France until the 1980s and in the Netherlands until the late 1980s and early 1990s.

In these different periods of problematisation and criminalisation, and under dramatically changing socioeconomic conditions, unemployment increased, and anti-immigrant political movements (outside and inside established political parties) began to attract support. State authorities and others increasingly expressed their concern about the immigration issue, leading in all three countries to restrictive policies. These processes contributed to the construction of racist violence as a social problem – directly by internal state actors and indirectly by external actors. Eventually, in all three countries (albeit at different times) this led to the inclusion of the issue of racist violence on the formal agendas (phase D). This occurred in a context in which emphasis was placed on the 'excluding recognition' type of state response, although some examples of 'including recognition' have been noted since.

Trends in state responses to racist violence

In the previous two sections, similarities and differences in state responses to racist violence since 1950 in Britain, France and the Netherlands have been presented. Increasingly, however, a trend has been notable in which the differences seem to vanish. Political and ideological discourses, in general, as well as state responses to racist violence in particular increasingly corresponded with each other in the three nation-states. There has been a dominant perception in Britain which presented the British situation in this respect as being just ahead of those in other Western European countries. This study has shown that this perception does not really hold.

Similarities between Britain, France and the Netherlands have been obvious, but differences have been so manifold and of such importance that one definitely cannot conclude that France and the Netherlands are 'moving on the same path' as Britain with the only difference a slight time lag. The three countries have their own specific histories with respect to the perception of racist violence and state responses to it. Of course the similarities should not be ignored, but neither should the differences which construct a major part of today's occurrences and responses.

Especially since the late 1980s and early 1990s one increasingly notices policy measures and alternatives converging in all three nation-states. One of the characteristics of the early 1990s is the representation of perceived and expected increases of demographic movements as threats to British, French and Dutch (i.e. 'European') 'ways of life'. Since the late 1980s, state authorities in the three countries involved were cooperating in, and implementing, measures to limit the entrance of new immigrants (see Joly and Cohen, 1989; Joly, 1992; Webber, 1993a; 1993b; Castles and Miller, 1993; Wrench and Solomos, 1993;

Cohen, 1994; Cornelius, Martin and Hollyfield, 1994). Frequently, these activities coincided with public and political debates about the 'threat of immigration which would also have an influence on the 'everyday life of groups of people of immigrant origin' already resident in these countries. Often these minority groups were at the core of the debates. On several occasions there was a problematisation and even criminalisation of specific communities. To summarise, all three countries have shown an increasingly dominant discourse presenting a link between immigration restrictions and 'good integration and community relations'.

This convergence is caused by globalisation in general, and the Europeanisation in particular, not only of the world economy, but also of political, environmental, military and demographic processes (Castles and Miller, 1993: 93). These processes are characterised by rapid and fundamental economic, social, political and ideological changes (Castles and Miller, 1993: 65). Increasingly, real and imagined problems in these fields shape the European political agenda and form the basis for relations and cooperation between individual European countries, including Britain, France and the Netherlands. This process of increasingly interwoven economic and political relations is reflected in the activities of the European Union. The changes and developments in Eastern Europe in 1989 and the need for, and trends in, restructuring self-perception and self-definition on both a European and a national level have been influential in this respect.

One of the characteristics of this present process consists of the emergence of, and increasing support for, nationalist and racist political ideas, slogans, programmes, discourses and parties. Another characteristic of these changing times is of the representation of real and expected increases in demographic movements as a threat to the 'European way of life'. A third characteristic consists of the intertwined or double-edged policies in all three countries directed towards the proclaimed desire for integration on the one hand and the perceived need for immigration control on the other. This double-edged path reinforces perceptions of immigration as potentially problematic, and certain groups of immigrants as not being included in society. Discriminatory immigration policies do not seem to stop at the immigration process, 'but they can be the first step towards the marginalisation of the future settlers' (Castles and Miller, 1993: 201).

Increasingly racist violence is reported in all three nation-states within this context, and the groups of people excluded from major areas of society (labour market, education, political participation) are reported as being the main targets of the violence. State responses increasingly have tended to be two-faced. Examples of the 'excluding recognition' of racist violence by state authorities have been numerous as shown in this study. However, nothing has led to the conclusion that possible actions of state authorities in this field have been exhausted. Every now and then, new subjects and targets for restrictive policies surface: from labour immigration, family reunion, and 'illegal residency', to asylum-seekers, 'marriages of convenience' and 'tourist asylum-seekers' (see Joly, 1992; Webber, 1993a–b; Cohen, 1994, among others). Often public and political debates and media panics have been followed by new restrictions and adjustments to existing legislation.

On the other hand, all three countries have increasingly provided examples of racist violence being recognised as constituting a serious problem. This, however, has not been a 'smooth' or gradual process. Individual incidents brought the topic of racist violence on to the various agendas temporarily, and policies were proposed or even implemented. The 'including recognition' of racist violence by state authorities has been demonstrated in all three countries, although many of the responses remained merely symbolic. However, practical actions to combat this violence and the circumstances in which it was perceived to flourish have increasingly been present in Britain, France and the Netherlands.

In other words, one may conclude that there is a trend of convergence in state responses to racist violence in Britain, France and the Netherlands. This trend surfaced in the early 1990s, so conclusions or predictions regarding its direction in the future are not possible. The history of the state responses in the three countries, however, makes it certain that these will include ambiguous and 'double-edged' measures in the near future.

Conclusion

Racist violence could be expected to be handled in a similar fashion to many other forms of crime in the three countries involved. At different times, many forms of crime have been defined as constituting a serious problem. Once the phenomenon has entered the formal agenda, specific legal measures are often introduced and implemented by the state to deal with the issue. The history of the phenomenon of racist violence in Britain, France and the Netherlands, however, does not confirm this expectation. The inclusion of the issue on the public and formal agendas has questioned the fundamental principles of the nation-states involved. These questions mainly concern the racist or anti-racist nature of society and state (self-image).

At first, state responses to racist violence mainly consisted of ignoring and denying the racist nature and/or the structural character of the reported violence (phase A). If this was no longer possible, due to mainly external pressure (phase B), the reported violence was associated and correlated with issues of immigration and 'integration' of victimised communities. These issues were, or became, the main ones within the debates and discussions, with the violence treated mainly as a side-effect. Racist violence was not a law and order problem, but a consequence of immigration. In the debates, the state authorities found themselves caught between racist and anti-racist pressure groups and movements. With the immigration issue constituting an increasingly dominant topic on the formal agenda, state responses to racist violence largely consisted of policies of immigration restriction ('excluding recognition'), although some state measures were noted concerning the broader field of anti-discrimination ('including recognition'). Increasingly a convergence in state responses can be seen among the three countries. This convergence is characterised by double-edge state responses with elements of the 'including recognition', as well as of the 'excluding recognition' of racist violence.

Different British, French and Dutch state responses have been reported. The number and importance of these differences have shown three nation-states moving on different paths slowly but steadily, heading towards convergence (of state responses). An important conclusion is that the reported differences are not explained by the processes of immigration, except partly in relation to the moment in time when the phenomenon of racist violence increasingly attracted attention and entered the public and formal agendas. Explanations of the differences in state responses are to be found in historical, political, socio-economical and ideological processes.

The British situation was principally characterised by the politicised public debates on 'race relations', migration and racist violence being shaped within the dominant *'race' discourse*. The British state was the first in this study in which 'racial' violence was recognised as forming a major social problem closely linked to the perceived increase of threats to state security (1980–81) and the politicisation of law and order. Examples of 'including recognition' state responses to racist violence were shown. In line with the mainstream political and ideological discourses, however, racist violence was mainly regarded and dealt with as a matter of law and order and policing specific communities.

The French situation was characterised by *the assimilative discourse* of 'one people, one culture', which hardly allowed the recognition of the phenomenon of racist violence other than as 'common crime'. The exception consisted of the period in which such violence constituted an alleged threat to state security and was perceived as 'political terrorism' in the light of the Algerian War of Independence. Since the late 1960s, the violence was predominantly perceived as 'just more proof' of the assumed existence of a *seuil de tolérance*, and was responded to according to the 'excluding recognition' type of state response. The late 1980s and 1990 showed instances of 'double edged' state responses to racist violence.

The Dutch situation was characterised by a *'paternalistic pragmatic' discourse* which always included double, contradicting strategies to respond to emerging issues and conflicts, with an important role for the so-called social midfield. On the one hand, these strategies consisted of statements and measures playing down possibly disturbing phenomenona, such as racist violence. On the other hand, they consisted of rather strong condemnation and repression to maintain the state's own non-racist, tolerant self-image. The Dutch state was the only one which frequently showed instances of the 'occasional recognition' of specific individual incidents. In the early 1990s, racist violence formed a public and political topic which could no longer be neglected. A 'two-faced' state response was registered, including two lines of response involving not only a front stage (preventing any panic) and a back stage (serious measures to prevent and suppress any occurrences) response, but also measures of the 'excluding recognition' type of state response.

Increasingly differences between the three countries appear to be vanishing. Political and ideological discourses as well as 'double edged' state responses to racist violence have increasingly corresponded with each other, including instances of 'including' and 'excluding recognition' of racist violence by state authorities. This convergence in state responses to racist violence is partly due to political and socioeconomical 'Europeanisation', as well as the European convergence of the so-called migration and integration issues. All three states increasingly have shown themselves to be caught between pressures from racist sentiments, parties and ideologies and pressures from anti-racism movements and ideologies. And state responses have functioned especially to define a self-perception of the nation-state.

Recorded racist incidents in Britain, France and the Netherlands, 1980–93

Britain[1]

	Metropolitan Police	Provinces	Total of Wales and England
1980	277		
1981[2]	727		
1982[3]	1,293		
1983	1,277		
1984	1,515	1,329	2,844
1985	1,945	1,626	3,571
1986	1,733	4,519	6,252
1987	2,179	2,965	5,144
1988	2,214	2,366	4,580
1989	2,697	2,347	5,044
1990	2,908	3,451	6,359
1991	3,373	4,509	7,882
1992	3,227	4,507	7,734
1993[4]	3,889	5,873	9,762

France[5]

	Racist actions	Racist threats	Anti-semitic actions	Total
1980	35	20	75	130
1981	23	23	26	72
1982	43	55	30	128
1983	68	96	21	185
1984	53	102	15	170
1985	70	98	11	179
1986	54	95	2	151
1987	46	80	13	139
1988	64	135	17	216
1989	54	237	18	309
1990	52	283	20	355
1991	51	317	24	392
1992	32	141	20	193
1993	37	134	14	185

The Netherlands[6]

	Right-wing extremist and racist actions[7]
1980	22
1981	13
1982	23
1983	57
1984	62
1985	37
1986	43
1987	13
1988	5
1989	30
1990	37
1991	40
1992	270
1993	352

Notes

1 *Sources*: Until 1982 by the Greater London Council Police Committee (1984: 4); from 1983 up to 1987 by the annual reports by the Commissioner of the Metropolitan Police; from Home Affairs Committee (1989: vi); from 1988 up to 1993 by Hansard, 26 April 1993 and Hansard, 24 June 1994 as cited by Virdee (1995: 15).
2 Until December 1981.
3 May to December 1982 after the introduction of a new system of registration.
4 Covers April 1993 to April 1994.
5 *Source: Commission Nationale Consultative des Droits de l'Homme* (1995: 27 and 37).
6 *Source*: Buis & van Donselaar (1993: 64).
7 Including besmirching actions.

References

Anderson, B. (1983) *Imagined Communities*, London: Verso.

Anne Frank Stichting (1985) *The Extreme Right in Europe and the United States*, Amsterdam.

Anne Frank Stichting (1987) *Vreemd Gespuis*, Amsterdam.

Anthias, F. and N. Yuval-Davis (1993) *Racialized Boundaries: Race, Nation, Gender, Colour and Class and the Anti-racist Struggle*, London: Routledge.

Banton, M. (1992) The Relationship between Racism and Antisemitism, *Patterns of Prejudice*, vol. 26, nos 1 and 2, pp. 17–27.

Barker, M. (1981) *The New Racism: Conservatives and the Ideology of the Tribe*, London: Junction Books.

Beetstra, T.A., C.D.C.J. van Mourik, J.M. Neefe and A.E.M. de Ridder (1994) De sociale constructie van georganiseerde criminaliteit in Nederland, in M. Moerings (1994) *Hoe Punitief Is Nederland?*, Arnhem: Gouda Quint, pp. 237–51.

Benyon, J. (1986) *A Tale of Failure: Race and Policing*, CRER Policy Paper no. 3, University of Warwick, Coventry.

Benyon, J. (1987a) Interpretations of Civil Disorder, in J. Benyon and J. Solomos (eds) *The Roots of Urban Unrest*, Oxford: Pergamon Press, pp. 23–38.

Benyon, J. (1987b) Unrest and the Political Agenda, in J. Benyon and J. Solomos (eds) *The Roots of Urban Unrest*, Oxford: Pergamon Press, pp. 165–79.

Benyon, J. and J. Solomos (eds) (1987) *The Roots of Urban Unrest*, Oxford: Pergamon Press.

Bethnal Green and Stepney Trades Council (BG & STC) (1978) *Blood on the Streets*, London: BG & STC.

Bhikhu Parekh (1994) *Racial Violence: A Separate Offence? A Discussion Paper*, The All-Party Parliamentary Group on Race and Community, Houses of Parliament, Session 1993/94, London: A Charta Mede Associate Company.

Bindman, G. (1994) A Racial Violence and Harassment Bill, *New Community*, vol. 20, no. 3, pp. 526–9.

Björgo, T. and R. Witte (eds) (1993) *Racist Violence in Europe*, London: Macmillan.

Bol, M.W. and B.J.W. Docter-Schamhardt (1993) *Politie en Openbaar Ministerie tegen Rassendiscriminatie*, WODC Onderzoek en Beleid, no. 123, Arnhem: Gouda Quint.

Bouzid (1984) *La Marche, traversée de la France profonde*, Paris: Sinbad.

Bovenkerk, F. (ed) (1978) *Omdat Zij Anders Zijn*, Meppel: Boom.

Bovenkerk, F. (1992) *Testing Discrimination in Natural Experiments:*

A *Manual for International Comparative Research on Discrimination on the Grounds of 'Race' and Ethnic Origin*, Geneva: International Labour Office.

Bovenkerk, F., F. Buijs and H. Tromp (eds) (1990) *Wetenschap en Partijdigheid: Opstellen voor Andre J.K. Köbben*, Assen: Van Gorcum.

Bovenkerk, F., R. Miles and G. Verbunt (1990a) Comparative Studies of Migration and Exclusionism on the Grounds of 'Race' and Ethnic-Background in Western Europe: A Critical Appraisal, *International Migration Review*, vol. XXV, no. 2, pp. 375–91.

Bovenkerk, F., R. Miles and G. Verbunt (1990b) Racism, Migration and the State in Western Europe: A Case for Comparative Analysis, *International Sociology*, vol. 5, no. 4, pp. 475–90.

Bowling, B. (1990) *Policing Racial Violence in Britain*, paper presented in the Learned Society, University of Victoria, British Columbia.

Bowling, B. (1993a) Racial Harassment and the Process of Victimisation: Conceptual and Methodological Implications for the Local Crime Survey, *British Journal of Criminology*, vol. 33, no. 2, pp. 231–49.

Bowling, B. (1993b) Policing Violent Racism: Policy and Practice in an East London Locality, unpublished thesis, Sociology Department, London School of Economics and Political Science.

Bowling, B. and W. Saulsbury (1993) A Local Response to Racial Violence, in T. Björgo and R. Witte (eds), *Racist Violence in Europe*, London: Macmillan, pp. 221–35.

Brants, C.H. and K.L.L. Brants (1991) *De Sociale Constructie van Fraude*, Arnhem: Gouda Quint.

Bridges, L. (1982) Racial Attacks, *Legal Action Group Bulletin*, January, pp. 9–11.

Brink, R. van den, J.M. Cuartes and J. Tanja (1988) *Racisme in Frankrijk: Le Pen in het Land van Vrijheid, Gelijkheid en Broederschap*, Amsterdam: Anne Frank Stichting.

Brown, C. (1984) *Black and White Britain: The Third PSI Survey*, London: Heinemann.

Brundtland, G.H. (1993) Address by the Prime Minister of Norway to the Fourth Part-Session of the 44th Ordinary Session of the Parliamentary Assembly of the Council of Europe, Strasbourg, 4 February.

Buis, F.J. and J. van Donselaar (1994) *Extreem-Rechts*, Leiden: Leids Instituut voor Sociaal Wetenschappelijk Onderzoek (LISWO).

Buis, H. (1988) *Beter Een Verre Buur. Racistische Voorvallen in Buurt en Straat*, Amsterdam: SUA.

Bunyan, T. (ed) (1993) *Statewatching the New Europe*, London: Statewatch.

CARF (Campaign Against Racism and Fascism)/Southall Rights (1981) *Southall: The Birth of a Black Community*, London: CARF/Southall Rights.

Cashmore, E. and E. McLaughlin (eds) (1991) *Out of Order: Policing Black People*, London: Routledge.

Castles, S. (1993) Migrations and Minorities in Europe. Perspectives for the 1990s: Eleven Hypotheses, in J. Wrench and J. Solomos (eds) *Racism and Migration in Western Europe*, Oxford: Berg, pp. 17–34.

Castles, S. and M.J. Miller (1993) *The Age of Migration*, London: Macmillan.

Castles, S., H. Booth and T. Wallace (1987) *Here For Good: Western Europe's New Ethnic Minorities*, 2nd edn, London: Pluto Press.

Cobb, R.W. and C.D. Elder (1983) *Participation in American Politics: The Dynamic of Agenda-Building*, 2nd edn, Baltimore, MD: Johns Hopkins University.

Cobb, R., J-K. Ross and M.H. Ross (1976) Agenda Building as a Comparative Political Process, *American Political Science Review*, vol. 70, no. 1, pp. 126–39.

Cohen, P. (1988) The Perversions of Inheritance: Studies in the Making of Multi-Racist Britain, in P. Cohen and H.S. Bains (eds) *Multi-Racist Britain*, London: Macmillan, pp. 9–118.

Cohen, P. and H.S. Bains (eds) (1988) *Multi-Racist Britain*, London: Macmillan.

Cohen, R. (1994) *Frontiers of Identity: The British and the Others*, London: Longman.

Cohn-Bendit, D. and T. Schmid (1992) *Heimat Babylon*, Hamburg: Hoffmann & Campe.

Commissioner of Police of the Metropolis, *Annual Reports 1983–1989*, London.

Commission for Racial Equality (1987) *Living in Terror*, London: CRE.

Commission for Racial Equality (1988) *Learning in Terror*, London: CRE.

Commission Nationale Consultative des Droits de l'Homme (CNCDH) (1994) *1993: La Lutte contre le racisme et la xénophobie*, Paris: La Documentation française.

Commission Nationale Consultative des Droits de l'Homme (CNCDH) (1995) *1994: La Lutte contre le racisme et la xénophobie*, Paris: La Documentation française.

Cook, D. (1993) Racism, Citizenship and Exclusion, in D. Cook and B. Hudson (eds) *Racism and Criminology*, London: Sage, pp. 136–57.

Cook, D. and B. Hudson (eds) (1993) *Racism and Criminology*, London: Sage.

Coppes, R. (1994) Niet zomaar een stukje stof: Hoofddoekjesaffaires in Frankrijk, Nederland en Groot-Brittannië, *Sociologische Gids*, no. 2 (jgXLI), pp. 130–43.

Cornelius, W.A., P.L. Martin and J.F. Holyfield (eds) (1994) *Controlling Migration: A Global Perspective*, Stanford, CA: Stanford University Press.

Costa-Lascoux, J. (1994) French Legislation against Racism and Discrimination, *New Community*, vol. 20, no. 3, pp. 371–9.

Cottaar, A. and W. Willems (1984) *Indische Nederlanders. Een onderzoek naar beeldvorming*, Den Haag: Moeson, 1984.

Cottaar, A. and W. Willems (1987) Indische Nederlanders, Een

Ondergeschoven Bevolkingsgroep, in Anne Frank Stichting, *Vreemd Gespuis*, Amsterdam: Anne Frank Stichting, pp. 121–33.

Department of the Environment (1989) *Tackling Racial Violence and Harassment in Local Authority Housing*, London: HMSO.

Desir, H. (1985) *Touche pas a mon pote*, Paris: Grasset.

Dobash, R.E. and R.P. Dobash (1992) *Women, Violence and Social Change*, London: Routledge.

Donselaar, J. van (1991) *Fout na de Oorlog. Fascistische en Racistische Organisaties in Nederland 1950–1990*, Amsterdam: Bert Bakker.

Donselaar, J. van (1993) The Extreme Right and Racist Violence in the Netherlands, in T. Björgo and R. Witte (eds) *Racist Violence in Europe*, London: Macmillan, pp. 46–61.

Donselaar, J. van (1995) *De Staat Paraat? De bestrijding van extreem-rechts in West-Europa*, Amsterdam: Babylon De Geus.

Dubbelman, J.E. (1987) De filosofie is: Indammen; De eerste reacties op de komst van de Tamils, in Anne Frank Stichting, *Vreemd Gespuis*, Amsterdam: Anne Frank Stichting, pp. 176–87.

Eijk, V. van der (1975) Politieke Participatie: Een overzicht van de recente literatuur, *Acta Politica*, vol. X, pp. 341–63.

Eijk, C. van der and W.J.P. Kok (1975) Nondecisions Reconsidered, *Acta Politica*, vol. X, pp. 277–301.

Elbers, F. and M. Fennema (1993) *Racistische Partijen in West-Eruopa*, Leiden: Stichting Burgerschapskunde.

Entzinger, H. (1984) *Het Minderhedenbeleid*, Meppel: Boom.

Fanon, F. (1952) *Peau noire, masques blancs*, Paris: Editions du Seuil.

Fanon, F. (1961) *Les Damnés de la terre*, Paris: François Maspero (Translated (1967) *The Wretched of the Earth*, Harmondsworth: Penguin).

Fascisme Onderzoek Kollektief (FOK) (1995) *Jaaroverzicht 1993–1994. Extreem-rechts in Nederland*, FOK-Dossier 9, Amsterdam: FOK.

Finer, S.E. (1970) *Comparative Government*, Harmondsworth: Penguin.

Forbes, D. (1988) *Action on Racial Harassment: Legal Remedies and Local Authorities*, London: Legal Action Group/London Housing Unit.

Ford, G. (1990) *Report on the Findings of the Committee of Inquiry into Racism and Xenophobia*, Strasbourg: European Parliament.

Freeman, Gary P. (1979) *Immigrant Labour and Racial Conflict in Industrial Societies*, Princeton, NJ: Princeton University Press.

Freeman, Gary P. (1992) The Consequence of Immigration Policies for Immigrant Status: A British and French Comparison, in L.A.M. Messina, L.R. Fraga, L.A. Rhodebeck and F.D. Wright (eds) *Ethnic and Racial Minorities in Advanced Industrial Democracies*, New York: Greenwood Press, pp. 17–32.

Fryer, P. (1991) *Staying Power*, 5th edn, London: Pluto Press.

Gordon, P. (1983) *White Law*, London: Pluto Press.

Gordon, P. (1990) *Racial Violence and Harassment*, 2nd edn, London: Runnymede Trust.

Gordon, P. (1993) The Police and Racist Violence in Britain, in

T. Björgo and R. Witte (eds) *Racist Violence in Europe*, London: Macmillan, pp. 167–78.

Graaf, H. van der and R. Hoppe (1989) *Beleid en Politiek*, Muiderberg: Coutinho.

Greater London Council Police Committee (1984) *Racial Harassment in London*, London: GLC.

Groenendijk, C.A. (1990) Verboden voor Tukkers: Reacties op Rellen tussen Italianen, Spanjaarden en Twentenaren in 1961, in F. Bovenkerk, F. Buijs and H. Tromp (eds) *Wetenschap en Partijdigheid: Opstellen voor Andre J.F. Köbben*, Assen: Van Gorcum, pp. 55–96.

Guidice, F. (1992) *Arabicides, une chronique française 1970–1991*, Paris: La Decouverte.

Guillaumin, C. (1991) 'Race' and Discourse, in M. Silverman (ed.) *Race, Discourse and Power in France*, Aldershot: Avebury, pp. 5–13.

Hall, P.A. (1993) Pluralism and Pressure Politics in France, in J.J. Richardson (ed.) *Pressure Groups*, Oxford: Oxford University Press, pp. 159–74.

Hall, S. (1978) Racism and Reaction, in Commission for Racial Equality (CRE), *Five Views of Multi-racial Britain*, London: CRE.

Hall, S., C. Critcher, T. Jefferson, J. Clarke and B. Roberts (1978) *Policing the Crisis: Mugging, the State, and Law and Order*, London: Macmillan.

Hamm, M.S. (ed.) (1994) *Hate Crime: International Perspectives on Causes and Control*, Cincinnatti: Anderson.

Hansson, N. (1991) France: The Carpentras Syndrome and Beyond, *Patterns of Prejudice*, vol. 25, no. 1, pp. 32–45.

Hargreaves, A.G. (1991) Political Mobilization among North Africans, *Ethnic and Racial Studies*, Vol. 14, no. 3, pp. 350–67.

Heijden, H.A. van der (1990) *Tussen Wetenschap en Politiek*, Kampen: Mondiss.

Hester, S. and P. Eglin (1992) *A Sociology of Crime*, London: Routledge.

Hiro, D. (1992) *Black British White British*, London: Paladin (original edn 1971).

Hisschemöller, M. (1993) *De Democratie van Problemen*, Amsterdam: VU-uitgeverij.

Holmes, C. (1981) *A Tolerant Country? Immigrants, Refugees and Minorities in Britain*, London: Faber & Faber.

Holthuizen, M. (1992) *De behandeling van discriminatiezaken door politie en justitie*, Utrecht: Wetenschapswinkel Rechten.

Holtrop A. and U. Den Tex (1984) Bij Ons In Holland, *Vrij Nederland* (bijlage), 30 June.

Home Affairs Committee (1986) *Racial Attacks and Harassment*, London: HMSO.

Home Affairs Committee (1989) *Racial Attacks and Harassment*, London: HMSO.

Home Office (1981) *Racial Attacks*, London: HMSO.

House of Commons (1982) Home Affairs Committee, *Racial Attacks*.

Second Report from the Home Affairs Committee, Session 1981–82, HC. 106, London: HMSO, 1982.

Hunte, J.A. (1966) *Nigger Hunting in England?*, London: West Indian Standing Conference.

Husbands, C.T. (1993) Racism and Racist Violence: Some Theories and Policy Perspectives, in T. Björgo and R. Witte (eds) *Racist Violence in Europe*, London: Macmillan, pp. 113–27.

Institute of Race Relations (IRR) (1979) *Police Against Black People*, London: IRR.

Institute of Race Relations (IRR) (1987) *Policing Against Black People*, London: IRR.

Institute of Race Relations (IRR) (1991) *Deadly Silence: Black Deaths in Custody*, London: IRR.

Inter-Departmental Racial Attacks Group (1989) *The Response to Racial Attacks and Harassment: Guidance for the Statutory Agencies*, London: HMSO.

Inter-Departmental Racial Attacks Group (1991) *The Response to Racial Attacks: Sustaining the Momentum*, London: HMSO.

Jansma, L. and J. Veenman (1977) De Schiedamse Rel, *Mens en Maatschappij*, 2.

Jenkins, S. and V. Randall (1970) *Here to Live: A Study of Race Relations in an English Town*, London: Runnymede Trust.

Joint Commission Against Racialism (1981) *Racial Violence in Britain 1980*, paper presented to the Home Secretary, 4 February, London.

Joly, D. (1992) *Refugees: Asylum in Europe?*, London: Minority Rights Publications.

Joly, D. and R. Cohen (eds) (1989) *Reluctant Hosts: Europe and its Refugees*, Aldershot: Avebury.

Joshua, H., T. Wallace and H. Booth (1983) *To Ride the Storm*, London: Heinemann.

Journal Officiel de la République Française, 14 July 1990.

Kay, D. and R. Miles (1993) *Migration, Racism and the Labour Market in Britain 1946–1951*, London: Routledge.

Kettle, M. and L. Hodges (1982) *Uprising*, London: Pan.

Klug, F. (1982) *Racist Attacks*, London: Runnymede Trust.

Koekebakker, O. (1990) *Immigrant in Europa*, Utrecht: Nederlands Centrum Buitenlanders.

Kushner, T. (1994) *The Holocaust and the Liberal Imagination: A Social and Cultural History*, Oxford: Blackwell.

Layton-Henry, Z. (1982) Racial Attacks in Britain, *Patterns of Prejudice*, vol. 16, no. 2, pp. 3–13.

Layton-Henry, Z. (1984) *Politics of Race in Britain*, London: George Allen & Unwin.

Layton-Henry, Z. (1992) *The Politics of Immigration*, Oxford: Blackwell.

Layton-Henry, Z. and P.B. Rich (eds) (1986) *Race, Government and Politics in Britain*, London: Macmillan.

Levin, J. and J. McDevitt (1993) *Hate Crimes: the Rising Tide of Bigotry and Bloodshed*, New York: Plenum Press.

Lijphart, A. (1979) *Verzuiling, Pacificatie en Kentering in de Nederlandse Politiek*, 3rd revised edn, Amsterdam: DeBussy.

Lloyd, C. (1991) Concepts, Models and Anti-Racist Strategies in Britain and France, *New Community*, vol. 18, no. 1, pp. 63–73.

Lloyd, C. (1993) Racist Violence and Anti-Racist Reactions: A View of France, in T. Björgo and R. Witte (eds) *Racist Violence in Europe*, London: Macmillan, pp. 207–20.

Lloyd, C. (1994) Universalism and Difference: The Crisis of Anti-racism in the UK and France, in A. Rattansi and S. Westwood (eds) *Racism, Modernity and Identity on the Western Front*, Cambridge: Polity Press, pp. 222–44.

Lloyd, C. and H. Waters (1991) France: One Culture, One People?, *Race and Class*, vol. 32, no. 3, pp. 49–65.

Lucassen, L. and R. Penninx (1985) *Nieuwkomers: Migranten en hun Nakomelingen in Nederland 1550–1985*, Amsterdam: Meulenhoff.

MacDonald, I., R. Bhavani, L. Khan and G. John (1989) *Murder in the Playground: The Burnage Report*, London: Longsight Press.

MacEwen, M. (1994) Anti-Discrimination Law in Great Britain, *New Community*, vol. 20, no. 3, pp. 353–70.

MacMaster, N. (1991) The 'seuil de tolérance': The Uses of a 'Scientific' Racist Concept, in M. Silverman (ed) *Race, Discourse and Power in France*, Aldershot: Avebury, pp. 14 28.

Mair, P. (ed.) (1990) *The West European Party System*, Oxford: Oxford University Press.

Mayer, N. (1992) Carpentras and the Media, *Patterns of Prejudice*, vol. 26, nos 1 and 2, pp. 48–63.

Mayhew, P., D. Elliott and L. Dowds (1989) *The 1988 British Crime Survey*, London: HMSO.

Mercer, Kobena, 'Powellism; Race, Politics and Discourse', unpublished Ph.D thesis, Goldsmith's College, University of London, 1990.

Messina, A.M., L.R. Fraga, L.A. Rhodebeck and F.D. Wright (1992) *Ethnic and Racial Minorities in Advanced Industrial Democracies*, New York: Greenwood Press.

Miles, R. (1982) *Racism and Migrant Labour*, London: Routledge & Kegan Paul.

Miles, R. (1984) The Riots of 1958: The Ideological Construction of 'Race Relations' as a Political Issue in Britain, *Immigrants and Minorities*, vol. 3, no. 3, pp. 252–75.

Miles, R. (1989) *Racism*, London: Routledge.

Miles, R. (1993) *Racism after 'Race Relations'*, London: Routledge.

Miles, R. (1994a) Explaining Racism in Contemporary Europe, in A. Rattansi and S. Westwood (eds) *Racism, Modernity and Identity on the Western Front*, Cambridge: Polity Press, pp. 189–221.

Miles, R. (1994b) A Rise of Racism and Fascism in Contemporary Europe? Some Sceptical Reflections on its Nature and Extent, *New Community*, vol. 20, no. 4, pp. 547–62.

Muus, P. (1993) *Internationale Migratie naar Europa*, Amsterdam: SUA.

Nederveen Pieterse, J.P. (1989) *Empire and Emancipation*, New York: Praeger.

Netherlands Scientific Council for Government Policy (NSCGP) (1979) *Ethnic Minorities*, Report no. 17, The Hague.

Netherlands Scientific Council for Government Policy (NSCGP) (1990) *Immigrant Policy*, Report no. 36, The Hague.

Newham Monitoring Project (1988) *Annual Report 1987*, London: NMP.

Newham Monitoring Project (1989) *Still Fighting: Annual Report 1988*, London: NMP.

Newham Monitoring Project (1990) *Racism and Racist Violence in Schools*, London: NMP.

Newham Monitoring Project/CARF (1991) *Newham: The Forging of a Black Community*, London: NMP/CARF.

Noriel, G. (1988) *Le Creuset français*, Paris, Seuil.

Oakley, R. (1992) *Report on Racial Violence and Harassment in Europe*, Strasbourg: Council of Europe.

Ogden, P.E. (1991) Immigration to France since 1945, *Ethnic and Racial Studies*, vol. 14, no. 3, pp. 294–318.

Penninx, R. (1979) Naar een algemeen etnisch minderhedenbeleid, in Wetenschappelijke Raad voor het Regeringsbeleid, *Etnische Minderheden*, no. 17, Staatsuitgeverij, 's-Gravenhage, pp. 1–174.

Phizacklea, A. and R. Miles (1980) *Labour and Racism*, London: Routledge & Kegan Paul.

Pilkington, E. (1988) *Beyond the Mothercountry*, London: IB Tauris.

Possel, A.C. (ed.) (1987) *Rechtspraak Rassendiscriminatie*, Lelystad: LBR/Vermande.

Possel, A.C. (ed.) (1990) *Met Recht Rassendiscriminatie Bestrijden*, Utrecht/Zwolle: Landelijk Bureau Racismebestrijding/Tjeenk Willink.

Possel, A.C. (ed.) (1991) *Rechtspraak Rassendiscriminatie 1988–1990*, Utrecht/Zwolle: Landelijk Bureau Racismebestrijding/Tjeenk Willink.

Rath, J. (1991) *Minorisering: De Sociale Constructie van 'Etnische Minderheden'*, Amsterdam: SUA.

Rath, J. (1993) The Ideological Representation of Migrant Workers in Europe: A Matter of Racialisation?, in J. Wrench and J. Solomos (eds) *Racism and Migration in Western Europe*, Oxford: Berg, pp. 215–32.

Rattansi, A. (1994) Western Racisms, Ethnicities and Identities in a 'Postmodern' Frame, in A. Rattansi and S. Westwood (eds) *Racism, Modernity and Identity on the Western Front*, Cambridge: Polity Press, pp. 15–86.

Rattansi, A. and S. Westwood (eds) (1994) *Racism, Modernity and Identity on the Western Front*, Cambridge: Polity Press.

Reenen, P. van (1979) *Overheidsgeweld: Een sociologische studie van de dynamiek van het geweldsmonopolie*, Alphen aan de Rijn: Samsom.

Rensen, P. (1994) *Dansen met de duivel*, Amsterdam: L.J. Veen.

Rex, J. (1983) *Race Relations in Sociological Theory*, London: Routledge & Kegan Paul.

Rex, J. (1986) *Race and Ethnicity*, Milton Keynes: Open University Press.

Richardson, J.J. (ed.) (1993a) *Pressure Groups*, Oxford: Oxford University Press.

Richardson, J.J. (1993b) Interest Group Behaviour in Britain: Continuity and Change, in J.J. Richardson (ed.) *Pressure Groups*, Oxford: Oxford University Press, pp. 86–99.

Rieu, A.M. and G. Duprat (eds) (1993) *What Is Europe? European Democratic Culture*, Milton Keynes/London: Open University/Routledge.

Rodrigues, P.R. (1994) Racial Discrimination and the Law in the Netherlands, *New Community*, vol. 20, no. 3, pp. 381–91.

Rose, D. (1992) *A Climate of Fear: The Murder of PC Blakelock and the Case of the Tottenham Three*, London: Bloomsbury.

Royal Commission on Population, Report of the, Cmnd 7695, London: HMSO, 1949.

Salt, J. (1976) International Labour Migration: The Geographical Pattern of Demand, in J. Salt and H. Clout (eds) *Migration in Post-War Period: Geographical Essays*, Oxford: Oxford University Press, pp. 80–125.

Salt, J. and H. Clout (1976) *Migration in Post-War Period: Geographical Essays*, Oxford: Oxford University Press.

Saulsbury, W. and B. Bowling (1991) *The Multi-Agency Approach in Practice: The North Plaistow Racial Harassment Project*, Research and Planning Unit Paper no. 64, London: Home Office.

Scarman, Lord (1981) *The Scarman Report on the Brixton Disorders*, Harmondsworth, Penguin.

Schmid, A.P. and A.J. Jongman (1988) *Political Terrorism: A Research Guide to Concepts, Theories, Data Bases and Literature*, revised, expanded and updated edn, Amsterdam: North-Holland Publishing Company, New Brunswick, NJ; Transaction Books.

Schmid, A.P., J.F.A. deGraaf, F. Bovenkerk, L.M. Bovenkerk-Teerink and L. Brunt (1982) *Zuidmoluks Terrorisme, de Media en de Publieke Opinie*, Amsterdam: Intermediair.

Schuster, J. (1996) *Poortwachters en Migranten*.

Sheptycki, J.W.E. (1993) *Innovations in Policing Domestic Violence*, Aldershot, Avebury.

Silverman, M. (ed.) (1991) *Race, Discourse and Power in France*, Aldershot: Avebury.

Singer, D. (1991) The Resistible Rise of Jean-Marie Le Pen, *Ethnic and Racial Studies*, vol. 14, no. 3, pp. 368–81.

Sivanandan, A. (1987) *A Different Hunger: Writings on Black Resistance*, London: Pluto Press.

Smith, A.M. (1994) *New Right Discourse on Race and Sexuality: Britain 1968–1990*, Cambridge: Cambridge University Press.

Smith, G. (1980) *Politics in Western Europe*, 3rd edn, London: Heinemann.

Solomos, J. (1988) *Black Youth, Racism and the State*, Cambridge: Cambridge University Press.

216   Racist Violence and the State

Solomos, J. (1989) *Race and Racism in Contemporary Britain*, London: Macmillan.

Solomos, J. and L. Back (1994) Conceptualising Racisms: Social Theory, Politics and Research, *Sociology*, vol. 28, no. 1, pp. 143–61.

Solomos, J. and T. Rackett (1991) Policing and Urban Unrest: Problem Constitution and Policy Response, in E. Cashmore and E. McLaughlin (eds) *Out of Order: Policing Black People*, London: Routledge, pp. 42–64.

Stouthuysen, P. (1993) *Extreem-Rechts in Na-Oorlogs Europa*, Brussels: VUB Press.

Studlar, D.T. (1986) Non-White Policy Preferences, Political Participation and the Political Agenda in Britain, in Z. Layton-Henry and P.B. Rich (eds) *Race, Government and Politics in Britain*, London: Macmillan, pp. 159–86.

Studlar, D.T. and Z. Layton-Henry (1990) Nonwhite Minority Access to the Political Agenda in Britain, *Policy Studies Review*, vol. 9, no. 2, pp. 372–93.

Stuurman, S. (1981) *Kapitalisme en Burgerlijke Staat*, 3rd edn, Amsterdam: SUA.

Stuurman, S. (1985) *De Labyrintische Staat*, Amsterdam: SUA.

Tahar Ben Jelloun (1984) *Hospitalité française: racisme et immigration maghrebine*, Paris: Seuil.

Tompson, K. (1988) *Under Siege: Racial Violence in Britain Today*, Harmondsworth: Penguin.

Van Amersfoort, J.M.M. (1974) *Immigratie en minderheidsvorming: een analyse van de Nederlande situatie 1945–1973*, Alphen aan den Rijn: Samson, 1974.

Viard, P. (1984) Les Crimes Racistes en France, *Les Temps Modernes*, vol. XL, nos 452–4, pp. 1942–52.

Virdee, S. (1995) *Racial Violence and Harassment*, London: Policy Studies Institute.

Webber, F. (1993a) The New Europe: Immigration and Asylum, In T. Bunyan (ed.) *Statewatching the New Europe*, London: Statewatch, pp. 130–41.

Webber, F. (1993b) European Conventions on Immigration and Asylum, in T. Bunyan (ed.) *Statewatching the New Europe*, London: Statewatch, pp. 142–55.

Wetenschappelijke Raad voor het Regeringsbeleid (WRR) (1979) *Etnische Minderheden*, Rapporten aan de Regering, no. 17, The Hague: Staatsuitgeverij.

Wetenschappelijke Raad voor het Regeringsbeleid (WRR) (1989) *Allochtonenbeleid*, Rapporten aan de Regering, no. 36, The Hague: Staatsdrukkerij/Uitgeverij (SDU).

Wihtol de Wenden, C. (1988) *Les Immigrés et la politique*, Paris: la Fondation Nationale des Sciences Politiques (FNSP).

Wihtol de Wenden, C. (1991) Immigration Policy and Nationality, *Ethnic and Racial Studies*, vol. 14, no. 3, pp. 319–32.

Witte, R. (1991) De Onbegrepen Verkiezingsuitslag voor Extreem-Rechts, *Acta Politica*, vol. XXVI, no. 4, pp. 449–70.

Witte, R. (1992) Ernst geweld tegen minderheden wordt onderschat, *de Volkskrant*, 10 March.

Witte, R. (1993a) Internationaal Vergelijkend Onderzoek naar Staatsreacties op Racistisch Geweld: Een Ontwerp voor een Analysekader, in G. Horeweg, C. van Montfort and P. Schreuder (eds) *Promotieonderzoek van de Faculteit der Sociale Wetenschappen: Verwantschap en Diversiteit*, Utrecht: Interdisciplinair Sociaal-Wetenschappelijk Onderzoeksinstituut van de Rijksuniversiteit Utrecht (ISOR), pp. 155–76.

Witte, R. (1993b) Racist Violence: An Issue on the Political Agenda?, in T. Björgo and R. Witte (eds) *Racist Violence in Europe*, London: Macmillan, pp. 139–53.

Witte, R. (1994a) Comparing State Responses to Racist Violence in Europe: A Model for International Comparative Analysis, in M.S. Hamm (ed.) *Hate Crime: International Perspectives on Causes and Control*, Cincinnatti: Anderson, pp. 91–103.

Witte, R. (1994b) The Nature and Causes of Racist and Xenophobic Violence in Europe, Paper presented at Council of Europe Meeting on Practical Measures for Tackling Racist and Xenophobic Violence, Strasbourg, 12 October (to be published by the Council of Europe in 1996).

Witte, R. (1995) Racist Violence in Western Europe, in *New Community*, 21(4): pp. 489–500.

Witte, R. and Y. Yesilgöz (1992) Etnische Minderheden: Misdadige Criminalisering, *LBR-Bulletin*, no. 4, pp. 21–3.

Woodall (1993) Arabicide in France: An Interview with Fausto Guidice, *Race and Class*, vol. 35, no. 2, p. 27.

Wrench, J. and J. Solomos (eds) (1993) *Racism and Migration in Western Europe*, Oxford: Berg.

Wright, V. (1983) *The Government and Politics of France*, London: Hutchinson (1st edn 1978).

Yeşilgöz, Y. (1993) A Double Standard: The Turkish State and Racist Violence, in T. Björgo and R. Witte (eds) *Racist Violence in Europe*, London: Macmillan, pp. 179–93.

INDEX